NATIONAL GEOGRAPHIC
KiDS

ALMANAC 2017

NATIONAL GEOGRAPHIC
WASHINGTON, D.C.

National Geographic Kids Books
gratefully acknowledges the following people for their help with the
National Geographic Kids Almanac 2017.

Anastasia Cronin of the
National Geographic Explorers program

Amazing Animals

Suzanne Braden, Director, Pandas International

Dr. Rodolfo Coria, Paleontologist, Plaza Huincul, Argentina

Dr. Sylvia Earle,
National Geographic Explorer-in-Residence

Dr. Thomas R. Holtz, Jr., Senior Lecturer, Vertebrate
Paleontology, Department of Geology, University of Maryland

Dr. Luke Hunter, Executive Director, Panthera

Dereck and Beverly Joubert,
National Geographic Explorers-in-Residence

Nizar Ibrahim, National Geographic Emerging Explorer

"Dino" Don Lessem, President, Exhibits Rex

Kathy B. Maher, Research Editor,
National Geographic magazine

Kathleen Martin, Canadian Sea Turtle Network

Barbara Nielsen, Polar Bears International

Andy Prince, Austin Zoo

Christopher Sloan

Julia Thorson, translator, Zurich, Switzerland

Dennis vanEngelsdorp, Senior Extension Associate,
Pennsylvania Department of Agriculture

Going Green

Eric J. Bohn, Math Teacher, Santa Rosa High School

Stephen David Harris,
Professional Engineer, Industry Consulting

Catherine C. Milbourn, Senior Press Officer, EPA

Brad Scriber, Senior Researcher, *National Geographic* magazine

Paola Segura and Cid Simões,
National Geographic Emerging Explorers

Dr. Wes Tunnell, Harte Research Institute for
Gulf of Mexico Studies, Texas A&M University–Corpus Christi

Natasha Vizcarra, Science Writer and Media Liaison,
National Snow and Ice Data Center

Culture Connection

Dr. Wade Davis, National Geographic Explorer-in-Residence

Deirdre Mullervy, Managing Editor,
Gallaudet University Press

Super Science

Tim Appenzeller, Chief Magazine Editor, *Nature*

Dr. Rick Fienberg, American Astronomical Society,
Press Officer and Director of Communications

Dr. José de Ondarza, Associate Professor,
Department of Biological Sciences, State University
of New York, College at Plattsburgh

Lesley B. Rogers, Managing Editor (former),
National Geographic magazine

Dr. Enric Sala, National Geographic Visiting Fellow

Abigail A. Tipton, Director of Research (former),
National Geographic magazine

Erin Vintinner, Biodiversity Specialist,
Center for Biodiversity and Conservation at the
American Museum of Natural History

Barbara L. Wyckoff, Research Editor (former),
National Geographic magazine

Wonders of Nature

Anatta, NOAA Public Affairs Officer

Dr. Robert Ballard,
National Geographic Explorer-in-Residence

Douglas H. Chadwick, wildlife biologist and contributor to
National Geographic magazine

Susan K. Pell, Ph.D., Science and Public Programs Manager,
United States Botanic Garden

History Happens

Dr. Sylvie Beaudreau, Associate Professor,
Department of History, State University of New York

Elspeth Deir, Assistant Professor, Faculty of Education,
Queens University, Kingston, Ontario, Canada

Dr. Gregory Geddes, Lecturer, Department of Global Studies,
State University of New York–Orange,
Middletown-Newburgh, New York

Dr. Fredrik Hiebert, National Geographic Visiting Fellow

Micheline Joanisse, Media Relations Officer,
Natural Resources Canada

Dr. Robert D. Johnston,
Associate Professor and Director of the
Teaching of History Program, University of Illinois at Chicago

Dickson Mansfield, Geography Instructor (retired),
Faculty of Education, Queens University,
Kingston, Ontario, Canada

Tina Norris, U.S. Census Bureau

Parliamentary Information and Research Service,
Library of Parliament, Ottawa, Canada

Karyn Pugliese, Acting Director, Communications,
Assembly of First Nations

Geography Rocks

Glynnis Breen, National Geographic Special Projects

Carl Haub, Senior Demographer,
Conrad Taeuber Chair of Public Information,
Population Reference Bureau

Dr. Mary Kent, Demographer, Population Reference Bureau

Dr. Walt Meier, National Snow and Ice Data Center

Dr. Richard W. Reynolds,
NOAA's National Climatic Data Center

United States Census Bureau, Public Help Desk

Dr. Spencer Wells,
National Geographic Explorer-in-Residence

NATIONAL GEOGRAPHIC KiDS

A mountain gorilla mother watches toddlers play in a bamboo forest in Parc National des Volcans, Rwanda.

Contents

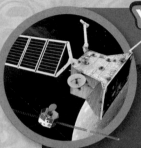

Culture Connection

96

Awesome Adventure

122

Fun and Games

142

Super Science

162

Wonders of Nature

198

History Happens

222

Geography Rocks

254

ALMANAC NEWSMAKER CHALLENGE

The Results are in!
Who Stepped Up to the
Plate to Fight Food Waste
in 2016? See page 89.

Want to become part of the
2017 Almanac Newsmaker Challenge?
Go to page 105 to find out more.

BepiColombo, a European Space Agency mission to check out the planet Mercury in collaboration with the Japanese space agency, JAXA, is scheduled to launch in early 2017. Composed of two orbiters and a carrier spacecraft, it is scheduled to reach Mercury in 2024.

SCIENTISTS IN DISGUISE

For these animal researchers, playing dress-up is part of the job.

At China's Wolong National Nature Reserve, a pair of large pandas gently tend to a tiny cub, first easing it onto a scale and then checking its temperature as a part of a physical examination. But look closely and you'll see that those aren't giant pandas examining their young—they're actually humans wearing fuzzy costumes. It's a funny scene, for sure, but these researchers are working to collect valuable data while minimizing the animal's stress and human attachment.

WILD PLAY

At this Chinese center in particular, where pandas are bred in captivity with the hopes of returning them to the wild, experts wear the costumes to help the animals acclimate to life on their own. The less obvious human interaction, they believe, the better equipped the cub will be to survive in the wild. And scientists don't stop at the costume: Researchers also sprinkle themselves with panda poop and pee to mask their human scent.

OTHER CLEVER COSTUMES

But it's not just panda people who play dress up. In Wyoming, U.S.A., a pair of scientists once donned moose suits created by a Star Wars designer to track the animal's interaction with natural predators, while employees at a whooping crane center in Wisconsin, U.S.A., use bird-shaped hand puppets to feed hatchlings. While these methods may seem fun for the humans involved, they are a necessary step to help the animals.

Battling DROUGHT

CALIFORNIA, U.S.A., is suffering its worst drought on record. And experts have come up with some clever and creative approaches to battle this devastating dry spell. One such solution? Turning the Los Angeles Reservoir into a giant ball pit. By filling the reservoir with millions of "shade balls"—four-inch (10-cm) black plastic spheres that provide shade to the water, reducing evaporation—experts expect to conserve up to 300 million gallons (1.1 billion L) of water each year. Meanwhile, other places in California are doing their part to save water. Dodger Stadium in Los Angeles has turned to low-flush toilets, while Exposition Park has removed some of its lush green lawns in favor of drought-tolerant plants and reduced watering times. Important steps in saving water—and, hopefully, securing the future of the state.

Meet Sparklemuffin
and Skeletorus

SKELETORUS

SPARKLEMUFFIN

These two spiders are sure to make you squeal ... with delight. Recently discovered in Australia, these two tiny peacock spiders—a species named for the "fan" on the male's abdomen that looks similar to the brightly colored bird's plumage—have unusual, bold markings. But that's not all that makes these spiders stand out: They dance, too! To get a female's attention, male peacock spiders perform a mesmerizing mating display, doing everything from a one-legged leg boogie to an elaborate tail wiggle. So even if you're afraid of arachnids, you have to admit that these crawlers are more cool than creepy.

LETTUCE IN SPACE

Traveling in outer space and craving a salad? No problem! NASA has revealed that it has been able to grow lettuce in the harsh, microgravity environment of space. In fact, astronauts recently munched on leaves of red romaine—the first food to be both harvested and consumed by NASA astronauts on the International Space Station. But this experiment (nicknamed "Veggie" by NASA) isn't just about getting astronauts to eat healthier. It's a push towards creating a more sustainable spacecraft, so that astronauts onboard can have access to fresh food. That's especially essential on lengthy deep space trips, like the planned mission to Mars set for some time in the 2030s.

YOU CAN EAT THIS CUP!

Edible CUPS

Why toss that cup away when you can eat it? To combat the worldwide issue of excess waste (the typical person in a developed country produces about 2.6 pounds [1.2 kg] of garbage a day), companies are coming up with eco-friendly edible cups and tableware. With flavors like vanilla bean and tart cherry, Loliware cups are made from seaweed, organic sweeteners, and flavors from fruit and vegetables. Or, you can sip milk in a crunchy cookie mug, which doubles as a sweet treat once you're down to the last drop. In Japan, one company sells edible dishes made of shrimp, salt, and potato starch that it hopes will be served at the 2020 Olympic Games in Tokyo. Soon you just may be able to clean your plate—and eat it, too.

New Human Ancestor
DISCOVERED

LEE BERGER
EXAMINES
A JAWBONE.

What began as an adventurous caving trip in the Rising Star cave near Johannesburg, South Africa, turned into a major archaeological discovery for a pair of spelunkers. In the cave, their eyes locked on what looked like human bones in the sediment below. They quickly snapped pictures and sent them to Lee Berger, a paleoanthropologist and a National Geographic Explorer who had been doing research in the area. Sensing that the cavers' sighting was significant, Berger launched an excavation that required a team of "underground astronauts"—highly qualified scientists small enough to slide through supernarrow passageways in order to reach the thousands of bones more than 100 feet (30.5 m) below.

The harrowing recovery process was worth it: Berger's squad eventually unearthed *Homo naledi*, a previously unidentified species of early humans. The discovery of these ancient fossils has been applauded around the world as it potentially gets us one step closer to truly understanding the beginnings of humankind.

Kermit's Twin

Kermit the Frog has a double!
Scientists recently discovered a real-life frog that resembles the famous character from the Muppets. Found in eastern Costa Rica's forests, the one-inch (2.5-cm)-long amphibian is named Diane's bare-hearted glass frog. Like other glass frogs, it has see-through skin covering its belly. The amphibian's back is lime-green, which helps the frog blend into its environment. And rather than croaking, this hopper whistles. Because of the frog's Kermit-like looks, it's winning many human fans. That makes it a little bit easier to be green!

DIANE'S
BARE-
HEARTED
GLASS
FROG

DOG SCREEN TIME

Sure, your dog is smart. But your pup may be more perceptive than you even realize—especially when it comes to watching TV. A recent study shows that most dogs can recognize onscreen images of other dogs as they would in real life and actually pay attention to whatever they're watching. This discovery is even linked to programs and channels made just for canines. (DOGTV, for example, shows images of pooches playing in grassy fields or shots of dogs surfing in southern California, U.S.A.) So is it OK to let your pet park it in front of the TV? Experts say that a little screen time here and there is OK—but a walk outside is still the best type of doggie entertainment, paws down.

HOT MOVIES in 2017*

STAR WARS

TOY STORY 4

DESPICABLE ME 3

- **Star Wars: Episode VIII**
- **Despicable Me 3**
- **LEGO Batman Movie**
- **Toy Story 4**
- **The Croods 2**
- **Get Smurfy**

*Release dates and titles are subject to change.

Camera Ball

THE BALL TOOK THIS PHOTO!

The Throwable Panoramic Ball Camera really gets the big picture. The ball's surface is embedded with 36 tiny cameras that snap simultaneously to create a 360-degree panoramic image. Chuck the ball into the air and the cameras automatically capture what's happening in all directions. Upload the images to your smartphone, tablet, or computer, and a software program weaves all the photos together to make one big image. Small and lightweight, it's tough enough to survive a drop if you don't catch it on the way down. Heads up!

Cat's Meow

What kind of tunes are music to your cat's ears?

Turns out it's not calming classical—rather, it's the sound of other cats. Scientists from the University of Wisconsin-Madison say that while cats typically ignore music made for humans, they become more at ease while listening to rhythms imitating purrs and the suckling sounds of kittens nursing. One musician has even recorded an album where he layered such sounds with melodies from a cello, creating soothing songs that are made for both feline and human listening pleasure. The ideal end result? That these tunes can help calm skittish shelter cats or anxious kitties left home alone. Scaredy cats, no more.

BACKYARD BEATS

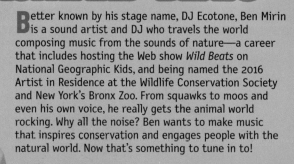

Better known by his stage name, DJ Ecotone, Ben Mirin is a sound artist and DJ who travels the world composing music from the sounds of nature—a career that includes hosting the Web show *Wild Beats* on National Geographic Kids, and being named the 2016 Artist in Residence at the Wildlife Conservation Society and New York's Bronx Zoo. From squawks to moos and even his own voice, he really gets the animal world rocking. Why all the noise? Ben wants to make music that inspires conservation and engages people with the natural world. Now that's something to tune in to!

Cool Events in 2017

Canada Turns 150

O Canada! Canada marks 150 years since Confederation with nationwide festivities.

July 1

Inauguration Day

The new AMERICAN PRESIDENT is sworn in on the steps of the U.S. Capitol building.

January 20

International Tiger Day

Sport your stripes today as you show love—and raise awareness— for these beloved (and endangered) big cats.

July 29

World Puppetry Day

Talk to the hand! Puppets get their time to shine today as we celebrate the mastery of this art form.

March 21

Amazon Day

Make some noise! Honor the Amazon—the world's largest rain forest—today.

September 5

Star Wars Day

May the *fourth* be with you! Celebrate all things from a galaxy far, far away today.

May 4

World Teacher Day

Honor the COOLEST PERSON in school today.

October 5

International Yoga Day

Try a DOWNWARD DOG or TREE POSE TODAY!

June 21

Punkin Chunkin World Championships

Using catapults, air cannons, and more, competitors in Delaware, U.S.A., attempt to launch their pumpkins THE FARTHEST.

Early November

Nutty Art

These are sure to, uh, *crack* you up.

Steve Casino, a self-proclaimed "peanut painter," creates tiny but totally lifelike replicas of famous figures from the shells of the popular nut (the peanuts are actually removed before he starts each sculpture). From Willy Wonka to Wonder Woman, and Taylor Swift to Snoopy, Casino intricately paints each peanut with acrylic paint and uses bamboo skewers for arms and legs—a process that can take up to ten hours per peanut. And he doesn't just do celebs: You can get your own face painted on a peanut. If, that is, you're willing to shell out big bucks for it.

TAYLOR SWIFT

THE HULK

PET SMUGGLER BUSTED!

Dangerous Decoys

When U.S. Fish and Wildlife Service (FWS) inspector Naimah Aziz searched through a wooden cargo crate at New York City's JFK International Airport from Guyana, a country in South America, she didn't expect to see live tarantulas crawling toward her. Alarmed, Aziz asked the owner to remove the tarantulas so she could finish her inspection. It turned out that the spiders were decoys—Aziz soon discovered several illegal caiman lizards, which were taken to a local zoo. It looks like there's no crawling away for these bad guys.

Amazing Animals

An emperor penguin and chicks gather on Snow Hill Island in Antarctica.

17 Cutest Animals of 2017

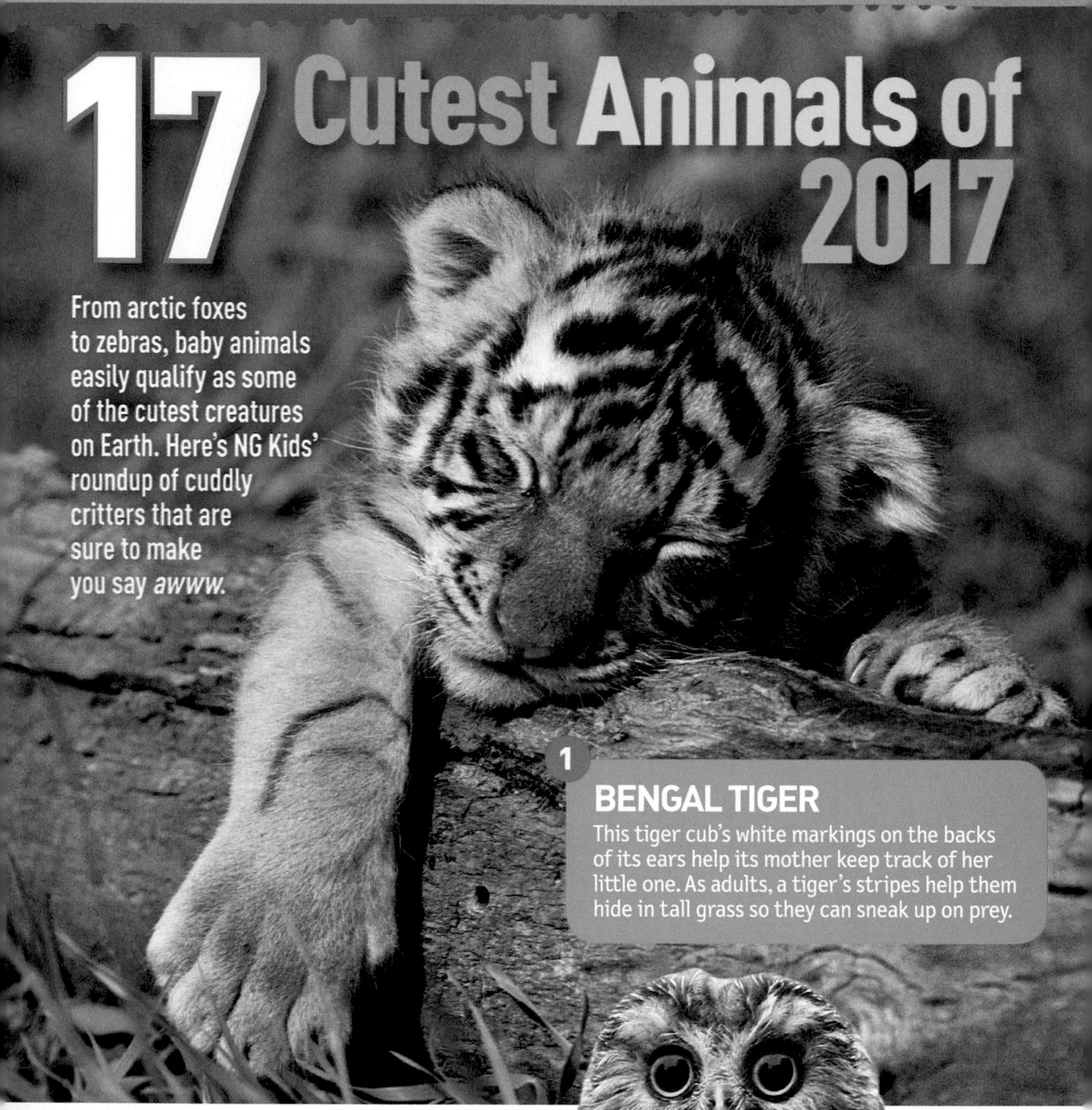

From arctic foxes to zebras, baby animals easily qualify as some of the cutest creatures on Earth. Here's NG Kids' roundup of cuddly critters that are sure to make you say *awww.*

1

BENGAL TIGER

This tiger cub's white markings on the backs of its ears help its mother keep track of her little one. As adults, a tiger's stripes help them hide in tall grass so they can sneak up on prey.

2

SAW-WHET OWL

Hear the sound of a saw being sharpened on a stone? If you're in the woods of the western and northeastern United States or Canada, it could be the alarm call of a saw-whet owl. This bird may be small, but the seven- to eight-inch (17- to 20-cm)-tall owl is a swift and fierce night hunter, swooping down on unsuspecting mice, chipmunks, and squirrels under the cover of darkness.

3 PYGMY SEAHORSE

Among seahorses, it's the males who carry the pair's eggs in a kangaroo-like pouch. When the babies hatch, they gallop out of the pouch in a wild herd of mini seahorses, with the smallest species only half an inch (1.5 cm) tall.

4 DIK-DIK

One of the smallest ungulates (animals with toed hooves, such as buffalo and deer), the dik-dik is a tiny antelope. It lives in parts of Africa with dense cover, where it's easy to find food, keep cool, and hide from predators such as lions and leopards.

5 WALLY THE BUNNY

Wally, an English Angora rabbit, is quite the funny bunny! With adorably giant ears and fur trimmed like a poodle, this famous rabbit has an Instagram account with more than 206,000 followers.

6

WHITE TERN

A white tern's mother balances her eggs on a tree branch or ledge, so these tropical birds are placed in a precarious perch as soon as they're born. Luckily, their strong feet help to keep a grip on things.

7

PATRICK THE WOMBAT

If wombats could talk, Patrick would have plenty of tales to tell! At over 30 years old and 79 pounds (36 kg), Patrick is believed to be the oldest and largest wombat living in captivity.

8

AMERICAN ALLIGATOR

Born at 6 to 8 inches (15 to 20 cm) long, a male baby alligator can grow to be about 11 feet (3.5 m) long and can weigh half a ton (453 kg).

9 STRIPED SKUNK

A wild skunk's ability to hit a target with its stinky spray doesn't come easy. Young skunks practice their moves by picking a target, stomping their feet, threatening with their tails, and letting out little toots.

10 SAND CAT

This rare, fluffy-faced feline lives wild in parts of Africa and Asia. Its soft coat provides camouflage and keeps it warm at night and cool during the day. A great sense of hearing helps this cat hunt for gerbils, reptiles, and insects.

11 KINKAJOU

The kinkajou looks like a little monkey but is actually related to the raccoon. This little mammal loves to slurp honey from beehives with its long, skinny tongue, earning it the nickname "honey bear." How sweet!

12

RED-EYED TREE FROG

When a hungry snake approaches a sleeping frog, one flash of its bright red eyes can startle the predator. Then, the frog can safely hop away.

13

DWARF FLYING SQUIRREL

With an elastic membrane between its forelegs and hind legs stretched out like a cape, this tiny flying squirrel flies from tree to tree to seek out seeds, fruits, and leaves.

14

AMERICAN PIKA

The American pika may look like a big mouse, but it's more closely related to the rabbit. As a baby, these animals are about as big as a walnut, and adults grow to be about as big as a baseball.

15

MOUNTAIN GORILLA

Young mountain gorillas spend their days having fun: climbing trees, chasing each other, and swinging from branches. This gentle species lives within family units and eats a mostly vegetarian diet.

16 PUDSEY

Give this pooch a bone! After winning *Britain's Got Talent* along with his human, Ashleigh, the dancing dog has starred in his own movie and even wrote an "autobi-*dog*-raphy" about his rise to fame.

17 LUNA THE SEA OTTER

Despite being abandoned on a California, U.S.A., beach at just one week old and weighing only two pounds (1 kg), Luna has made a remarkable recovery. Now living in an aquarium in Chicago, Illinois, U.S.A., the lively otter loves to play with everything from plastic toys to ice cubes.

ANIMAL RASCALS

5 mischief-makers you'll never forget

Do you know people who are clever or sneaky, who enjoy pulling crazy pranks or fooling you? Sometimes animals exhibit this same type of behavior. See for yourself with these five stories about animal tricksters.

1

UP AND OVER

One day, Mavis Knight, of Toronto, Canada, spots a raccoon on her garage roof. From there the raccoon climbs a nearby tree until he reaches the utility lines. Then he stands up on the bottom of the wire, holds the top one, and sidesteps across—all the way to a neighbor's backyard. A week later, he does it again.

Why? A tall, wooden fence separates the properties. Instead of taking time to run around the barrier, this furry daredevil has found a quicker "highway" over the top. "He's very clever," Knight says. "I'm no longer angry at him. I just enjoy him." It's like having front-row seats at the circus.

A RACCOON USES A HIGH WIRE TO GET FROM YARD TO YARD.

2

PULLING TEETH

Bill Exner of Waterville, Maine, U.S.A., is eating a peanut butter sandwich in bed when he gets sleepy. So he takes out his false teeth, sets them on the nightstand, and falls asleep.

The next morning, his teeth are gone! He searches under the bed and behind the dressers. No pearly whites. Then, Exner remembers seeing a mouse near his bed the night before. He pries off the baseboard, shines a flashlight into the space behind the wall, and ... aha! Exner spots his dentures—safe and licked clean. He livetraps two sneaky little mice, then releases them on a college campus. Luckily, it's not a law school.

GONE FISHIN'

Bailey the Labrador retriever has eaten something he shouldn't. "His owners see it poking out behind his rib cage, but they don't know what it is," says Gary Sloniker, a veterinarian in Spooner, Wisconsin, U.S.A. The vet takes the dog in for an x-ray. What do they see? A 24-inch (61-cm) ice-fishing pole!

Sloniker thinks Bailey was chewing the handle when he stretched his neck, making the pole slide right into the puppy's mouth. His swallowing reflex kicked in, and down it went.

The vet reaches down Bailey's throat with long-handled tweezers and "fishes" out the hookless pole.

THIS X-RAY OF BAILEY'S INNARDS SHOWS THE ICE-FISHING POLE HE SWALLOWED.

THE ROD THAT BAILEY SWALLOWED WAS SIMILAR TO THIS ONE BUT DIDN'T HAVE THE REEL ATTACHED.

SWEET THIEF

Huh? Jo Adams opens her candy store in Estes Park, Colorado, U.S.A., to find dirt on the checkout counter and a candy tin on the floor. Curious, she plays the video from her surveillance cameras.

A small black bear can be seen sliding his claws under the locked front door and jiggling it open. The store is packed with yummy treats, but the bear chooses to chow down on only peanut butter cups, English toffee, fudge balls, and rice cereal treats. Then he tops it all off with four big cookies called—drumroll, please—cookie bears.

NIGHT MUSIC

It's a humid July evening in Katonah, New York, U.S.A. At the Caramoor Music Festival, an opera is being performed on an outdoor stage. The audience falls silent as one of the female stars begins to sing. *Tra-la-la ... CROAK! Tra ... CROAK! La ... CROAK!*

Operagoers look at each other. They shift in their seats. "The croaking sounds very loud and very close," says Paul Rosenblum, managing director of the festival. By Act 2, Michael Barrett, head of Caramoor at the time, can't stand it anymore. Wearing dress clothes, he leaves his seat and goes backstage. He climbs a ladder onto the roof of the nearest building. And there's the culprit: a lone frog no bigger than a golf ball. Barrett catches the little loudmouth and releases him in the woods. The opera continues. And the famous soloist no longer sounds like she has a frog in her throat.

EXTRAORDINARY Animals

SEA OTTER SHOOTS HOOPS

LEBRON JAMES "OTTER" WATCH OUT.

Portland, Oregon, U.S.A.
Someone alert the NBA: Eddie the sea otter is ready to go pro. His keepers at the Oregon Zoo taught the 18-year-old marine mammal to play basketball as a way to keep his arthritis from getting worse. Since he learned to shoot hoops, Eddie tosses anything he can get his paws on—especially his doggie chew toys—into the basket.

"In the wild, sea otters like Eddie would do a similar behavior we call the spy hop," says Jenny DeGroot, Eddie's keeper and trainer. "They come straight up out of the water, above the waves, to get a look around."

But at the zoo, Eddie's on the lookout for something else. If he scores a basket he gets a tasty treat, such as shrimp or clams. Swish!

I'M A GREAT NEIGH-BOR!

HORSE LIVES IN HOUSE

Holt, Germany

Who needs a pasture? Nasar the Arabian horse spends his days in his owner's house, snacking in the kitchen or listening to classical music in the living room.

Owner Stephanie Arndt often caught the horse looking through the windows into her home, but it wasn't until a major storm hit town that the animal was let inside. Worried a tree might fall on Nasar's barn, Arndt allowed him in for shelter. The horse quickly adapted to his new surroundings. Nasar even has his own bathroom—a spare room covered with straw.

Nasar can drop by the house anytime during the day, but Arndt makes him sleep in the barn at night. Sounds like a stable living arrangement.

MEOW-ABUNGA, DUDE.

SKATEBOARDING CAT

Coolangatta, Australia

Didga the tabby cat leaps from her moving skateboard and lands on top of a surprised dog out for a walk. The cat quickly jumps back onto her board, which has passed under the big pooch, and continues rolling down the crowded sidewalk.

Didga was at first more interested in eating than skateboarding. "I had a skateboard in the kitchen that she kept climbing on, so I put food on it," owner Robert Dollwet says. Dollwet decided to train Didga to ride the skateboard, So is Didga a naturally gifted skateboarder? Sort of—but veterinarian E. Kathryn Meyer thinks Dollwet's reward system has something to do with her talent. Whatever she's skating for, Didga is one paw-some cat.

WHAT IS
Taxonomy?

Since there are billions and billions of living things, called organisms, on the planet, people need a way of classifying them. Scientists created a system called **taxonomy**, which helps to classify all living things into ordered groups. By putting organisms into categories we are better able to understand how they are the same and how they are different. There are seven levels of taxonomic classification, beginning with the broadest group, called a domain, down to the most specific group, called a species.

Biologists divide life based on evolutionary history, and they place organisms into three domains depending on their genetic structure: Archaea, Bacteria, and Eukarya. (See p. 169 for "The Three Domains of Life.")

SAMPLE CLASSIFICATION
RING-TAILED LEMUR

Kingdom:	Animals
Phylum:	Chordata
Class:	Mammalia
Order:	Primates
Family:	Lemuridae
Genus:	*Lemur*
Species:	*catta*

Where do animals come in?

Animals are a part of the Eukarya domain, which means they are organisms made of cells with nuclei. More than one million species of animals have been named, including humans. Like all living things, animals can be divided into smaller groups, called phyla. Most scientists believe there are more than 30 phyla into which animals can be grouped based on certain scientific criteria, such as body type or whether or not the animal has a backbone. It can be pretty complicated, so there is another, less complicated system that groups animals into two categories: vertebrates and invertebrates.

Chinese stripe-necked turtle

TIP
Here's a sentence to help you remember the classification order:
King **P**hillip **C**ame **O**ver **F**or **G**ood **S**oup.

BY THE NUMBERS

There are 11,877 vulnerable or endangered animal species in the world. The list includes:

- **1,200 mammals**, such as the snow leopard, the polar bear, and the fishing cat.
- **1,373 birds**, including the Steller's sea eagle and the Madagascar plover.
- **2,248 fish**, such as the Mekong giant catfish.
- **931 reptiles**, including the American crocodile.
- **1,011 insects**, including the Macedonian grayling.
- **1,961 amphibians**, such as the Round Island day gecko.
- **And more**, including 164 arachnids, 727 crustaceans, 239 sea anemones and corals, 173 bivalves, and 1,771 snails and slugs.

Vertebrates
Animals WITH Backbones

Fish are cold-blooded and live in water. They breathe with gills, lay eggs, and usually have scales.

Amphibians are cold-blooded. Their young live in water and breathe with gills. Adults live on land and breathe with lungs.

Reptiles are cold-blooded and breathe with lungs. They live both on land and in water.

Birds are warm-blooded and have feathers and wings. They lay eggs, breathe with lungs, and usually are able to fly. Some birds live on land, some in water, and some on both.

Mammals are warm-blooded and feed on their mothers' milk. They also have skin that is usually covered with hair. Mammals live both on land and in water.

Bird: Bald eagle

Fish: Clown anemonefish

Invertebrates
Animals WITHOUT Backbones

Sponges are a very basic form of animal life. They live in water and do not move on their own.

Echinoderms have external skeletons and live in seawater.

Mollusks have soft bodies and can live either in or out of shells, on land or in water.

Arthropods are the largest group of animals. They have external skeletons, called exoskeletons, and segmented bodies with appendages. Arthropods live in water and on land.

Worms are soft-bodied animals with no true legs. Worms live in soil.

Cnidaria live in water and have mouths surrounded by tentacles.

Cnidaria: West Coast sea nettle

Worm: Earthworms

Cold-blooded versus Warm-blooded

Cold-blooded animals, also called ectotherms, get their heat from outside their bodies.

Warm-blooded animals, also called endotherms, keep their body temperature level regardless of the temperature of their environments.

NATIONAL GEOGRAPHIC KiDS
MISSION ANIMAL RESCUE
Save ANIMALS >>
Save the WORLD

RHINO

A threatened calf is flying high after he gets airlifted to a new, safe home.

A 15-month-old white rhinoceros gobbles grass next to his mother on a plain in South Africa. Everything appears calm, but the rhinos aren't safe. Poachers, which kill the rhinos for their horns, tend to lurk here. Last year more than 1,000 rhinos were killed in South Africa alone.

A HEAVY LIFT

Suddenly, a helicopter approaches. The pilot and passenger, a veterinarian, work for Rhinos Without Borders. This program plans to airlift a hundred rhinos from their current habitat to a protected reserve in the neighboring country of Botswana. They'll first be driven to a nearby refuge, where staff can make sure they're healthy enough for the trip.

The chopper nears, and the vet leans out and shoots a tranquilizer dart at each rhino. Both drop to the ground, completely sedated. Staff from Rhinos Without Borders rush over to give the rhinos a quick checkup. They then wake the drowsy animals to lead them into big crates. A crane on one truck must lift the heavy crates onto the other vehicle. Then the trucks and chopper take off.

RHINO REST STOP

Fifteen minutes later, the rhinos arrive at the two-acre (0.8-ha) refuge where they'll spend their "layover" in enclosures called bomas (BOH-mas) before going to Botswana. Staff monitor each rhino—if one gets sick, it can't travel.

For the next few weeks the rhinos—now named Kass and Draegon—rest and eat grass mixed with a plant called alfalfa. "We limit their contact with humans," says National Geographic Explorer-in-Residence Dereck Joubert, who founded an organization called Great Plains Conservation with his wife, National Geographic Explorer-in-Residence Beverly Joubert. Great Plains Conservation partnered with a group called andBeyond to launch Rhinos Without Borders and its rescue mission

WELCOME HOME

After two months, the rhinos are ready to go to Botswana. They're loaded onto a plane in crates, and arrive in their new home—a guarded reserve on a stretch of grassland—just two hours later.

Once staff open the crates, Draegon and his mother walk off into the wild. "They're much safer here," Beverly says. "We were so happy to give them a lift."

INTO THE CRATE

CHECKUP TIME

The term rhinoceros combines two Greek words meaning "nose" and "horn."

Adult white rhinos can weigh 5,000 pounds (2,268 kg).

MISSION: LION RESCUE

ALL ABOUT LIONS AND HOW TO SAVE THEM

SAVE ANIMALS, SAVE THE WORLD!

National Geographic Kids has an initiative called **Mission Animal Rescue** to show kids how to save endangered animals. You can help, too! Try out these cool rescue activities.

Write a script for a podcast on rhinos. Include fun facts about the animals and how people can help protect them. Record the podcast and play it for others.

Do the **Mission Animal Rescue challenge!** In November, go to our site **natgeo.com/kids/mission-animal-rescue** and take the "Which Wild Cat Are You?" personality quiz in support of Big Cat Week.

Create a rhino family photo album with pictures of the world's five rhino species. Add facts about each species to the album.

Check out the Nat Geo Kids book series **Mission Animal Rescue.** For more details or to donate to the cause, grab a parent and go online. **natgeo.com/kids/mission-animal-rescue**

Wild Hamsters

FARMERS TRY TO MAKE PEACE WITH THESE PESKY CRITTERS.

In a sun-dappled wheat field in France, a prowling barn cat meets a black-bellied hamster. Too far from her burrow to run for shelter, the wild hamster rises on her hind legs to face her enemy. She puffs out her cheeks, flashes her black underbelly, growls, and bares her teeth. The cat backs away. That black-bellied hamster is one tough rodent.

"They're afraid of nothing," says Alexandre Lehmann, a biologist who has worked with these wild hamsters for the past 12 years. "They fight against cars and dogs and even farmers. They try to fight against tractors. The Germans call them small bears."

Good thing the black-bellied hamster won't go down without a fight. Because in France, where only 500 to 1,000 remain in the wild, these cranky critters are in a fight for their lives.

During hibernation a hamster's heart beats only about six times a minute.

There are around 25 different species of wild hamsters.

TWO-DAY-OLD HAMSTERS

34

The earliest hamsters lived more than 2.5 million years ago.

ENTRANCE TO A HAMSTER BURROW

CAPTIVE-BRED HAMSTERS ARE READY FOR RELEASE INTO THE WILD.

A NEST INSIDE A BURROW

FEISTY RODENTS

Don't confuse the black-bellied hamster with its puny tame relative, the golden hamster. At about 12 inches (30 cm) long, the black-bellied hamster is twice as big. And it's way more feisty.

In fact, black-bellied hamsters historically have been considered public enemy number one—rodents on the wrong side of the law. Ranging from the eastern steppes of Russia to the plains of Alsace in France, black-bellied hamsters have long been seen as pests because of their appetites for farmers' grains, beets, and cabbage. And since mother hamsters can give birth to as many as 14 babies a year, sometimes the population has exploded. The hamsters earned a bad rap, and humans tried everything to get rid of them. Some older farmers remember a time when, as kids, they were paid as bounty hunters to kill hamsters and bring their tails to city hall.

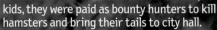

FRANCE — EUROPE
ATLANTIC OCEAN

The war on hamsters continued until just a few decades ago, when naturalists noticed the rodents were in trouble. Although plenty of hamsters were in Russia and the Ukraine, their numbers had been dwindling in western Europe. A movement began to save the hamsters. In 1993 France passed a law protecting them as an endangered species.

HELPING HANDS

At the Stork and Otter Reintroduction Centre in Alsace, Lehmann and his colleagues breed captive hamsters and release their pups into the wild. But breeding black-bellied hamsters isn't easy. Remember, these critters have attitude. Forget humans—they don't even like each other.

If all goes well, the mother hamster will give birth to a litter of about seven pups in three weeks' time. One year later the pups will be ready for release into the wild.

GROWING HABITAT

Black-bellied hamsters might think of themselves as tough guys. But to a fox or an eagle, they're just a four-legged snack. To survive, hamsters need to be released into a field with lots of leafy hiding places. That's a problem in Alsace, where most farmers plant corn. The corn hasn't sprouted in early spring, when hamsters come out from winter hibernation. In the bare fields the hamsters are easy targets for predators.

Some older farmers don't want hamsters on their property because of their reputation as pests. But most are willing to help, especially since the French government will pay farmers to grow early-sprouting crops such as alfalfa and winter wheat and allow hamsters to be released on their lands. It's a way to protect not just the hamsters, but also other small animals that thrive in a landscape of leafy fields.

Sounds like the bad beast on the block is up to some good after all.

According to an ancient Indian legend, the Raven turned one out of every ten bears white to remind people of a time when Earth was covered by snow and ice.

Secrets of the Spirit Bear

A rare animal creates a mysterious sight in the forest.

On a cold, rainy October night in the rain forest, a hulking white form with a ghostly glow appears in the distance. No, it's not the ghost of a black bear. It's a spirit bear, also called a Kermode bear, which is a black bear with white hair. Kermode bears live almost exclusively in one place: the Great Bear Rainforest along the coast of British Columbia, Canada. Researchers want to figure out why the bears with white coats have survived here. Fewer than 200 spirit bears call this area home.

WHITE COAT CLUES

For many animals, unusual white coloration can make it hard to survive since they may have trouble hiding from predators. But the Kermode bears' coloring may actually help them survive and give them an edge while catching salmon.

"A white bear blends into the background during the day and is more successful catching fish," explains biologist Thomas Reimchen. "There is an advantage to one bear in some conditions and to the other in different conditions."

TALE OF TWO ISLANDS

Canada's Gribbell Island has the highest concentration of Kermode bears, followed by neighboring Princess Royal Island. These isolated islands may be another key to the bears' survival since there's no competition from grizzly bears, and wolves are the only natural threat. The islands' trees provide shelters, and rivers are filled with salmon.

Even though spirit bears have flourished on these islands, new threats such as logging worry scientists and the members of the Native American Gitga'at First Nation, who have lived with and protected spirit bears for centuries. That's why researchers are working hard to understand the biology of the spirit bear. As they do, they can find the best ways to ensure its survival.

TOUGH CATS

COUGAR KITTENS WATCH MOM TO SURVIVE.

Snowy footprints wind through the trees in Wyoming's Teton Mountains. They are the paw prints of a mother mountain lion following the scent of an elk. Her seven-month-old kittens romp alongside her. They're supposed to be learning to hunt by watching their mom. Shh! Mom chirps at her kittens to tell them to hide, then she freezes. She crouches down, ready to pounce. Then, the skillful hunter takes down the elk in a cloud of snow, and just a few seconds later dinner is served for this feline family.

TRACKING CATS

How young cougars learn to hunt is one of the things cougar researchers like Mark Elbroch of Panthera, a conservation organization, are working to figure out. They're keeping track of the mother cougar—who they call F51—using the satellite signal from her electronic collar. When she gave birth to her kittens, Elbroch put expandable tracking collars on them, too.

RAISING THE FAMILY

As the kittens grew older and stronger, they learn how to search for food by following their mother, watching her select an animal to stalk, and observing how she caught her prey. They also learn that sometimes meal plans change quickly. Sometimes, wolves chase F51 and her kittens away from kills, and they also compete with coyotes, bears, wolves, and, in Wyoming, even other cougars for elk and mule deer.

Luckily F51 is able to provide plenty of food for her kittens. Her territory overlaps with another female's, and they are friendly with each other, often sharing food.

FINAL CHALLENGE

In the spring, one of the researchers watches a couple of one-year-old cougars with a fawn they don't quite know what to do with. Their mother likely injured the fawn so that her kittens could use it to practice hunting skills. These two are just beginning to figure out how to make a kill. Like these young cats, F51's kittens had watched their mom to learn survival skills. Elbroch's team spots one kitten, now on her own. The team is relieved to see her kill a ground squirrel by herself. Now they're hopeful that this tough young cat will survive.

5 COOL THINGS ABOUT KOALAS

A koala doesn't look like the kind of creature that keeps campers awake at night or dines on food that would give you a serious stomachache. There's a lot more to these living "teddy bears" than cotton-ball ears and a laid-back lifestyle. Check out five amazing things about these wild, loud, and lovable creatures from Australia.

1. Loudmouths

Imagine a burp so loud it brings you to your knees, followed by a snore that rattles the rafters. Combine them and you have the typical bellow of a koala. Why so noisy? Male koalas grunt with gusto to broadcast their whereabouts to distant females or to scare rivals.

2. Toxic Diet

Koalas eat one to two pounds (450 to 900 g) of eucalyptus leaves each day. The leaves are not only poisonous—they're also tough to digest and provide little nutrition. But koalas have a specially adapted digestive system that extracts every drop of energy from the leaves while neutralizing their toxins.

3. Mistaken Identity

The Europeans who first settled in Australia mistook these tree dwellers for a type of bear, and the name "koala bear" stuck. However, a koala is actually a marsupial—a type of mammal that protects and nurtures its tiny newborns in a pouch.

4. Feisty Guys

A koala may look like a stuffed animal, but you'd be sorry if you tried to cuddle a wild one. Their long, sharp claws—supremely adapted for climbing trees— are used as daggers when two male koalas argue over territory or a mate.

5. Awesome Moms

Born blind, hairless, and no bigger than a jelly bean, a baby koala, or joey, spends six months sleeping and drinking milk in its mother's pouch. Eventually, it will poke its head out to eat pap—a poopy soup from its mother that builds resistance to eucalyptus poison. When the joey leaves the pouch, the mama koala carries it on her back or belly as she climbs trees and teaches the tiny koala by example.

FOXES ON ICE

Clever arctic foxes survive snow, ice, and freezing cold temperatures.

Not far from the North Pole, an arctic fox trots across the endless sea ice on a winter walkabout. It's been days since her last meal, and the whipping wind is relentless. She digs a hollow in the snow, curls up her cat-size body, and wraps her tail across her body and face to stay warm. Her fur acts like a warm sleeping bag, keeping her snug as temperatures dip below zero degrees. But warm fur alone might not keep this fox alive during the polar winter. Other freeze-defying strategies make this animal a champion of the cold.

FINDING FOOD

Arctic foxes prefer to eat small rodents called lemmings, but when times are tough, they'll take what they can get. This may be scraps of a seal that a polar bear has killed, or crabs and algae stuck to the bottom of ice. Sometimes, they'll stash dead lemmings near their dens for leaner times.

LEMMING

KEEPING WARM

In the toughest temps, this female fox digs a snow den and hunkers down for up to two weeks. She can slow her heart rate and metabolism to avoid burning more energy—similar to hibernation but not as long lasting. The fox's short legs provide heat exchange between warm blood flowing down from the body and cold blood flowing up from the legs.

When the fox emerges, she listens for scurrying sounds under the snow. Quietly, she takes a few steps, and then dives into the snow. Her head emerges with a brown fur ball in her mouth. With the energy tank refilled, this arctic fox has a better chance of making it through the long, dark winter.

Bet you didn't know

8 fab facts about bats

1 Ghost bats may be named for their translucent **wings** and ghostlike color.

2 The pallid bat is immune to **scorpion venom.**

3 **Bat** hibernation caves are called **hibernacula.**

4 Some **bats** can **live** for **30 years.**

5 Certain bats can **eat** more than **500 mosquitoes** in an hour.

6 The Malaysian flying fox's **wingspan** stretches up to **6 feet.** (1.8m)

7 Chiropto-phobia is the **fear** of **bats.**

8 The **spotted bat's** ears are about one-**third** the length of its **body.**

WOLVERINE!

How to track a wild, mysterious super-predator

Wolverines are small but ferocious bearlike animals. They're so mysterious that scientists don't even know how many there are in the wild. But researchers like Gregg Treinish are working to help this wild species continue to survive.

"It's February and I'm on the top of a mountain in Montana, U.S.A., all alone. The snow-caked forest is silent. All of a sudden I spot a wolverine track. I start following his trail.

"Tracking a wolverine is like following a ghost through the forest. They're so fast—covering 20 miles (32 km) in a day—and stealthy that I've never seen one in the wild. But if I pay close attention to the trail this one left, I can learn a lot about him.

"The tracks are grouped side by side instead of one after the other, showing that the wolverine was bounding fast, hunting something. I see another set of wolverine tracks. Then two more, crossing each other. Something was going on here. Ahead, I spot a four-foot (1.2-m) hole in the snow. Dirt and blood are scattered around the edge. I peer in to see an elk leg—a tasty meal for the wolverine.

"I search the hole and find two wolverine hairs, which I place in a bag. Later, scientists will extract DNA from the hairs and that will help them discover how many wolverines live in this area, what they're eating, and how far they're traveling.

"As climate change warms the planet, wolverines' snowy habitat is disappearing. The clues I find will help scientists track the population to learn whether we need to take action to prevent these phantoms of the forest from disappearing forever."

Wolverines are highly intelligent. People have reported seeing them climb trees, wait, and then pounce on deer that walk by.

A WOLVERINE CHOWS DOWN ON A LARGE ANIMAL'S LEG BONE.

41

FREAKY frogs!

Over 6,000 species of frogs hop, burrow, climb, swim, and even soar in exotic ecosystems around the world—and your own neighborhood. Their sometimes startling adaptations make them remarkable survivalists. Here are some frogs whose freakish good looks and bizarre lifestyles will make you become a frog fan.

WARNING LABEL

From the top, the Oriental fire-bellied toad from Korea, China, and southeastern Russia appears to be a mild-mannered frog. If threatened, though, it flashes its brightly colored belly to warn predators, "Look but don't touch." Not only is it toxic, it's also covered with sharp warts.

An amphibian is a **frog, toad,** newt, **salamander,** or caecilian.

CLEARLY SEE-THROUGH

From Central and South America, glass frogs are translucent (kind of see-through, like fogged glass). This type of camouflage makes them appear nearly invisible or like a bump on a leaf. Some even have green bones to blend in and trick predators. If you flip over a glass frog, you can see its heart beating through its skin.

FROG-ZILLA!

At 7 pounds (3.2 kg) and with a sitting length of 12.5 inches (31.8 cm), the Goliath frog from Cameroon and Equatorial Guinea is bigger than a Chihuahua. The world's largest frog, it can leap ten times its body length, or about 10 feet (3 m) each hop. Its body and legs can stretch 29.5 inches (7.5 cm) long, a little longer than a tennis racket.

FLYING FROG

Why hop when you can fly? These amphibians, which live high up in the rain forest canopy in Indonesia, Malaysia, and Thailand, glide from tree to tree to escape predators or search for food. With its webbed feet and side skin flaps, this four-inch (10-cm)-long frog can glide up to 50 feet (15 m). That's like flying from the pitcher's mound to home plate on a Little League field.

Frogs live on **every** continent **except** Antarctica.

BIG GULP

Go ahead and yell, "Hey, bigmouth!" The Amazon horned frog won't be offended. That's because its mouth is 1.6 times wider than its entire body length. It eats anything it can fit inside that mega-mouth, including rodents, snakes, lizards, and even other frogs. And it swallows the prey whole. Sometimes its eyes are bigger than its stomach. Some Amazon horned frogs have attempted to eat prey that was larger than themselves.

KISS ME AND CROAK

A golden poison frog has enough poison on its skin to kill several men. This tiny toxic frog from Colombia doesn't make its own poison. It absorbs toxins from the insects that it eats. Unlike most frogs, it boldly rests out in the open for everyone to see. Its color warns enemies to leave it alone. Being armed with enough poison to drop half a football team means there's no need to hide.

BURPING UP BABY

The male Darwin's frog of Argentina and Chile gives "birth," but in his own weird way. After the female lays eggs, the male guards them for about 20 days. Then he swallows them, and the tadpoles grow and morph into frogs inside his throat pouch. After 50 to 60 days, Daddy belches up more than a dozen baby frogs. Yum!

THE BIGGEST SMALLEST DISCOVERY

In 2009, on the rain forest floor in Papua New Guinea, scientists discovered the planet's smallest frog species, known only by its scientific name, *Paedophryne amauensis*. How small is it? A couple of them could sit on a dime and still have room!

GOOFBALLS

THE WAY ARMADILLOS BEHAVE WILL CRACK YOU UP.

If you held a contest for the funniest animal on the planet, the prize would have to go to an armadillo. Get ready to LOL as NG shows off the silly side of armadillos.

Armadillos live mostly in Central and South America. Only the nine-banded armadillo lives in the United States.

An armadillo looks hilarious.

Armadillos look like a mixture of a huge roly-poly, a pig, and a medieval knight—with a bit of giant insect mixed in. But they're actually mammals, closely related to anteaters and sloths. They have long snouts and piglike ears, and their bodies are covered with protective bony plates that look like a knight's armor.

Armadillos are mostly nocturnal. They stay inside their burrows when it's hot and come out at dawn or dusk or at night to look for food.

They turn into balls.

Armadillos usually aren't fighters. When threatened, the three-banded armadillo protects itself by rolling into a ball. The result looks so much like a soccer ball that a three-banded armadillo named Fuleco was the mascot of the 2014 World Cup in Brazil.

They leap straight up when startled.

If something startles a nine-banded armadillo by touching it on the back, it responds by jumping straight up into the air, sometimes as high as four feet (1.2 m). It's a reflex that probably helps them get away from predators. (Or maybe it just makes the predators laugh so hard they forget to chase the armadillo.)

They're likely to get into traffic jams.

If you frighten an armadillo, it might run away to hide in the nearest burrow. But sometimes when one armadillo is trying to get into the burrow, another armadillo (or two!) is trying to get out. They get stuck!

Armadillos have been around for at least 65 million years.

They stick out their tongues to eat.

Armadillos use their long, sticky tongues to feel around in ant nests, slurping up lots of ants at a time. A nine-banded armadillo can eat thousands of ants at one meal. Ants may not be *your* favorite food, but don't make fun of an armadillo's snack— it might stick out that extra-long tongue at you!

TONGUE

A nine-banded armadillo uses its huge front claws to dig its burrow. It might have several burrows but uses only one for its babies. That burrow is up to 25 feet (7.6 m) long and can have several rooms and connecting tunnels.

ROOM

TUNNEL

BIG CATS

A young male jaguar

Not all wild cats are big cats, so what are big cats? To wildlife experts, they are the four living members of the genus *Panthera:* tigers, lions, leopards, and jaguars. They can all unleash a mighty roar and, as carnivores, they survive solely on the flesh of other animals. Thanks to powerful jaws; long, sharp claws; and daggerlike teeth, big cats are excellent hunters.

WHO'S WHO?

BIG CATS MAY HAVE a lot of features in common, but if you know what to look for, you'll be able to tell who's who in no time.

FUR

Most tigers are orange-colored with vertical black stripes on their bodies. This coloring helps the cats blend in with tall grasses as they sneak up on prey. These markings are like fingerprints: No two stripe patterns are alike.

TIGERS

JAGUARS

A jaguar's coat pattern looks similar to that of a leopard, as both have dark spots called rosettes. The difference? The rosettes on a jaguar's torso have irregularly shaped borders and at least one black dot in the center.

LEOPARDS

A leopard's yellow coat has dark spots called rosettes on its back and sides. In leopards, the rosettes' edges are smooth and circular. This color combo helps leopards blend into their surroundings.

LIONS

Lions have a light brown, or tawny, coat and a tuft of black hair at the end of their tails. When they reach their prime, most male lions have shaggy manes that help them look larger and more intimidating.

JAGUAR
100 to 250 pounds
(45 TO 113 KG)

5 to 6 feet long
(1.5 TO 1.8 M)

LEOPARD
66 to 176 pounds
(30 TO 80 KG)

4.25 to 6.25 feet long
(1.3 TO 1.9 M)

BENGAL TIGER
240 to 500 pounds
(109 TO 227 KG)

5 to 6 feet long
(1.5 TO 1.8 M)

AFRICAN LION
265 to 420 pounds
(120 TO 191 KG)

4.5 to 6.5 feet long
(1.4 TO 2 M)

47

NATIONAL GEOGRAPHIC KiDS

MISSION ANIMAL RESCUE

Save ANIMALS >>
Save the WORLD

LION

Caged and neglected, an orphaned cub gets a second chance.

The female lion cub cowers in the corner of a cramped cage in a village in Ethiopia, Africa. People are paying money to see her up close, and she's hissing and snarling out of fear. While visiting the village, American humanitarian aid worker Jane Strachan hears rumors about the cub. When she catches sight of the terrified animal huddled on the dirt floor, Strachan becomes very worried. There's a chain circling the cub's neck, held by a padlock, and no one can find the key. One day the leash will interfere with her breathing. "If she stays here, she'll die," Strachan says.

SAVING THE LION

Rushing back to Ethiopia's capital, Addis Ababa, Strachan contacts the Born Free wildlife rescue team and tells them about the captive lioness. Soon after, a rescue worker and a federal wildlife officer confront the feline's keepers, informing them that it's illegal to house a lion. The keepers hand over the cub, and the worker places her in a pet carrier, then drives her to his rescue center.

Caretakers name the cub Safia and perform a checkup. They're concerned that the cub hasn't received enough calcium. "It's likely that Safia's mom was killed by hunters before the cub was done nursing, so she didn't get all the nutrients she needed," says Stephen Brend, who runs the center. Otherwise the 60-pound (27-kg) seven-month-old seems healthy.

CAGED CUB

LET FREEDOM ROAR

Since Safia never learned survival skills from her mom, she can't be released back into the wild. But her new home at the center will be a grassy area with bushes and trees, similar to a lion's natural habitat. When Safia is placed in her enclosure, she cautiously explores, diving for cover at every little noise. Soon, she gets playful, chasing birds and batting a plastic ball. Gobbling up two meat meals a day with calcium supplements helps Safia gain strength.

After nearly a year and a half, the now 275-pound (125-kg) Safia is released into another, permanent home. Safia meets Dolo, her big cat "roommate." Soon the two are close friends and spend their days playing and lounging together. And when Dolo lets out a mighty roar, Safia joins in. "Safia's finally happy in the way she deserves," Strachan says.

The largest population of wild lions is in Tanzania, Africa.

PLAY BALL!

Lions spend about 20 hours a day resting.

THE LION QUEEN

Male lions live 10 to 12 years. Females can live up to 16 years.

NATIONAL GEOGRAPHIC KIDS
MISSION: LION RESCUE

ALL ABOUT LIONS AND HOW TO SAVE THEM

SAVE ANIMALS, SAVE THE WORLD!

National Geographic Kids has a new initiative called **Mission: Animal Rescue** to show kids how to save lions and other threatened animals. Try out these activities to help the majestic lion.

Create a photo album of pet cats and lions from a local zoo. Share the album with friends to teach them about lions.

Find celebs with pet cats. Write a letter asking them to join the effort to help save their pets' big-cat relatives.

Get more lion rescue activities in the National Geographic Kids book *Mission: Lion Rescue.* To make a contribution in support of the mission initiative, grab a parent and go online. kids.nationalgeographic.com/mission-animal-rescue/

CHEETAHS: Built for SPEED

This wild cat's body makes it an incredible predator.

Breathing deeply, the cheetah prepares her body for the chase. Head low, eyes focused on an impala, she slowly inches forward. In three seconds this streamlined, superfast cat is sprinting at 60 miles an hour (96 km/h), eyes locked, laserlike, on the fleeing impala.

Most other cats can retract their claws when they're not using them. Cheetahs' claws stick out all the time, like dogs' claws. Cheetahs use these strong, blunt claws like an athlete uses cleats on track shoes—to help push off and quickly build up speed. The large center pad on the cheetah's foot is covered with long ridges that act like the treads on a car tire. A sprinting cheetah needs to be able to stop fast, too. It is able to spread its toes wide, and its toe pads are hard and pointed. This helps a cheetah turn

Long, muscular tail for balance in tight turns

Strong, blunt claws and ridged footpads to grip the ground

The legendary Jamaican runner Usain Bolt is the world's fastest human. Bolt ran 200 meters in 19.19 seconds, about 23 miles an hour (37 km/h), but that's slow compared with the cheetah. Cheetahs can run about three times faster than Bolt. At top speed a sprinting cheetah can reach 70 miles an hour (113 km/h). Next time you're in a car on the highway, imagine a cheetah racing alongside you. That will give you an idea of how fast this speedy cat can run.

Several adaptations help cheetahs run so fast. A cheetah has longer legs than other cats. It also has a

quickly and brake suddenly. It can stop in a single stride from a speed of more than 20 miles an hour (32 km/h).

All of these body adaptations add up to extraordinary hunting abilities. A cheetah stalks up close to a herd of impalas, then streaks forward with lightning speed. As the herd bolts, the cat singles out one individual and follows its twists and turns precisely. As it closes in on its prey the cheetah strikes out with a forepaw, knocks the animal off its feet, and clamps its jaws over the prey's throat.

Small, short face with enlarged nostrils to take in lots of air

long, extremely flexible spine. These features work together so a running cheetah can cover up to 23 feet (7 m) in one stride—about the length of five ten-year-olds lying head to feet in a row.

Snow Leopard SECRETS

High-tech tools help scientists understand how to save these big cats.

On a cool summer night, a snow leopard curiously sniffs an overhanging boulder for a strong scent sprayed by other cats. He rubs his cheeks on the boulder, scrapes the ground with his hind paws, and then urinates.

This act—called scraping—is how snow leopards communicate with one another. A scrape tells other snow leopards what they're doing and may reveal whether a snow leopard is male or female, has cubs, or is looking for a mate.

Recently, researchers studying the 4,000 to 6,500 snow leopards in the wild have set up motion-activated cameras at scraping sites in an effort to gather more information on these elusive cats and expose new details about how many snow leopards there are, how long they live, and how we can protect them.

Even though snow leopards live in some of the most rugged mountain terrain on Earth, people pose the biggest threat to their survival. Poachers can sell a snow leopard's hide and bones for thousands of dollars. Herders often kill any snow leopard that attacks their livestock. Hunters target ibex, wild sheep, and other animals for food and trophies— removing important snow leopard prey.

Like a snow leopard reality show, the cameras expose everything that happens. The images also help researchers count the number of snow leopards in an area and reveal whether prey animals, livestock, or poachers are nearby.

Other researchers will gently trap the wild cats and put satellite radio collars on them to track where the cats roam and to learn new things about how and where they live. Technology like this is essential to help researchers protect snow leopards in the wild and preserve their habitat.

Despite their name, snow leopards are not snow-colored. Their spotted gray or beige fur actually stands out against a snowy background—but blends in with rocks.

MARKING TERRITORY

TWO CUBS

CHASING DOWN PREY

SEA TURTLE

A lost and freezing loggerhead gets help from warmhearted volunteers.

The freezing sea turtle can barely manage another stroke as she struggles to keep herself warm in the frigid waters of Cape Cod Bay off Massachusetts, U.S.A. The reptile is suffering from the turtle version of human hypothermia—when body temperature falls below normal levels. Her strength is fading fast.

She bobs lifelessly on the surface of the water before a gust of wind propels her toward land. Washed up on the shore of Crosby Landing Beach, she lies motionless in the sand, bitterly cold. If she doesn't get help soon, she won't have a chance.

LIFEGUARDS ARRIVE

Taking a morning stroll along the beach, Brian Long spots the large turtle. He can't tell if she's alive, so he immediately phones the Massachusetts Audubon Society, a conservation organization. The call reaches director Bob Prescott, who rushes to the beach in a pickup truck and identifies the two-and-a-half-foot (0.76-m)-long creature as a loggerhead sea turtle. An endangered species, they spend their summers in the north and their winters in warmer southern waters, but this turtle likely got lost while navigating down the coast and missed the chance to migrate before cold weather set in. The animal's eyes are closed, and she's not visibly breathing. But when

Some Pacific loggerheads migrate over 7,500 miles (12,000 km) between nesting beaches.

A cooler loggerhead nest will produce more male hatchlings, while a warmer one will produce more females.

THE WEAK TURTLE ARRIVES AT THE REHAB CENTER.

Prescott gently touches her neck, the big-beaked reptile slowly raises her head. She's hanging on but urgently needs medical care. The two men hoist the huge animal onto the bed of the truck, and she's taken to New England Aquarium in Boston, Massachusetts. Here, she can begin her recovery.

SHELL-SHOCKED

At the aquarium's marine animal rehabilitation center, staff name the turtle Biscuits and give her an exam. She weighs in at 165 pounds (75 kg) —slightly underweight for a loggerhead of Biscuits's age. She has developed open wounds, she's dehydrated, and she has pneumonia. She is also cold-stunned, a condition that affects reptiles if their temperatures drop too low. As their bodies cool, the animals' blood circulation slows, causing the animals to enter a coma-like state, practically unable to move.

Now her caretakers' goal is to raise her body temperature from an extremely low 48°F (9°C) to between 70°F and 80°F (21°C and 25°C). But it won't be easy—warming her too quickly could be deadly. She's moved into a temperature-controlled pool set to 55°F (13°C).

These turtles may live for 50 years or more in the wild.

GEORGIA SEA TURTLE CENTER STAFF UNLOAD BISCUITS FROM THE PLANE.

TURTLE TAKEOFF

Soon, Biscuits is ready for to be moved to the Georgia Sea Turtle Center on Jekyll Island, which is located closer to her release site. Here the staff will continue to prepare her for reentry into the wild. Along with three other recovering turtles, she's flown to Georgia, U.S.A., on a private jet. Once there, Biscuits is placed in a tank where she can continue practicing her swimming strokes. Caretakers also put live blue crabs and horseshoe crabs in her tank so she can get used to catching prey again. These critters are some of a loggerhead's favorite foods in the wild, and Biscuits quickly remembers how to snatch up the tasty treats in her beak.

CARETAKERS LIFT BISCUITS INTO HER POOL AT THE AQUARIUM'S REHAB CENTER.

BISCUITS RETURNS TO THE SEA.

Each day the rehabbers raise the thermostat a little higher. As the temperature rises, Biscuits begins to move normally again.

To help her regain energy, the staff offer healthy meals of fish and squid, and they rehydrate her with daily injections of nutrient-filled fluids. Biscuits also receives antibiotics for her pneumonia and soothing ointment for her skin.

BACK TO THE SEA

A month later Biscuits is ready to return to the ocean. She's heavier, now weighing 180 pounds (82 kg), and has proven she can catch live prey. She's driven by her rehabilitation team to a release site in Florida, U.S.A. When the team lowers her onto the sand at the water's edge, she immediately crawls into the crashing waves and swims off, healthy and happy at last.

Bottlenose dolphins live all over the world—near shore, far out to sea, and in warm water in both hemispheres.

Talking
Dolphin

Surprising new evidence suggests that each bottlenose dolphin creates its own name.

With a flick of its tail, a young bottlenose dolphin races through the ocean. The powerful dolphin easily cuts through water. At the surface, where it's sunny and clear, visibility is great—it's easy to see for miles. But deeper underwater, where the dolphin swims, visibility is down to a few feet. Yet the dolphin swiftly and easily zooms around boulders, dodges puffer fish, and avoids an enormous sea turtle without hesitation.

When it discovers a huge school of fish, the hungry dolphin whistles excitedly. In the distance a dolphin trills a reply. The two whistle back and forth, as the second dolphin rushes to locate its friend. Soon the two share a secret communication as they twist and turn in unison, eating, leaping, and gliding through the school with the perfect precision of ballet dancers.

Dolphins live in a dark, murky, underwater world. It's often impossible to see each other or anything else around them, so sound plays an essential role in their survival. To communicate with each other,

Bottlenose dolphins eat fish, squid, and shrimp.

A bottlenose dolphin is 8 to 12 feet (2.4 to 3.7 m) long.

dolphins produce a variety of whistles, squeaks, trills, and clicks.

Only other dolphins understand what the squeaks and squawks mean. Biologists haven't cracked their secret communication, except for one kind of whistle. It might last less than a second, but this whistle is a big deal. Why? Because these whistles are actually names of dolphins—and every bottlenose dolphin has one.

DOLPHIN RINGTONE

Think of a signature whistle as a special ringtone. When other dolphins hear it, they know which dolphin is calling or chattering. It's sort of a "Yo, it's Bob. I'm over here" kind of message. Other group members may reply with their own signature whistles, like a dolphin's version of Marco Polo.

Dolphins often hunt and explore solo, but they need to stay connected to the group. Their signature whistles allow them to check in with other dolphins who may be nearly five football fields away.

BABY NAMES

Many animal species have distinctive or shared calls. But a specific name for an individual is

A mother dolphin whistles repeatedly to her newborn for several days after it's born. Biologists believe that this enables the calf to learn to recognize her through sound.

rare. Only humans, some parrot species, and a few other kinds of dolphins are known to have names for individuals.

Scientists believe that the calf itself comes up with the signature whistle. Like human babies, a calf plays with sounds throughout its first year, and dolphins have their own version of baby babble. So, while testing its sound skills, a baby dolphin is actually figuring out its signature whistle—and it may be nothing like its mother's or a group member's whistles. By the time the calf is a year old, its signature whistle is set.

Deciphering dolphin names is just the beginning of figuring out what dolphins communicate about with all their trills and squeaks. Do they chat about sharks? Discuss the tides? Maybe they even have a name for people. Someday scientists hope to decipher the rest of the mysteries of dolphin communication.

Dolphin Dictionary

BEHAVIOR	RUBBING FINS AFTER BEING APART	S-SHAPED BODY POSTURE	APPROACH FROM BEHIND	TAIL-SLAPPING	TOUCHING FIN TO SIDE OF ANOTHER DOLPHIN
WHAT THE DOLPHIN IS SAYING	HELLO! I MISSED YOU.	WATCH OUT!	LET'S PLAY!	BACK OFF!	HEY, GIVE ME A HAND.
SIMILAR BEHAVIOR IN HUMANS	SHAKING HANDS	WAVING CLENCHED FIST IN THE AIR	STARTING A GAME OF TAG	HAND UP, SIGNALING "STOP, KEEP AWAY"	TAPPING SOMEONE ON THE SHOULDER

Parenting, PUFFIN Style

Tips for bringing up these little clowns of the sea

There comes a time, if you're a puffin, that **your beak changes** from dull gray to outrageous orange. **Your feet, too.** That means one thing—it's time to become a puffin parent. Here are **six pointers** for new puffin moms and dads.

① Touch Down Carefully

When you're ready to become a parent, return to the islands of the North Atlantic where you hatched years before. Remember, landing on rocks isn't like your usual soft watery splashdown. So don't fly in at your full speed of 55 miles an hour. (88 km/h).

② Show Your Affection

Sometime, maybe in the last year, you met that special someone. Each April you'll reunite. After racing toward each other, show your devotion by rubbing and tapping beaks. Other puffins will gather to enjoy this public display of affection.

3 **Develop a Routine**

Fly, dive, fly back, drop off fish. Repeat. Each day, you and your mate will make several trips to sea, easily diving 276 times. The usual catch is about ten fish per trip. By the time the chick is ready to leave the nest, each of you will have made 12,420 dives.

4 **Land and Run**

When returning from sea with a beak full of fish, don't forget to land close to the burrow, then race inside. Herring gulls would rather steal a quick meal from you than hunt for their own food.

"FLYING" THROUGH WATER

5 **Prepare for Lots of Fishing**

Congratulations! It's a *puffling!* This little fluffy ball of feathers needs you. It can't fly, swim, or hunt. To keep up with its ravenous appetite, it will take both you and your mate to bring it enough baby food: fish.

6 **Let Your Puffling Go**

You did it.—you raised a puffling. Now it must survive on its own, so you have to let it leave the nest. Plus it's time for you to return to life at sea. See you next year!

A MESSAGE TO PUFFLINGS:

You're 45 days old; it's time to leave Mom and Dad. You've got sturdy, smooth feathers now—perfect for flying or diving into the cold sea. To avoid predators hanging around the burrow, be sure to fly or swim away in the dark. In four to six years, you'll return and become a puffin parent, too.

Name That
TIDE POOL ANIMAL

When the tide goes out in rocky, coastal areas, some water gets left behind in pools and crevices. These spots are called tide pools and many different creatures like to hang out in them. See if you can name these tide pool animals.

A

This creature is always on the lookout for a new home. Snail shells are usually its preference, but with five pairs of legs, you can't call it a slowpoke!

A tide pool is one tough neighborhood! When the tide is in, waves come crashing; when the tide is out, animals are exposed to sun, cold weather, and even fresh water from rain. When you look closely at tide pool creatures you'll find they all have adaptations to survive these harsh conditions.

C

The webbing between this animal's short, triangular arms is a clue to its name. Sensors on the end of each of its arms can sense light and detect prey.

B

These drifters don't have much say about where they end up, but often they show up in tide pools. They may be soft and squishy, but their tentacles are stunning.

D

Nemo and his father lived inside one of these. When their tentacles are open they are ready for food; when they're folded in, they're likely munching.

E

After grazing on algae, this tide pool creature finds the perfect parking spot on a rock and hunkers down, sealing water underneath itself to keep its body moist during low tide.

F

Call it a tide pool salad. This leafy green creature can get dry and stiff at low tide, but it bounces right back once the water comes in.

Awesome
INSECT AWARDS

We're buggin' out! Our earth is crawling with over 800,000 species of insects. And whether they're teeny-tiny or superstrong, some of those six-legged species certainly stand out. Here are seven of the biggest, baddest, ickiest bugs out there!

Heavy Lifter

Sharp Shooter

The *rhinoceros beetle*, which gets its name from the hornlike structure on the male's head, is capable of carrying up to 850 times its own body weight.

If you spot a *bombardier beetle*, look out! When threatened, the bug shoots stinky, boiling-hot liquid out of its rear end at a distance up to eight inches (20 cm).

Is it a bird? A bat? No, it's the *Atlas moth*, who has a wingspan wider than a dinner plate—the largest moth wings on the planet.

Biggest Wings

They don't call it a *fly* for nothing! By beating its wings at over 200 times a second, a fly can pick up speeds faster than you can walk.

Fast Flier

Sharpest Defense

Coolest Camo

It's common to mistake the *walking leaf* for an actual leaf, thanks to its large, feathery wings. This clever camouflage provides protection from potential predators.

When clustered with others on a branch, a tiny *thorn bug* becomes part of a prickly pack no bird wants a bite of!

Colossal Crawler

The *Goliath beetle* weighs about as much as a quarter-pounder hamburger, making it one of the heaviest bugs on earth.

Monarchs Hit the Road!

Why did the monarch cross the road? To boost its population! At least that's what the U.S. Fish and Wildlife Service is hoping to do by creating a "Butterfly Highway" along U.S. Interstate 35, which runs between Texas and Minnesota.

Due to loss of habitat and food from herbicides that kill milkweed, the monarchs' numbers in North America have dramatically dwindled from 1 billion to about 100 million. But experts believe that they can bolster the butterfly's numbers to 225 million by 2020 by helping them out along their epic 2,000-mile (3,219-km) migration each September and October from Canada and the northern United States to Mexico. Because I-35 follows the same route as the migration, researchers hope that lining the road with milkweed

To stay warm, thousands of monarchs gather together to "roost" on trees.

Monarchs can't fly if their body temperature is less than 86°F (30°C).

will provide a much-needed food source for the winged insects.

Plans for the Butterfly Highway are underway, and experts hope that the effort will extend beyond the interstate. People living within 100 miles (161 km) of I-35 are encouraged to plant milkweed and flowering plants in their yards so the butterflies can refuel during their migration. Simple steps like these will ensure that the majestic monarchs will be protected wherever they roam.

One monarch traveled 265 miles (427 km) in one day during migration.

MILKWEED'S MAGIC

Why is milkweed so important for monarchs? Not only does the plant keep them fueled for their epic migration, but it also serves as a host for the butterfly's eggs. Once they hatch, the caterpillars chomp on milkweed leaves, and toxins in the plant make the species foul-tasting and poisonous to predators. Simply put, without milkweed, there would be no monarchs.

Prehistoric
TIME LINE

HUMANS HAVE WALKED on Earth for some 200,000 years, a mere blip in Earth's 4.5-billion-year history. A lot has happened during that time. Earth formed, and oxygen levels rose in the millions of years of the Precambrian time. The productive Paleozoic era gave rise to hard-shelled organisms, vertebrates, amphibians, and reptiles.

Dinosaurs ruled the Earth in the mighty Mesozoic. And 64 million years after dinosaurs became extinct, modern humans emerged in the Cenozoic era. From the first tiny mollusks to the dinosaur giants of the Jurassic and beyond, Earth has seen a lot of transformation.

THE PRECAMBRIAN TIME

4.5 billion to 542 million years ago
- The Earth (and other planets) formed from gas and dust left over from a giant cloud that collapsed to form the sun. The giant cloud's collapse was triggered when nearby stars exploded.
- Low levels of oxygen made Earth a suffocating place.
- Early life-forms appeared.

THE PALEOZOIC ERA

542 million to 251 million years ago
- The first insects and other animals appeared on land.
- 450 million years ago (m.y.a.), the ancestors of sharks began to swim in the oceans.
- 430 m.y.a., plants began to take root on land.
- More than 360 m.y.a., amphibians emerged from the water.
- Slowly the major landmasses began to come together, creating Pangaea, a single supercontinent.
- By 300 m.y.a., reptiles had begun to dominate the land.

What Killed the Dinosaurs?

It's a mystery that's boggled the minds of scientists for centuries: What happened to the dinosaurs? While various theories have bounced around, a new study confirms that the most likely culprit is an asteroid or comet that created a giant crater. Researchers say that the impact set off a series of natural disasters like tsunamis, earthquakes, and temperature swings that plagued the dinosaurs' ecosystem and disrupted their food chain. This, paired with intense volcano eruptions that caused drastic climate changes, is thought to be why half of the world's species—including the dinosaurs—died in a mass extinction.

DINO TIMES

THE MESOZOIC ERA

251 million to 65 million years ago
The Mesozoic era, or the age of the reptiles, consisted of three consecutive time periods (shown below). This is when the first dinosaurs began to appear. They would reign supreme for more than 150 million years.

TRIASSIC PERIOD

251 million to 199 million years ago
- Appearance of the first mammals. They were rodent-size.
- The first dinosaur appeared.
- Ferns were the dominant plants on land.
- The giant supercontinent of Pangaea began breaking up toward the end of the Triassic.

JURASSIC PERIOD

199 million to 145 million years ago
- Giant dinosaurs dominated the land.
- Pangaea continued its breakup, and oceans formed in the spaces between the drifting landmasses, allowing sea life, including sharks and marine crocodiles, to thrive.
- Conifer trees spread across the land.

CRETACEOUS PERIOD

145 million to 65 million years ago
- The modern continents developed.
- The largest dinosaurs developed.
- Flowering plants spread across the landscape.
- Mammals flourished, and giant pterosaurs ruled the skies over the small birds.
- Temperatures grew more extreme. Dinosaurs lived in deserts, swamps, and forests from the Antarctic to the Arctic.

THE CENOZOIC ERA—TERTIARY PERIOD

65 million to 2.6 million years ago
- Following the dinosaur extinction, mammals rose as the dominant species.
- Birds continued to flourish.
- Volcanic activity was widespread.
- Temperatures began to cool, eventually ending in an ice age.
- The period ended with land bridges forming, which allowed plants and animals to spread to new areas.

DINO Classification

Classifying dinosaurs and all other living things can be a complicated matter, so scientists have devised a system to help with the process. Dinosaurs are put into groups based on a very large range of characteristics.

Scientists put dinosaurs into two major groups: the bird-hipped ornithischians and the reptile-hipped saurischians.

Ornithischian

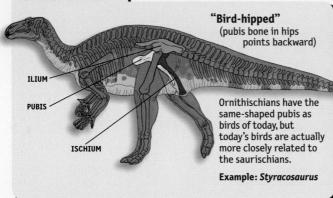

"Bird-hipped"
(pubis bone in hips points backward)

ILIUM
PUBIS
ISCHIUM

Ornithischians have the same-shaped pubis as birds of today, but today's birds are actually more closely related to the saurischians.

Example: Styracosaurus

Saurischian

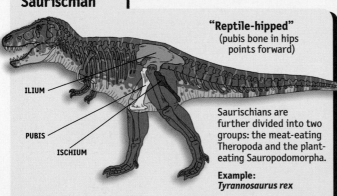

"Reptile-hipped"
(pubis bone in hips points forward)

ILIUM
PUBIS
ISCHIUM

Saurischians are further divided into two groups: the meat-eating Theropoda and the plant-eating Sauropodomorpha.

Example:
Tyrannosaurus rex

Within these two main divisions, dinosaurs are then separated into orders and then families, such as Stegosauria. Like other members of the Stegosauria, *Stegosaurus* had spines and plates along the back, neck, and tail.

Who Ate What?

Herbivores
- Primarily plant-eaters
- Weighed up to 100 tons (91 t)—the largest animals ever to walk on Earth
- Up to 1,000 blunt or flat teeth to grind vegetation
- Many had cheek pouches to store food.
- Examples: *Styracosaurus, Mamenchisaurus*

Carnivores
- Meat-eaters
- Long, strong legs to run faster than plant-eaters; ran up to 30 miles an hour (48 km/h)
- Most had good eyesight, strong jaws, and sharp teeth.
- Scavengers and hunters; often hunted in packs
- Grew to 45 feet (14 m) long
- Examples: *Velociraptor, Gigantoraptor, Tyrannosaurus rex*

4 NEWLY DISCOVERED DINOS

Humans have been searching for—and discovering—dinosaur remains for hundreds of years. In that time, at least 1,000 species of dinos have been found all over the world, and thousands more may still be out there waiting to be unearthed. Recent discoveries include the *Dreadnoughtus schrani*. Found in Argentina, it is one of the world's largest dinosaurs. For more exciting dino discoveries, read on.

3 *Regaliceratops peterhewsi*
(Ornithischian)

Royal horned face, geologist Peter Hews

Length: 16 feet (5 m)

Time Range: Late Cretaceous

Where: Alberta, Canada

1 *Chilesaurus diegosuarezi*
(Ornithischian)

Chile dinosaur and Diego Suárez, the 7-year-old who helped discover it

Length: 9.8 feet (3 m)

Time Range: Late Jurassic

Where: Chile

2 *Qijianglong guokr*
(Saurischian)

Dragon of Qijiang

Length: 50 feet (15 m)

Time Range: Late Jurassic

Where: China

4 *Yi qi*
(Saurischian)

Strange wing

Length: 2.1 feet (63 cm)

Time Range: Late Jurassic

Where: China

DINOSAUR FAMILY TREE

Experts believe the first dinosaurs to roam the planet some 230 million years ago were dog-size carnivores with reptilian traits. Eventually, those early dinosaurs changed enough to be divided into two groups based on the design of their hip bones: Ornithischia (bird-hipped) and Saurischia (reptile-hipped). Over time, these groups continued to branch out, and, as Earth's environment shifted, the size and shape of dinosaurs did, too.

ANKYLOSAURS
As big as a tank, slow-moving with short front legs.
PLANT

SMALL & LARGE CERATOPSIANS
Covered in bony plates with a birdlike beak.
PLANT

STEGOSAURS
Armored herbivore with bony plates along its spine and a powerful spiked tail.
PLANT

PACHYCEPHALOSAURS
Dome-headed, thick-skulled plant-eaters that lived in packs.
PLANT

ORNITHISCHIA (Bird-Hipped Dinosaurs)

EARLY DINOSAURS
Dog-sized, two-legged meat-eaters.
MEAT

DINOSAURIA

SAUROPODS
Large four-legged plant-eaters with small head, and a long neck and tail.
PLANT

CERATOSAURIANS
These "horned lizards" had sharp teeth and claws.
MEAT

PROSAUROPODS
The biggest plant-eaters of their time; walked on two legs.
PLANT

SAURISCHIA (Reptile-Hipped Dinosaurs)

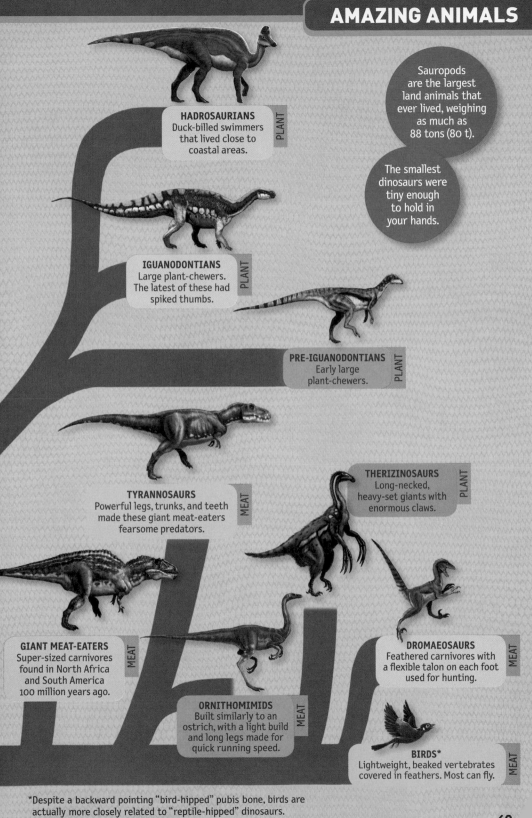

HADROSAURIANS
Duck-billed swimmers that lived close to coastal areas.

PLANT

Sauropods are the largest land animals that ever lived, weighing as much as 88 tons (80 t).

The smallest dinosaurs were tiny enough to hold in your hands.

IGUANODONTIANS
Large plant-chewers. The latest of these had spiked thumbs.

PLANT

PRE-IGUANODONTIANS
Early large plant-chewers.

PLANT

TYRANNOSAURS
Powerful legs, trunks, and teeth made these giant meat-eaters fearsome predators.

MEAT

THERIZINOSAURS
Long-necked, heavy-set giants with enormous claws.

PLANT

GIANT MEAT-EATERS
Super-sized carnivores found in North Africa and South America 100 million years ago.

MEAT

DROMAEOSAURS
Feathered carnivores with a flexible talon on each foot used for hunting.

MEAT

ORNITHOMIMIDS
Built similarly to an ostrich, with a light build and long legs made for quick running speed.

MEAT

BIRDS*
Lightweight, beaked vertebrates covered in feathers. Most can fly.

MEAT

*Despite a backward pointing "bird-hipped" pubis bone, birds are actually more closely related to "reptile-hipped" dinosaurs.

1

A fossil IS THE REMAINS OF AN ANCIENT ANIMAL OR PLANT THAT HAS BEEN PRESERVED.

2
FOSSILS SHOW THAT EEL-LIKE HAGFISH HAVE BEEN LIVING ON EARTH FOR 330 MILLION YEARS.

4
HORSESHOE CRABS, which are living fossils, are not crabs at all. They're actually in the spider family.

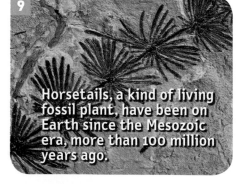

3
A LIVING FOSSIL is an animal or plant that hasn't changed much from its prehistoric ancestors.

5
Amber, FOSSILIZED TREE RESIN FROM AS LONG AS 70 MILLION YEARS AGO, SOMETIMES CONTAINS INSECTS THAT WERE TRAPPED IN THE STICKY STUFF.

17 AGE-OLD FACTS ABOUT

6
The skull of a 246-million-year-old marine animal called a placodont was discovered in the Netherlands in 2013.

7

Australia's famous koalas are living fossils that have been around for at least 20 million years.

8

AARDVARKS have an ancient arrangement of chromosomes—the material in cells that determines what an animal looks like—that make this **ONE-OF-A-KIND** animal a living fossil.

9

Horsetails, a kind of living fossil plant, have been on Earth since the Mesozoic era, more than 100 million years ago.

10 A population of living fossils, eight-inch (20-cm)-long fluorescent pink slugs, has been isolated for millions of years atop Mount Kaputor in Australia.

11 THE PURPLE FROG, A LIVING FOSSIL FOUND IN INDIA, HAS BEEN DESCRIBED AS LOOKING LIKE A "BLOATED DOUGH-NUT." IT EVOLVED FROM A CREATURE THAT LIVED ABOUT 130 MILLION YEARS AGO.

12 A fossil of an **elephant bird egg** sold at auction for over $100,000. It's so large, 120 chicken eggs could fit inside it.

13 Most of America's 50 states have an official state fossil. Alaska, Nebraska, and Washington gave this honor to the **MAMMOTH.**

14 The first discovery of **fossilized tree stumps** in the United States was made in 1850 by an amateur naturalist in the town of Gilboa, New York.

FOSSILS

15 **BODY FOSSILS** contain the remains of creatures that were once alive. Trace fossils are signs of prehistoric creatures, like footprints.

16 ONE OF THE MOST BEAUTIFUL SEASHELLS IS HOME TO A KIND OF CEPHALOPOD CALLED A NAUTILUS. THIS LIVING FOSSIL HAS BEEN AROUND FOR AT LEAST **500 million years.**

17 THE BIGGEST FOSSIL OF A SPIDER— MEASURING ONE INCH (2.5 CM) IN LENGTH—WAS FOUND IN CHINA AND IS 165 MILLION YEARS OLD.

HoW TO
SPEAk
CaT

COME ON, LET'S PLAY!

CHECK OUT THE BOOK!

HoW TO SPEAk CaT
A GUIDE TO DECODING CAT LANGUAGE

Cats are on a roll. All around the globe, kitties now rank as the most popular pet. And no wonder: Everyone feels good when a friendly cat purrs, rubs against their legs, or snuggles in their lap.

But let's get one thing straight. Cats are not dogs! They look, act, and (we're pretty sure) think differently. Dogs depend on us to take care of them; cats maintain a lot of their wildness.

Because they're so independent, cats hide their feelings. Unless you know exactly what to look for, a happy cat and a miserable one can look very much the same. But cats do communicate. Check out how to read your cat's moods by recognizing five ways it "talks" to you.

AAH. THIS IS THE LIFE.

THE PLAYFUL KITTEN

Kittens are always in the mood for fun. They spend almost every waking minute playing. They love to run and chase, pounce and wrestle, attack and retreat. At about seven weeks old, kittens learn the signs for inviting each other to play. Watch for a kitten with a relaxed, content look. That's its play face. Rolling onto its back or standing up on its hind legs are also signs that a cat's ready for fun. Holding its tail like a question mark and hopping sideways might be other ways of telling a playmate to let the games begin!

HAPPY CAT

You can tell a happy cat by its relaxed body, half-perked ears, and droopy whiskers. He'll greet you with a chipper "Hi, there" meow and a straight-up tail. Then he'll jump on your lap, purr loudly, and move his body under your hand. Keep your cat happy by petting him—just where he likes it.

Some of the best cat toys are free: a crumpled-up newspaper or a paper bag.

All cats, no matter the breed, are born with blue eyes. Their true color appears at about 12 weeks.

CAT ON THE HUNT

Shh! This cat is after something. You can tell by his intense stare, twitching tail, and forward-pointing ears and whiskers. All his senses are alert as he crouches low to the ground and pads silently toward his prey. Hunting is difficult, dangerous work. Humans have long admired cats for their courage and predatory skills. Without cats, early Egyptians would have lost much of their food supply to rats. So would sailors, who took the little rodent killers with them to sea, spreading the animals around the world. Your cat can hunt pesky houseflies or other insects that sneak into your home—keeping both you and your cat happy.

Cats hunt what they can get: rats in New York City, lizards in Georgia, U.S.A., and baby turtles on Africa's Seychelles islands.

HEH, HEH. HE CAN'T HEAR ME COMING.

THE FRUSTRATED FELINE

A frustrated cat will have wide eyes and forward, pricked ears. It'll bat its paws, its teeth might chatter, and it may slowly thrash its tail. Like humans, cats get frustrated when they don't get what they expect. For instance, an indoor cat stares out the window at a bird, but she can't reach the prey outside. The longer the cat sits and watches, the greater her frustration, until she's ready to attack someone.

A cat can get frustrated often. But if you know the signs, you can turn your irritated cat into a contented kitty. When she's annoyed that she can't get to a bird, distract your feline by playing with a fishing-pole toy. Let your kitty catch the "mouse" at the end, and that bird will soon be forgotten.

The word for "cat" is *mio* in Chinese, *gatto* in Italian, *poes* in Dutch, and *kedi* in Turkish.

I'D RATHER BE HUNTING.

CAUGHT ON CAMERA

ONCE I SCALE THIS TREE, WALKING ON THE CEILING SHOULD BE EASY.

IF YOU DON'T LIKE DOGGY DROOL, YOU MIGHT WANT TO SLEEP ON THE COUCH.

NAME Smoochiepoo

FAVORITE ACTIVITY
Washing the sheets with his slobber

FAVORITE TOY
Chewy pillows

PET PEEVE
Alarm clocks

NAME Master Meow

FAVORITE ACTIVITY
Competing in the Extreme Cat Olympics

FAVORITE TOY
Half-pipe litter box

PET PEEVE Gravity

THE PILLOW STARTED IT.

NAME Weasley

FAVORITE ACTIVITY
Pillow fights with imaginary pooch pals

FAVORITE TOY
A blanket—it's for playing tug-of-war, right?

PET PEEVE
Time-outs in his crate

REAL ANIMAL HEROES!

THESE ANIMALS SHOW AMAZING BRAVERY.

DOG SAVES KID FROM TRUCK

Geo the German shepherd mix follows ten-year-old Charlie Riley everywhere. Naturally the pup goes along on family walks.

One day Charlie, his mom, and two younger brothers are standing at a street corner. Geo is sitting at Charlie's side. Suddenly ...

"We hear a roar," Charlie's mother says. An out-of-control pickup jumps the curb. It's heading straight for Charlie!

But Geo makes a flying leap. "He hits me so hard I fall over," Charlie says. The speeding truck slams into Geo instead. They rush an injured Geo to the animal hospital for emergency surgery.

"My dog could have died," Charlie says. *And my son could have too,* thinks his mother. But he didn't—thanks to Geo.

CAT DETECTS LOW BLOOD SUGAR

Patricia Peter is asleep when her cat, Monty, bites her hand. "It's the hand I poke to test my blood sugar level," she says. Peter has diabetes, a serious disease that requires frequent blood testing. Peter pushes the cat away, but Monty bites harder. Peter gets up and Monty leads her to the kitchen, then jumps on the counter beside Peter's testing kit.

Peter tests, and her sugar level is dangerously low. She pops some sugar pills, and her level returns to normal. According to Peter's doctor, Monty knew something was wrong by smelling her breath and tasting her skin. "He's my guardian angel," Peter says.

PUP DETECTS SEIZURES

Zoe the pit bull mix is Gretchen Jett's best gift ever. Born deaf, the 11-year-old girl from Nevada, U.S.A., also has epilepsy, a brain disease that causes seizures. Because of this, she usually has to play indoors. So her dad gets a dog to keep his daughter company.

Just two nights later, Zoe bursts into Gretchen's parents' room. "I get up, thinking she needs to go outside," Gretchen's dad says. "Instead, Zoe runs in a circle and bolts straight into Gretchen's room. She's suffering a bad seizure." Circling and running becomes Zoe's signal. "When she does that we know something is wrong with Gretchen," her dad says. Zoe knows that Gretchen needs her.

Lifestyles of the RICH and FURRY

OUTRAGEOUS WAYS TO PAMPER YOUR PET

From canine country clubs to tabby tiaras, pets today are living in the lap of luxury. In 2014, pet owners spent about $58 billion—almost twice what they spent in 2002—on supplies and services to pamper their pets. "Pets improve our lives," says Bob Vetere of the American Pet Products Association. "So we want to improve theirs." *NG Kids* tracks just how far some owners go to give their pets the royal treatment.

WHAT TO WEAR

When Selena Gomez and Amanda Seyfried need fashion for their dogs, they don't have to look far. That's because many stores now cater exclusively to the pampered pet. At Fifi & Romeo (left) in Los Angeles, California, dogs in handmade cashmere sweaters and colorful raincoats are considered fashionable, not funny-looking, and are sure to please the most finicky pooch.

Will your pet be less happy if you don't shower it with expensive stuff?

Absolutely not! "As long as your pet has food, comfort, and friendship, that's what's most important," says pet psychologist John C. Wright.

IN THE HOUSE

Skeeter the cairn terrier hangs out in a two-story doghouse with floor-to-ceiling windows, and heated floors. It's just one of many custom-made cribs owners are building for their pets. "One owner asked for a cat house with a separate dining room, litter box room, and bedroom," says Michelle Pollak of La Petite Maison, which builds luxury pet homes (above). "Some pet owners spare nothing to make sure their pets are comfortable and happy."

KENNEL—OR VACATION?

Sampson the Yorkshire terrier loves a good massage. His sister, Delilah, likes to get her toenails painted. They can do it all at the Olde Towne Pet Resort in Virginia, U.S.A. (below), one of many "pet spas" around the country that act more like luxury hotels than kennels.

CHOW TIME

Plain old dog chow just won't do for canines like Clementine the beagle. Gourmet pet food has become all the rage. Places like Three Dog Bakery offer biscuits made of carob chips, apples, oatmeal, and peanut butter, and cats munch on Alaskan salmon bites.

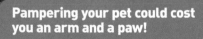

Pampering your pet could cost you an arm and a paw!

LUXURY SUITE AT PET SPA	**$110** A NIGHT
PROFESSIONAL MASSAGE	**$35**
CUSTOM-BUILT DOGHOUSE	**$10,000**
HAND-KNITTED SWEATER	**$280**
GOURMET DOG TREATS	**$6.99**

PET TECH

Think you're tech-savvy? With all the gadgets owners are buying for their pets, some animals may have you beat. Some owners set up webcams so their pets can watch them at work. And Petzila, a company dedicated to connecting pets with their owners, offers a device that allows away-from-home owners to see, talk to, and surprise a pet with a treat—all through Wi-Fi and the click of an app.

QUIZ WHIZ

How much do you know about all things animals? Quiz yourself!

ANSWERS BELOW

① **True or false?** Male seahorses carry eggs in a kangaroo-like pouch.

② **Which of the following is not an invertebrate?**
a. sponge
b. worm
c. echinoderm
d. Minion

③ **Bat hibernation caves are called _____.**
a. dens
b. grottoes
c. labyrinths
d. hibernacula

④ **What name do Kermode bears also go by?**
a. Kermit the Frog bears
b. brown bears
c. spirit bears
d. white bears

⑤ **Koalas eat one to two pounds (450 to 900 g) of_____ in a day.**
a. eucalyptus leaves
b. bamboo
c. grass
d. potato chips

Not **STUMPED** yet? Check out the *NATIONAL GEOGRAPHIC KIDS QUIZ WHIZ* collection for more crazy **ANIMAL** questions!

ANSWERS: 1. True; 2. d; 3. d; 4. c; 5. a

HOMEWORK HELP

Wildly Good Animal Reports

beluga whale

Your teacher wants a written report on the beluga whale. Not to worry. Use these organizational tools so you can stay afloat while writing a report.

STEPS TO SUCCESS: Your report will follow the format of a descriptive or expository essay (see p. 141 for "How to Write a Perfect Essay") and should consist of a main idea, followed by supporting details and a conclusion. Use this basic structure for each paragraph as well as the whole report, and you'll be on the right track.

1. Introduction
State your **main idea.**
The beluga whale is a common and important species of whale.

2. Body
Provide **supporting points** for your main idea.
The beluga whale is one of the smallest whale species.
It is also known as the "white whale" because of its distinctive coloring.
These whales are common in the Arctic Ocean's coastal waters.

Then **expand** on those points with further description, explanation, or discussion.
The beluga whale is one of the smallest whale species.
Belugas range in size from 13 to 20 feet (4 to 6.1 m) in length.
It is also known as the "white whale" because of its distinctive coloring.
Belugas are born gray or brown. They fade to white at around five years old.
These whales are common in the Arctic Ocean's coastal waters.
Some Arctic belugas migrate south in large herds when sea ice freezes over.

3. Conclusion
Wrap it up with a **summary** of your whole paper.
Because of its unique coloring and unusual features, belugas are among the most familiar and easily distinguishable of all the whales.

KEY INFORMATION

Here are some things you should consider including in your report:

What does your animal look like?
To what other species is it related?
How does it move?
Where does it live?
What does it eat?
What are its predators?
How long does it live?
Is it endangered?
Why do you find it interesting?

SEPARATE FACT FROM FICTION: Your animal may have been featured in a movie or in myths and legends. Compare and contrast how the animal has been portrayed with how it behaves in reality. For example, penguins can't dance the way they do in *Happy Feet.*

PROOFREAD AND REVISE: As with any great essay, when you're finished, check for misspellings, grammatical mistakes, and punctuation errors. It often helps to have someone else proofread your work, too, as he or she may catch things you have missed. Also, look for ways to make your sentences and paragraphs even better. Add more descriptive language, choosing just the right verbs, adverbs, and adjectives to make your writing come alive.

BE CREATIVE: Use visual aids to make your report come to life. Include an animal photo file with interesting images found in magazines or printed from websites. Or draw your own! You can also build a miniature animal habitat diorama. Use creativity to help communicate your passion for the subject.

THE FINAL RESULT: Put it all together in one final, polished draft. Make it neat and clean, and remember to cite your references.

Plastic bottles can be creatively reused as hanging cactus planters.

Going
Green

WHERE HAVE THE ANIMALS GONE?

All around the world, animals face threats to their habitat, many of which are caused by humans. Read on about two animals and their fight for survival.

The name "jaguar" comes from the Native American word *yaguar*, which means "he who kills with one leap."

Jaguars are good swimmers.

Jaguars have specialized eyes that are nearly twice as powerful at night as during the day to stalk and ambush prey in the dark.

Jaguars live to be 12 to 15 years old in the wild.

SAVING THE JAGUARS

JAGUAR CUB

Deep in the rain forest of Paraguay, jaguars stealthily sneak through the lush green plants and trees, stalking prey like peccaries and tapir, or take a cooling dip in the river. Here, the government and other organizations are striving to protect the forests in which the jaguars live. Other parts of the jaguar's range have not fared as well. Deforestation—humans chopping down trees to build farms, ranches, roads, and subdivisions—is destroying the jaguars' habitat and blocking their migration routes. This is leaving the cats stranded and vulnerable in the wild throughout their range—which extends through parts of North, South, and Central America—where they're exposed to humans who hunt them to protect their livestock. Facing this and other threats, jaguars have been all but eliminated in the United States, and experts estimate fewer than 15,000 remain in the wild.

In Paraguay, people are working to protect the forests of San Rafael National Park, a sanctuary for the hundreds of species of animals that live there, including jaguars. Further north, in Sonora, Mexico, six former cattle ranches have been combined to create 90 square miles (235 sq km) of rugged wilderness, known as the Northern Jaguar Reserve. Still, many jaguars live outside the protected boundaries, exposing them to human threats. Fortunately, conservation groups like the Northern Jaguar Project and Naturalia are stepping in to educate locals on the importance of saving the species and to stop illegal killing. And as their efforts intensify, the focus remains on securing a brighter future for the spotted cats.

Destruction

MANATEE RESCUE!

DRINK UP!

Swimming along a river in western Florida, U.S.A., a female manatee floats just beneath the water's surface. Dark in color and moving slowly, the manatee is hard to spot. Above the surface, a boat is heading straight toward her. The people on the boat don't see the manatee just below the surface. Suddenly, the boat collides with the manatee.

Luckily, this manatee, named Della, is rescued and treated at a rehabilitation center. Caretakers determine that she's just weeks away from having a baby. Soon, Della gives birth to a calf, named Pal. She also becomes an adoptive mom to Kee, a rescued orphaned calf. Della regains strength as she spends her days with the two calves, gliding around the water with them, and even napping with them at the bottom of their pool.

Five months later, it's time to release the trio back into the wild. Once submerged in their new stream, the manatee family happily paddles away.

Della, Pal, and Kee are lucky. They were rescued, treated, and given a new home. But that's not always the case. People are living in manatees' habitats. They are driving boats, fishing, and swimming in the water. That puts manatees at risk. Learning to share space with animals is important. Driving boats slowly and carefully in manatee habitats can help save these gentle giants.

When resting, manatees can stay submerged for up to 20 minutes.

Average adult manatees are about 10 feet (3 m) long and weigh 1,000 pounds (454 kg).

Manatees breathe only through their nostrils.

83

1

YOU CAN BUY JEANS MADE FROM PLASTICS FOUND FLOATING IN THE SEA.

2

Dogs have been trained to sniff out pollutants in waterways so the waste can be removed.

3

Scientists are trying to **convert sugar** into **clean fuel.**

4

Turning off the **tap** while **brushing your teeth** can conserve up to **eight gallons (30 L) of water** a day.

17 COOL THINGS ABOUT

5

The "Great Green Wall," a 4,400-mile (7,080-km)-long line of trees and vegetation, is being planted along the edge of Africa's Sahara.

8

In its lifetime, one reusable bag can prevent the use of 600 plastic bags.

6

A COMPANY IN DENMARK MAKES PLASTIC DINNER PLATES FROM RECYCLED PIG URINE.

7

The FIRST recorded PAPER RECYCLING happened in JAPAN in 1031.

9 THE *FASTEST* ELECTRIC CAR CAN TRAVEL OVER 300 MILES AN HOUR (483 KM/H).

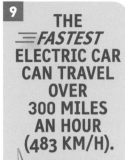

10 Shower water at a Chumbe Island eco-resort in Zanzibar, Africa, comes from filtered rainwater.

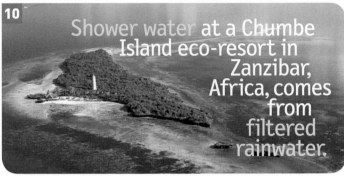

11 An airport in England collects chewed gum that's RECYCLED INTO TOYS AND TIRES.

12 CITIES MAY ONE DAY BUILD FARMSCRAPERS—HIGH-RISES IN WHICH FARMERS GROW CROPS—TO CONSERVE LAND.

GOING GREEN

13 RECYCLING ONE CAN OF SODA WILL SAVE ENOUGH ENERGY TO POWER A TV FOR THREE HOURS.

14 **Environmentalists** sometimes use mushrooms to soak up oil spills and toxic waste.

15 IN 2014 THE UNITED STATES CREATED A PACIFIC OCEAN MARINE RESERVE NEARLY TWICE THE SIZE OF TEXAS.

16 The **TOKELAU ISLANDS** in the Pacific Ocean **RUN ON SOLAR POWER** AND COCONUT OIL.

17 A VERMONT, U.S.A., TOWN USES GRAZING SHEEP TO REDUCE THE NEED FOR GAS-GUZZLING LAWN MOWERS.

THE ARCTIC'S DISAPPEARING ICE

In the past few decades, sea ice cover in the Arctic has shrunk because of global climate change. Arctic sea ice freezes up and expands in the winter and melts and shrinks in the summer. It typically reaches its smallest size every September. Scientists call this the "Arctic sea ice minimum." This minimum has shrunk from 3.02 million square miles (7.83 million sq km) in 1980 to about 1.4 million square miles (3.62 million sq km) in 2012. The change is so significant that cartographers at the National Geographic Atlas of the World redrew the map of the Arctic to reflect the smaller sea ice coverage. So what's behind this ice loss in the Arctic? Scientists point to a phenomenon known as the "positive feedback loop."

Sea ice's bright surface reflects sunlight back into space. This means icy areas absorb less solar energy and remain cool. But when air and ocean temperatures rise over time and more sea ice melts, fewer bright surfaces reflect sunlight back into space. The ice and exposed seawater absorb more solar energy, and this causes a feedback loop of more melting and more warming.

If the ice loss continues at the current rate, scientists are concerned the Arctic will become ice free during the summer at some point within this century. As the ice melts, it's essential that we find ways to protect the indigenous people and animals—such as polar bears and seals—that rely on the Arctic's ice for food and survival.

ARCTIC SEA ICE MINIMUM IN 1980

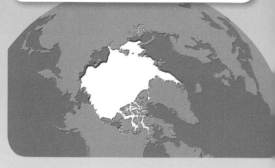

ARCTIC SEA ICE MINIMUM IN 2012

COMPARISON OF ARCTIC SEA ICE MINIMUMS

Arctic sea ice minimum in 1980

Arctic sea ice minimum in 2012

Pollution
Cleaning Up Our Act

So what's the big deal about a little dirt on the planet? Pollution can affect animals, plants, and people. In fact, some studies show that more people die every year from diseases linked to air pollution than from car accidents. And right now nearly one billion of the world's people don't have access to clean drinking water.

A LITTLE POLLUTION = BIG PROBLEMS
You can probably clean your room in a couple of hours. (At least we hope you can!) But you can't shove air and water pollution under your bed or cram them into the closet. Once released into the environment, pollution—whether it's oil leaking from a boat or chemicals spewing from a factory's smokestack—can have a lasting environmental impact.

KEEP IT CLEAN
It's easy to blame things like big factories for pollution problems. But some of the mess comes from everyday activities. Exhaust fumes from cars and garbage in landfills can seriously trash the Earth's health. We all need to pitch in and do some house-cleaning. It may mean bicycling more and riding in cars less. Or not dumping water-polluting oil or household cleaners down the drain. Look at it this way: Just as with your room, it's always better not to let Earth get messed up in the first place.

What a Prince!

The heir to the British throne is doing his part to save Earth's oceans. Working to combat both overfishing and the amount of plastic that lands in the ocean every year—8.8 million tons (8 million t) by some estimates—Prince Charles is leading a charitable drive to protect the seas with a focus on sustainable fishing. We'd say that's a quite a royal effort.

87

FOOD FOR THOUGHT

It may seem as if the world's oceans are so vast that nothing could hurt them. Unfortunately, that's not true. The oceans suffer from people dumping stuff in them that they don't want (pollution) and taking too much from them that they do want (overfishing). You can help turn this problem around.

BE AN OCEAN HERO!

You can be part of the solution if you carefully choose what fish to eat. Some are okay to eat; others you should avoid because they're overfished or caught in ways that harm the ocean. Check out the list below to help guide your seafood choices. To get the most up-to-date info, check out our Seafood Decision Guide at www.natgeoseafood.com. Ask your parents to consult it when they buy fish at the market or order it at a restaurant. Ask the grocer or chef where and how the fish was caught. Saving marine life is hard, but if everyone helps, it will make a difference.

BEST CHOICES

- abalone (farmed)
- catfish (U.S.)
- clams (farmed)
- clams, softshell
- crab, Dungeness
- crab, stone
- crawfish (U.S.)
- halibut, Pacific
- lobster, spiny (Australia, Baja, U.S.)
- mackerel, Atlantic
- mahimahi (U.S. troll)
- mullet (U.S.)
- mussels (farmed)
- oysters (farmed)
- pollock, Alaska
- sablefish/black cod (Alaska, Canada)
- salmon (Alaska wild)
- salmon, canned pink/sockeye
- sardines (U.S.)
- scallops, bay (farmed)
- shrimp, pink (Oregon)
- shrimp (U.S. farmed)
- squid, longfin (U.S.)
- striped bass (farmed)
- tilapia (U.S.)
- trout, rainbow (farmed)
- tuna, albacore (Canada, U.S.)
- tuna, yellowfin (U.S. troll)

WORST CHOICES

- cod, Atlantic
- crab, king (imported)
- crawfish (China)
- flounder/sole (Atlantic)
- grouper
- haddock (trawl)
- halibut, Atlantic
- mahimahi (imported longline)
- orange roughy
- salmon (farmed or Atlantic)
- shark
- shrimp/prawns (imported)
- swordfish (imported)
- tilapia (Asia)
- tuna, bigeye (longline)
- tuna, bluefin
- tuna, yellowfin (imported longline)

NATIONAL GEOGRAPHIC KIDS ALMANAC NEWSMAKER CHALLENGE 2016

In the first ever Almanac Newsmaker Challenge, we asked kids to Step Up to the Plate to Fight Food Waste. National Geographic Explorer Tristram Stuart inspired kids with the facts—*Enough food is wasted to feed all the 1 billion malnourished people on the planet three times over!*—and offered ideas on how we can all make a difference. Hundreds of kids from around the world went to our website and took the pledge to waste less food and inspire others to do the same. Here's who stepped up.

COUNTRIES REPRESENTED

15 countries were represented. Top countries: U.S., Canada, India, Japan, Philippines, and Vietnam. Top U.S. states: California and Florida.

Ireland
Canada
United States
California
Mexico
Florida
Trinidad & Tobago
Italy   Libya   Uganda   Egypt   India
Japan
Hong Kong
Vietnam
Philippines
Singapore

BOYS VS GIRLS

30% more girls than boys participated.

AGES

11

Newsmakers were as young as 4 and as old as 68. The average age was 11.

FAMILIES

Average number of people in household: 4.3
Two families had 13 people!

FAVORITE VEGETABLE*

Broccoli 20%   Carrots 15%   Potatoes 9%

Corn 7%   Cucumber 6%   Spinach 6%

Beans 5%   Peas 3%   Other 30%

This survey question was open-ended, so we got lots of responses!

FIGHTING FOOD WASTE

About one-third of the world's food is wasted. And National Geographic Emerging Explorer Tristram Stuart wants to do something about that. To feed some of the one billion hungry people in the world, Stuart has started a global movement against food waste. This includes the campaign Feeding the 5,000, which offers free feasts featuring foods salvaged from farm waste piles, like surplus veggies, imperfect apples, and dinged-up tomatoes. With these types of events, Stuart hopes that everyone around the world will become just as fed up as he is about food waste and do something about it.

TRISTRAM STUART

6 TIPS to Save the Earth

The Earth needs your help! Here are six ways to protect our planet.

1 Take a Walk – Usually get a ride to your friend's house down the street? Ask your parents if you can walk or ride your bike there instead. Skipping the car ride not only saves gas, but it also cuts back on air pollution. Just make sure to always have an adult with you on longer walks or rides, and stick to the sidewalks—especially on busy roads.

2 Fill It Up – Of the billions of bottles of water consumed in the United States every year, only about 30 percent of those are actually recycled. The rest clog up landfills or wind up in the ocean, where they may harm sea animals. An easy fix? Drink from a reusable water bottle. Experts say tap water is totally safe to drink, and you'll do your part to reduce the waste.

3 Bag It – Like water bottles, plastic grocery bags are likely to become hazards to the environment, as they take many years to degrade. Next time you go the grocery store with Mom or Dad, remind them to bring along reusable shopping totes.

4 Eat Up – Mom's right: You really should eat everything on your plate! Around the world, 1.4 billion tons (1.3 billion t) of food is lost or wasted every year. And all of that rotting food is filling up landfills and releasing harmful greenhouse gases into the environment. Coming up with creative ways to use up food that would otherwise be tossed—like making muffins out of ripe bananas—can make a big impact on the future of our planet.

5 Go Portable – Laptop computers use 50 to 90 percent less energy than desktop computers.

6 Pick It Up – Every year, people around the world generate 2.6 trillion pounds (1.2 trillion kg) of garbage—equal to the weight of more than 6 million blue whales. And some of that will wind up in your local creeks and playgrounds. So grab some gloves and a trash bag and pick up trash. You'll get some fresh air and exercise—and help the environment, too.

DID YOU KNOW?
If food waste were a country, it would be the third largest emitter of greenhouse gases behind China and the United States.

TRY MAKING YOUR OWN SOAP

Don't trash your leftover bits of soap! Combine soap slivers to keep pieces of soap from going into the garbage—and adding to landfill. Squish the slivers into cool shapes when they're wet.

By the NuMbErs

TRASH BREAKDOWN

After you toss out a banana peel, a soda can, or a smelly sock, it's out of sight, but it's still around— sometimes for weeks, and other times for hundreds of years! Here's a timeline of how long it takes everyday trash to decompose— or completely break down—in a landfill.

BANANA PEEL
2–5 WEEKS

APPLE CORE
2 MONTHS

WOOL SOCKS
1–5 YEARS

PLASTIC BAG
10–20 YEARS

LEATHER
50 YEARS

RUBBER BOOT SOLE
50–80 YEARS

ALUMINUM CAN
80–200 YEARS

GLASS BOTTLE
1 MILLION YEARS OR MORE

PLASTIC FISHING LINE
600 YEARS

91

GREEN Extremes

THESE OVER-THE-TOP IDEAS TAKE ECO-FRIENDLY TO A WHOLE NEW LEVEL. FIND OUT HOW FAR SOME PEOPLE WILL GO TO REUSE AND RECYCLE.

Recycled Art

This may look like a regular portrait, but look closely and you'll see it's actually made of discarded pieces of junk. Artist Zac Freeman collects objects like buttons, bike chains, and safety pins, and then glues them to a wooden canvas to create giant works of eco-friendly art.

Green Mile

A company in the Netherlands has plans to turn trash fished from the ocean into roads. Made from recycled plastic, the roads will provide an eco-friendly alternative to asphalt, which generates 1.6 million tons (1.5 million t) of CO_2 per year. Even cooler? The roads come in connectable pieces like Legos, so installing and fixing them will be a snap.

Cool **Capsule**

With the Ecocapsule, you can live anywhere in the world and leave no carbon footprints behind. This egg-shaped home—complete with a fold-up bed, mini kitchen, dining area, a toilet, and shower—generates its own clean energy, thanks to solar cells on the roof and a retractable wind turbine. As for running water? That comes from rain, captured and filtered from the capsule's curved roof.

No-Waste **Home**

This house is made completely out of recycled products and trash, including 4,000 VHS tapes, 500 bike tires, and 20,000 toothbrushes.

WASTE

93

QUIZ WHIZ

What's your eco-friendly IQ? Find out with this quiz!
ANSWERS BELOW

1 It can take up to _____ years for an aluminum can to decompose in a landfill.
a. 2
b. 20
c. 200
d. 2,000

2 True or false?
Jaguars are poor swimmers.

3 An airport in England makes recycled toys and tires out of which found items?
a. safety pins
b. coins
c. batteries
d. used chewing gum

4 About how many people around the world are lacking access to clean drinking water?
a. one billion
b. one million
c. one thousand
d. one hundred

5 Which famous royal figure is taking a stand to protect Earth's oceans?
a. Queen Elizabeth
b. King Kong
c. Prince Charles
d. Catherine Middleton

Not **STUMPED** yet? Check out the *NATIONAL GEOGRAPHIC KIDS QUIZ WHIZ* collection for more crazy **ENVIRONMENT** questions!

ANSWERS:
1. c; 2. False; 3. d; 4. a; 5. c

HOMEWORK HELP

Write a Letter That Gets Results

Knowing how to write a good letter is a useful skill. It will come in handy anytime you want to persuade someone to understand your point of view. Whether you're emailing your congressperson or writing a letter for a school project or to your grandma, a great letter will help you get your message across. Most important, a well-written letter leaves a good impression.

Check out the example below for the elements of a good letter.

Your address

Date

Salutation
Always use "Dear" followed by the person's name; use Mr., Mrs., Ms., or Dr. as appropriate.

Introductory paragraph
Give the reason you're writing the letter.

Body
The longest part of the letter, which provides evidence that supports your position. Be persuasive!

Closing paragraph
Sum up your argument.

Complimentary closing
Sign off with "Sincerely" or "Thank you."

Your signature

Abby Jones
1204 Green Street
Los Angeles, CA 90045

March 31, 2017

Dear Mr. School Superintendent,

I am writing to you about how much excess energy our school uses and to offer a solution.

Every day, we leave the computers on in the classroom, the TVs are plugged in all the time, and the lights are on all day. All of this adds up to a lot of wasted energy, which is not only harmful for the Earth, as it increases the amount of harmful greenhouse gas emissions into the environment, but is also costly to the school. In fact, I read that schools spend more on energy bills than on computers and textbooks combined!

I am suggesting that we start an Energy Patrol to monitor the use of lighting, air-conditioning, heating, and other energy systems within our school. My idea is to have a group of students dedicated to figuring out ways we can cut back on our energy use in the school. We can do room checks, provide reminders to students and teachers to turn off lights and computers, replace old lightbulbs with energy-efficient products, and even reward the classrooms that do the most to save energy.

Above all, I think our school could help the environment tremendously by cutting back on how much energy we use. Let's see an Energy Patrol at our school soon. Thank you.

Sincerely,

Abby Jones

Abby Jones

COMPLIMENTARY CLOSINGS

Sincerely, Sincerely yours, Thank you, Regards, Best wishes, Respectfully,

Stilt fishermen wait for their catch among the reefs of the Sri Lankan coast. They fish from narrow bamboo benches built between two stilts.

Culture Connection

CELEBRATIONS

1 CHINESE NEW YEAR
January 28
Also called Lunar New Year, this holiday marks the new year according to the lunar calendar. Families celebrate with parades, feasts, and fireworks. Young people may receive gifts of money in red envelopes.

2 HOLI
March 13
This festival in India celebrates spring and marks the triumph of good over evil. People cover one another with powdered paint, called *gulal*, and douse one another with buckets of colored water.

3 NAURYZ
March 21
This ancient holiday is a major moment on the Kazakhstan calendar. To usher in the start of spring, the people of this Asian country set up tentlike shelters called yurts, play games, go to rock concerts, and feast on rich foods.

4 QINGMING FESTIVAL
April 5
Also known as "Grave Sweeping Day," this Chinese celebration calls on people to return to the graves of their deceased loved ones. There, they tidy up the grave, as well as light firecrackers, burn fake money, and leave food as an offer to the spirits.

5 EASTER
April 16
A Christian holiday that honors the resurrection of Jesus Christ, Easter is celebrated by giving baskets filled with gifts, decorated eggs, or candy to children.

6 KONINGSDAG
April 27
Orange you glad it's King's Day? People across the Netherlands celebrate the monarchy with street parties and by wearing all things orange.

7 VESAK DAY
May 10
Buddhists around the world observe Buddha's Birthday with special rituals including chanting and prayer, candlelight processions, and meditation.

8 RAMADAN AND EID AL-FITR
May 27*–June 26**
A Muslim holiday, Ramadan is a month long, ending in the Eid Al-Fitr celebration. Observers fast during this month—eating only after sunset. People pray for forgiveness and hope to purify themselves through observance.

9 TANABATA
July 7
To commemorate this Star Festival, people in Japan first write wishes on colorful strips of paper. Then, they hang the paper on bamboo branches in their yards and around their homes in the hopes that their wishes will come true.

10 BASTILLE DAY
July 14
The French call this day *La Fête Nationale*, as it is the celebration of the start of the French Revolution in 1789. In Paris, fireworks light up the night skies while dance parties spill into the streets.

*Begins at sundown.
**Dates may vary slightly by location.

Around the World

⑪ NAG PANCHAMI
July 27
In Nepal and India, Hindus worship snakes—and keep evil spirits out of their homes— by sticking images of serpents on their doors and making offerings to the revered reptiles.

⑫ VERSLUNARMANNAHELGI
August 4–5
During Verslunarmannahelgi—also known as Iceland's Labor Day—people head to the great outdoors for camping trips, cookouts, and massive music festivals.

⑬ ROSH HASHANAH
September 20*–22
A Jewish holiday marking the beginning of a new year on the Hebrew calendar. Celebrations include prayer, ritual foods, and a day of rest.

⑭ HANUKKAH
December 12*–20
This Jewish holiday is eight days long. It commemorates the rededication of the Temple in Jerusalem. Hanukkah celebrations include the lighting of menorah candles for eight days and the exchange of gifts.

⑮ CHRISTMAS DAY
December 25

A Christian holiday marking the birth of Jesus Christ, Christmas is usually celebrated by decorating trees, exchanging presents, and having festive gatherings.

2017 CALENDAR

JANUARY
S	M	T	W	T	F	S
1	2	3	4	5	6	7
8	9	10	11	12	13	14
15	16	17	18	19	20	21
22	23	24	25	26	27	28
29	30	31				

FEBRUARY
S	M	T	W	T	F	S
			1	2	3	4
5	6	7	8	9	10	11
12	13	14	15	16	17	18
19	20	21	22	23	24	25
26	27	28	29			

MARCH
S	M	T	W	T	F	S
			1	2	3	4
5	6	7	8	9	10	11
12	13	14	15	16	17	18
19	20	21	22	23	24	25
26	27	28	29	30	31	

APRIL
S	M	T	W	T	F	S
						1
2	3	4	5	6	7	8
9	10	11	12	13	14	15
16	17	18	19	20	21	22
23	24	25	26	27	28	29
30						

MAY
S	M	T	W	T	F	S
	1	2	3	4	5	6
7	8	9	10	11	12	13
14	15	16	17	18	19	20
21	22	23	24	25	26	27
28	29	30	31			

JUNE
S	M	T	W	T	F	S
				1	2	3
4	5	6	7	8	9	10
11	12	13	14	15	16	17
18	19	20	21	22	23	24
25	26	27	28	29	30	

JULY
S	M	T	W	T	F	S
						1
2	3	4	5	6	7	8
9	10	11	12	13	14	15
16	17	18	19	20	21	22
23	24	25	26	27	28	29
30	31					

AUGUST
S	M	T	W	T	F	S
		1	2	3	4	5
6	7	8	9	10	11	12
13	14	15	16	17	18	19
20	21	22	23	24	25	26
27	28	29	30	31		

SEPTEMBER
S	M	T	W	T	F	S
					1	2
3	4	5	6	7	8	9
10	11	12	13	14	15	16
17	18	19	20	21	22	23
24	25	26	27	28	29	30

OCTOBER
S	M	T	W	T	F	S
1	2	3	4	5	6	7
8	9	10	11	12	13	14
15	16	17	18	19	20	21
22	23	24	25	26	27	28
29	30	31				

NOVEMBER
S	M	T	W	T	F	S
			1	2	3	4
5	6	7	8	9	10	11
12	13	14	15	16	17	18
19	20	21	22	23	24	25
26	27	28	29	30		

DECEMBER
S	M	T	W	T	F	S
					1	2
3	4	5	6	7	8	9
10	11	12	13	14	15	16
17	18	19	20	21	22	23
24	25	26	27	28	29	30
31						

HOWL-OWEEN PET PARTY

You expect to see ghosts, vampires, and pirates on Halloween. What you *don't* expect is for those creatures to have four legs. Millions of pets will be dressed up for the holiday—here are some of the funniest getups.

BARK! I MEAN, BOO!

LANEY THE POMERANIAN ISN'T FOOLING ANYONE IN HER GHOST GETUP.

I THINK I COULD USE MORE HAIR SPRAY.

These pets like wearing costumes but yours may not. Never force your pet to do something it doesn't want to do.

FORGET BATMAN, I'M BATDOG!

MASON THE CHIHUAHUA MAKES GOING BATTY LOOK SUPERCUTE.

TOBY THE ENGLISH BULLDOG IS HAVING A SERIOUSLY AWESOME HAIR DAY.

THERE'S NO PLACE LIKE THE DOGGIE PARK!

DRESSED AS DOROTHY FROM *THE WIZARD OF OZ*, NELLIE THE MIXED BREED IS ON THE LOOKOUT FOR A YELLOW BRICK ROAD.

I NOW PRONOUNCE ME THE CUTEST PUP EVER.

TINSLEY THE TERRIER TAKES THE CAKE IN HER WEDDING-THEMED COSTUME.

TREAT YOUR PET

Instead of candy, which will hurt your pet's tummy, give your furry friend its own Halloween snack. Check out pet stores for ideas, or grab a parent and try one of the recipes below from the American Society for the Prevention of Cruelty to Animals.

CREEPY CAT COOKIES

- ¼ cup (60 ml) of warm water
- 5 tablespoons (75 ml) of grated Parmesan cheese
- 3 tablespoons (45 ml) of margarine
- 1 tablespoon (15 ml) of cod liver oil
- 1 cup (240 ml) of white flour
- ¼ cup (80 ml) of soy flour

Preheat the oven to 300°F (150°C). Combine the water, cheese, margarine, and oil, then add the flour. Roll the dough ¼ inch (6 mm) thick and cut it with spooky-shaped cookie cutters. Bake the cookies on an ungreased cookie sheet for 20 to 25 minutes.

PUMPKIN POOCH BITES

- 2½ cups (600 ml) of whole wheat flour
- ½ cup (120 ml) of fresh or canned pumpkin
- ½ cup (120 ml) of peanut butter
- 2 teaspoons (10 ml) of cinnamon
- 1 teaspoon (5 ml) of baking powder
- ½ cup (120 ml) of water

Preheat the oven to 350°F (180°C). In a bowl, whisk together the flour, pumpkin, peanut butter, cinnamon, and baking powder. Add water as needed, but the dough should be stiff and dry. Roll the dough until it's ½ inch (1¼ cm) thick and cut it with cookie cutters. Bake the treats for about 40 minutes.

If you dress up your pet, check that the outfit is comfortable and allows the animal to breathe and walk safely.

These recipes should not replace your pet's regular meals. Check with your veterinarian if your pet has special dietary needs or food allergies.

What's Your Chinese Horoscope?
Locate your birth year to find out.

In Chinese astrology the zodiac runs on a 12-year cycle, based on the lunar calendar. Each year corresponds to one of 12 animals, each representing one of 12 personality types. Read on to find out which animal year you were born in and what that might say about you.

RAT
1972, '84, '96, 2008
Say cheese! You're attractive, charming, and creative. When you get mad, you can have really sharp teeth!

RABBIT
1975, '87, '99, 2011
Your ambition and talent make you jump at opportunity. You also keep your ears open for gossip.

HORSE
1966, '78, '90, 2002, '14
Being happy is your "mane" goal. And while you're smart and hardworking, your teacher may ride you for talking too much.

ROOSTER
1969, '81, '93, 2005, '17
You crow about your adventures, but inside you're really shy. You're thoughtful, capable, brave, and talented.

OX
1973, '85, '97, 2009
You're smart, patient, and as strong as an ... well, you know what. Though you're a leader, you never brag.

DRAGON
1976, '88, 2000, '12
You're on fire! Health, energy, honesty, and bravery make you a living legend.

SHEEP
1967, '79, '91, 2003, '15
Gentle as a lamb, you're also artistic, compassionate, and wise. You're often shy.

DOG
1970, '82, '94, 2006, '18
Often the leader of the pack, you're loyal and honest. You can also keep a secret.

TIGER
1974, '86, '98, 2010
You may be a nice person, but no one should ever enter your room without asking—you might attack!

SNAKE
1977, '89, 2001, '13
You may not speak often, but you're very smart. You always seem to have a stash of cash.

MONKEY
1968, '80, '92, 2004, '16
No "monkey see, monkey do" for you. You're a clever problem-solver with an excellent memory.

PIG
1971, '83, '95, 2007
Even though you're courageous, honest, and kind, you never hog all the attention.

Make a 3-D Valentine!

Be sweet to your loved ones and the Earth this Valentine's Day by turning everyday items around your house into something heartfelt. Show how much you care about the environment by creating recycled cards for your family and friends.

YOU WILL NEED

Old newspaper or leftover tissue paper

Heart-shaped cookie cutter

A clean plate

Bowl of water

Paintbrush

Glue wash (equal parts glue and water)

An old greeting card

WHAT TO DO

1 Tear newspaper or tissue paper into small pieces. Place the cookie cutter on the plate. Making sure each piece overlaps, position a few pieces of the paper inside the cookie cutter to create a thin layer. Dip your finger into the bowl of water and then press it gently on the paper layer, making the paper damp. Continue layering,

dipping, and pressing until the cookie cutter is about half full. Let it dry for at least a day.

2 When the paper mold is completely dry, gently press down on the mold and carefully lift off the cookie cutter. Using a clean paintbrush, apply a light coat of glue wash to the mold. As it dries, move on to Step 3.

3 Cover an old greeting card with things from around the house—such as construction paper, magazines, newspapers, or doilies. Write a poem or message inside the card and then glue your 3-D heart to the front. Now you're ready to give this Earth-friendly valentine to someone you love!

Archaeologist Fred Hiebert
digs the past

Imagine traveling to a far-flung destination and searching for artifacts in some of the planet's most remote places: deep, dark caves, desert oases, and even the bottom of the ocean.

That's just what Fred Hiebert does as a National Geographic explorer and archaeologist. His mission? Exploring the world in the hopes of unearthing artifacts so he can piece together critical information about the past.

Hiebert's work has spanned from Asia—where he led excavations along the Silk Road—to South America as he searched for signs of submerged settlements in Lake Titicaca, the continent's highest lake. His excavations have been applauded for unlocking mysteries surrounding ancient cultures, giving us a deeper understanding of what life was like thousands of years ago.

TIMELESS TREASURES

In many ways, archaeologists—and anthropologists, who study human civilization and cultures—are like treasure hunters. But the bounty isn't always shiny pieces of gold or glittering jewels. Many times, the most impressive artifacts are extremely simple, like a

piece of pottery. Hiebert's current excavations are at an ancient palace submerged along the edge of a lake in Kyrgyzstan, west of China.

"Along the ancient Silk Road in Central Asia is a valley where caravans and armies had to go around a lake. At one place along the lakeshore, the locals told us stories of a fantastic building underwater. Too good to be true?" Hiebert says.

NATIONAL GEOGRAPHIC KiDS

ALMANAC NEWSMAKER CHALLENGE

A Present for the Future

Calling all future explorers! Help us preserve our past by participating in the 2017 Almanac Newsmaker Challenge, led by Fred Hiebert. What you'll do: Create a virtual time capsule with up to ten key items that tell us about you, your family, friends, or community. Photograph it, then submit your shot by March 1, 2017, to ngkidsmyshot.com with the hashtag #timecapsule. Highlights will be featured in the 2018 National Geographic Kids' Almanac.

Time Capsule
Buried November 2000
Open on Veterans Day
November 11, 2050
Sponsored by Veterans of the Tri-State
And
The Greater Huntington Park and Recreation District

What items (or "artifacts") represent the things that are important to you today and would tell kids in 2050 about what life was like in 2017?

"Our underwater archaeological expedition is finding actual remains of a huge building which is 600 years old. It was built along the shore when the lake level was lower. This expedition is proving that sometimes legends are true!"

Unexpected discoveries like these can offer archaeologists and anthropologists the key to understanding ancient cultures. And it's the work of experts like Hiebert that brings to light new stories and details that might otherwise remain buried in the past.

World's Wackiest
HOUSES

Check out these not-so-humble abodes from around the globe.

Your house is a place to kick back and get cozy. But what if it also had 27 floors, a replica of King Tut's burial chamber, or an indoor garden? Make yourself at home in some of the coolest dwellings from around the world.

Nearly 30,000 registered archaeological sites are spread across Mexico.

SEA CREATURE SHACK

Naucalpan, Mexico
Here's what it'd be like to dwell in a shell. Architect Javier Senosiain designed this home to look like a real shelled sea creature called the nautilus. The house has curved rooms and looping hallways, plus a large front window with multicolored glass. There's even an indoor garden. The center of the house holds a circular TV room lined with soft couches. If you lived here, you'd never want to come out of your shell.

HOBBIT HOME

Pembrokeshire, Wales

Not all hobbit houses are located in mythical Middle Earth. Simon Dale constructed a family home that looks as if it came straight from *The Lord of the Rings* movies. The grass-covered dwelling was made from scrap wood, twisty tree limbs, and plaster. Inside, floor-to-ceiling tree trunks hold up the roof. Dale built the home in four months with mainly a hammer, chain saw, and chisel—no wizards necessary.

> Wales is said to have more castles per square mile than any other European country.

TOWER POWER

Mumbai, India

For a billionaire looking for new digs, the sky's the limit. One wealthy businessman even had a 27-story skyscraper built as a private home for his family of five. The tower—which supposedly cost one billion dollars—boasts a spa, ballroom, movie theater, and yoga studio. Literally living the high life comes at a price, though. The building's first electric bill reportedly totaled $115,000!

> Some 447 languages are spoken in India.

> Brazil's soccer team has won five World Cups—that's more than any other nation.

ROUND RESIDENCE

São Paulo, Brazil

Sculpted from cement and iron by Eduardo Longo, the 32-foot (9.8-m)-tall house known as the Sphere has three stories and a sleek interior. Instead of a staircase, levels are linked by a winding ramp. For outdoor fun, you can grab onto a rope swing attached to the exterior and go flying around the orb. Longo hopes to create neighborhoods of stacked Sphere houses as a way to save space in his jam-packed city.

17 ZANY FACTS ABOUT

1 You can find "Sunday Best Roast Chicken" and "Chilli & Chocolate" **POTATO CHIPS** in Great Britain.

WALKERS
Chilli & Chocolate
flavour potato crisps
VOTE FOR ME!

2 IF YOU THINK YOU'VE TRIED EVERY KIND OF POPSICLE, THINK AGAIN: YOU CAN BUY A **pickle-flavored** ONE IN THE UNITED STATES!

3 **BEEF TONGUE** is a popular flavor of ice cream in Tokyo, Japan.

4 THE "FAT ELVIS ON-A-STICK" IS A DEEP-FRIED, BANANA-BATTERED PEANUT BUTTER CUP WITH BACON.

5 You can order **FRIED WILD EEL SPINE** at a restaurant in New York City, U.S.A.

6 Silkworm larvae are steamed or boiled and sold at street markets in South Korea. In China and Vietnam, they're fried.

7 **BIRD'S NEST SOUP,** a Chinese delicacy, is made with a swiftlet's nest floating in broth. Swiftlets make their nests entirely out of sticky saliva.

8 During Roman times, people ate dormice—as appetizers and for dessert!

9

Oreo cookies

TASTE—AND LOOK—DIFFERENT AROUND THE GLOBE. IN INDONESIA, SOME ARE FLAVORED LIKE BLUEBERRY ICE CREAM.

IN ARGENTINA, OREOS "x3" HAVE 3 COOKIES AND 2 LAYERS OF FILLING.

10

Fried Kool-Aid balls— MADE WITH A DEEP-FRIED COMBO OF FLOUR, WATER, AND KOOL-AID MIX—ARE SOLD AT SOME U.S. COUNTY FAIRS.

11

TUNA EYEBALLS
are served up with garlic and soy sauce in Japan.

12

Fairgoers in Arizona, U.S.A., can buy caramel apples dipped in **MEALWORMS!**

FAR-OUT FOOD

13

At a restaurant in Taiwan, food is **SERVED IN MINI-TOILETS.**

14

You can buy jam infused with sand from near the Great Pyramid at Giza, Egypt.

15

Bananas, curry, and mashed potatoes are **TOPPINGS** served on pizza in Sweden.

16

WASABI-INFUSED KIT KAT CANDY BARS ARE SOLD IN JAPAN.

17

ROCKET FIZZ SODA POP OFFERS UP SODA FLAVORS RANGING FROM PEANUT BUTTER AND JELLY TO BACON!

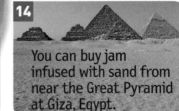

CHEW ON THIS

SUSHI!
"Sushi" means "raw fish," right? Wrong! It's believed to come from the Japanese word su, meaning "vinegar," and meshi, the Japanese word for "rice." So sushi is really "vinegar rice," or sticky rice. Some sushi has raw fish in it, but plenty has no seafood at all. You can roll in whatever ingredients you want—chicken, vegetables, even candy!

WASABI, the spicy green herb eaten with sushi, is sometimes faked using horseradish and food coloring.

GINGER has been used to treat things such as bellyaches and burns.

Ancient Japanese warriors called samurai were paid with **RICE.**

SEAWEED has been used to polish shoes.

CUCUMBERS are 96 percent water.

CHECK OUT THE BOOK!

NATIONAL GEOGRAPHIC KIDS

COOK BOOK

COOL THINGS ABOUT JAPAN

The first known people to live in Japan arrived about 35,000 years ago.

The capital city of Tokyo was once a small fishing village named Edo.

It's considered polite to slurp your noodles in Japan.

In 2012 more than 50,000 people in Japan were at least 100 years old.

More pets live in Japan than children.

CREPES!

It might sound fancy, but the crepe is basically a paper-thin take on the pancake. The French dish was once served in place of bread, but today it's topped or stuffed with a variety of sweet or savory ingredients. Bon appétit!

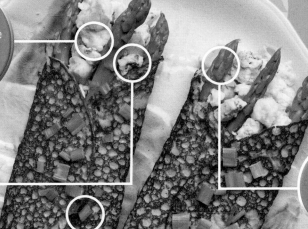

In 1493, Christopher Columbus took chickens on his second voyage to the New World so his sailors would have **EGGS** to eat during their travels.

The old London Stock Exchange was nicknamed **"GORGONZOLA** Hall" because its marble walls resembled the Italian cheese.

In the 18th century, **ASPARAGUS** was called "sparrow-grass."

Europeans once believed that dried bunches of **CHIVES** hanging in a home would drive away evil influences.

The world record for the most slices of **HAM** cut in one hour is 2,160.

MAKE YOUR OWN CREPES

Get a parent's help to whip up some delicious crepes.

1 Mix 1½ cups (240 ml) of flour, 1 tablespoon (15 ml) of sugar, 1 teaspoon (5 ml) of baking powder, ½ teaspoon (2.5 ml) each of salt and vanilla, and 2 cups (480 ml) of milk into a large mixing bowl.

2 In a smaller bowl, beat 2 eggs, breaking up the yolks. Pour them into the large bowl, and whisk with the other ingredients until the batter is smooth.

3 Add 1 teaspoon (5 ml) of margarine to a medium-size frying pan and heat until bubbly. Add ½ cup (120 ml) of the crepe batter, covering the bottom of the pan.

4 Cook for 30 seconds until lightly browned. Use a spatula to flip and cook the other side. Repeat until you run out of batter.

5 Roll the crepes with ham, egg, cheese, or any other filling you'd like. Sprinkle a handful of chopped chives on top.

MONEY Around the World!

Jordan's **HALF-DINAR COIN** has seven sides.

TO SPEND **$1 BILLION** A DOLLAR AT A TIME, YOU'D HAVE TO PAY A BUCK A SECOND FOR NEARLY 32 YEARS.

IN THAILAND, OVAL BARS OF SILVER ONCE USED AS MONEY WERE CALLED **"TIGER TONGUES."**

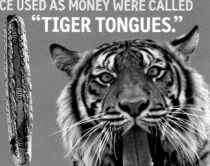

IN ARGENTINA, **"MANGO"** IS SLANG FOR **"PESO."**

A **20,000**-PESO BANKNOTE FROM CHILE CONTAINS INK THAT CHANGES **COLOR** WHEN TILTED.

The INCA called gold **"THE SWEAT OF THE SUN"** and silver **"THE TEARS OF THE MOON."**

DENMARK'S 50-ORE COIN has a HEART on it.

I KNEW I SHOULD'VE TRIED A FAKE ATM INSTEAD.

IN 2002, A MAN OPENED A FAKE BANK AND TOOK IN **$650,000** BEFORE HE WAS CAUGHT.

POTATOES were once used as **CURRENCY** on the **SOUTH ATLANTIC ISLAND** of **TRISTAN DA CUNHA.**

A 1913 U.S. LIBERTY HEAD NICKEL—ONE OF ONLY FIVE IN EXISTENCE— **SOLD AT AUCTION FOR MORE THAN $3.1 MILLION.**

THE PHRASE **"BRING HOME THE BACON"** STARTED AFTER A 12TH-CENTURY PRIEST REWARDED A MARRIED COUPLE **WITH A SIDE OF BACON.**

BRICKS OF COMPRESSED TEA LEAVES WERE ONCE USED AS CURRENCY IN SIBERIA, MONGOLIA, AND CHINA.

MONEY TIP!

ANYTIME YOU BUY SOMETHING **ON SALE,** PUT WHAT YOU SAVED IN YOUR PIGGY BANK.

12 Ways to Say Friend

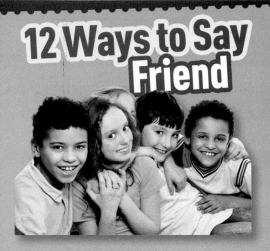

1. **AFRIKAANS: vriend** (male)/**vriendin** (female)
2. **CANTONESE: pung yau**
3. **GERMAN: Freund** (male)/**Freundin** (female)
4. **HAWAIIAN: hoaloha**
5. **HINDI: dost**
6. **ICELANDIC: vinur** (male)/**vinkona** (female)
7. **MALAY: kawan**
8. **SPANISH: amigo** (male)/**amiga** (female)
9. **SWAHILI: rafiki**
10. **TAGALOG** (Filipino): **kaibigan**
11. **AKUAPIM TWI** (Ghana): **adamfo**
12. **WELSH: ffrind**

LANGUAGES IN PERIL

TODAY, there are more than 7,000 languages spoken on Earth. But by 2100, more than half of those may disappear. In fact, experts say one language dies every two weeks, due to the increasing dominance of larger languages, such as English, Spanish, and Mandarin. So what can be done to keep dialects from disappearing? Efforts like National Geographic's Enduring Voices Project are now tracking down and documenting the world's most threatened indigenous languages, such as Tofa, spoken only by people in Siberia, and Magati Ke, from Aboriginal Australia. The hope is to preserve these languages— and the cultures they belong to.

10 LEADING LANGUAGES

Approximate population of first-language speakers (in millions)

1. Chinese*	1,197
2. Spanish	414
3. English	335
4. Hindi	260
5. Arabic	237
6. Portuguese	203
7. Bengali	193
8. Russian	167
9. Japanese	122
10. Javanese	83

Some languages have only a few hundred speakers, while Chinese has nearly one billion two hundred million native speakers worldwide. That's about triple the next largest group of language speakers. Colonial expansion, trade, and migration account for the spread of the other most widely spoken languages. With growing use of the Internet, English is becoming the language of the technology age.

*Includes all forms of the language.

Bet you **didn't know**

6

epic facts
about mythology

1 One **cyclops** from Greek mythology **liked to snack** on **humans.**

2 To live **forever,** gods in ancient Chinese myths **ate** peaches from a **magic tree.**

3 An Irish folklore **hero** carried a **spear** made of **sea monster bones.**

4 The spirits of **old umbrellas** appear in some **Japanese myths.**

5 Certain African tales feature a **snake** that **belches out rainbows.**

6 According to **Viking** lore, the god Odin rode an **eight-legged horse.**

MONSTER MYTHS

5 TERRIFYING TALES DEBUNKED

BUSTED!

Are monsters more than just the stuff of freaky films? Some people think so. They believe that big, bad beasts—hairy giants, pterodactyl-like brutes, and more—lurk just out of sight in areas around the world. Luckily scientists have explanations that bust these tales. Check out five monster myths that have been defanged.

The Nepali name for Mount Everest in the Himalaya means "Forehead of the Sky."

MYTH 1

THE LOVELAND FROG, A BIG AMPHIBIOUS CREATURE, PROWLS AN OHIO, U.S.A., TOWN.

HOW IT MAY HAVE STARTED
This slimy, froglike beast is said to stand four feet (1.2 m) tall and walk on two legs. In 1972 a police officer claimed he caught sight of it on a roadside while driving through Loveland, Ohio, U.S.A. at night. When another officer also reported seeing the freaky frog, the rumor took off.

WHY IT'S NOT TRUE
An investigation by local police found no evidence of the creature. Later, one of the police officers stated that he didn't actually believe that he had seen a monster, and that people had exaggerated his story. It's probable that the Loveland Frog was actually an escaped pet monitor lizard—some types can stretch ten feet (3 m).

SHAGGY-HAIRED BEASTS CALLED YETIS ROAM ASIA'S PEAKS.

HOW IT MAY HAVE STARTED
Yetis are allegedly hairy ogres that look like a human-bear hybrid with jagged fangs. The legend of the yeti probably originated in Tibet, a territory nestled near Asia's Himalaya mountain range. Sherpas, a once-nomadic people from the area, may have spread the myth during their travels in the 16th century. People still claim to see yetis today.

WHY IT'S NOT TRUE
In 2014 scientists did DNA tests on strands of hair found where yetis were supposedly spotted. Results showed that the hairs came not from an unknown beast, but from a rare sub-species of brown bear that lives in the area. It's likely that those who claimed to have seen a yeti really just saw this bear.

MYTH 2

MYTH 3

Lough Corrib, a huge lake in western Ireland, contains more than 360 islands.

THE DOBHAR-CHÚ—PART DOG, PART OTTER, ALL MONSTER—LURKS IN IRELAND.

HOW IT MAY HAVE STARTED

An otter-dog mix, the Dobhar-Chú (Gaelic for "water hound") supposedly inhabits Ireland's lakes. It's known for unleashing eerie whistles and having an appetite for humans. No one knows where the legend of this beast came from, but it dates back to at least the 1700s, when a carved image of the creature appeared on the tombstone of one of its alleged victims.

WHY IT'S NOT TRUE

It's more likely that Dobhar-Chú is a Eurasian otter. The animal is found in Ireland's rivers and lakes and often whistles to communicate.

MYTH 4

The wetlands of Lake Bangweulu in Zambia are home to roughly 390 species of birds.

THE KONGAMATO, A FLYING REPTILIAN MONSTER, ATTACKS BOATERS IN AFRICA.

HOW IT MAY HAVE STARTED

Reportedly seen soaring over southern and central African swamps, the Kongamato is said to have leathery wings, sharp teeth, and a bad habit of swooping down to smash boats that paddle into its territory. Some say the creature is a pterodactyl—a prehistoric flying reptile. Although the myth has circulated for about a century, its origins are unknown.

WHY IT'S NOT TRUE

Scientists know the Kongamato couldn't be a long-extinct pterodactyl. It's more likely a swamp-dwelling hammerhead bat, the largest bat in Africa. It could also be a big type of stingray that tips boats as it leaps from the water.

MYTH 5

IN THE AMERICAS, THE BEASTLY CHUPACABRA DRINKS THE BLOOD OF FARM ANIMALS.

HOW IT MAY HAVE STARTED

When several goats and chickens in areas of Puerto Rico turned up dead with their blood seemingly drained in the 1990s, rumors spread that the culprit was a vampire-like monster with fangs, a forked tongue, and quills running down its back. A rash of similar deaths that occurred a few years later in Texas were also blamed on the Chupacabra (which roughly translates to "goat sucker" in Spanish).

WHY IT'S NOT TRUE

Investigators looking into the deaths of chickens in Texas found no real evidence that the animals' blood had been drained, making the possibility of a vampire-like slayer way less likely. And sightings of the Chupacabra have usually turned out to be sickly coyotes or dogs suffering from mange, a skin condition that gives them a sinister appearance.

117

World Religions

Around the world, religion takes many forms. Some belief systems, such as Christianity, Islam, and Judaism, are monotheistic, meaning that followers believe in just one supreme being. Others, like Hinduism, Shintoism, and most native belief systems, are polytheistic, meaning that many of their followers believe in multiple gods.

All of the major religions have their origins in Asia, but they have spread around the world. Christianity, with the largest number of followers, has three divisions—Roman Catholic, Eastern Orthodox, and Protestant. Islam, with about one-fifth of all believers, has two main divisions—Sunni and Shiite. Hinduism and Buddhism account for almost another one-fifth of believers. Judaism, dating back some 4,000 years, has more than 13 million followers, less than one percent of all believers.

CHRISTIANITY

Based on the teachings of Jesus Christ, a Jew born some 2,000 years ago in the area of modern-day Israel, Christianity has spread worldwide and actively seeks converts. Followers in Switzerland (above) participate in an Easter season procession with lanterns and crosses.

BUDDHISM

Founded about 2,400 years ago in northern India by the Hindu prince Gautama Buddha, Buddhism spread throughout East and Southeast Asia. Buddhist temples have statues, such as the Mihintale Buddha (above) in Sri Lanka.

HINDUISM

Dating back more than 4,000 years, Hinduism is practiced mainly in India. Hindus follow sacred texts known as the Vedas and believe in reincarnation. During the festival of Navratri, which honors the goddess Durga, the Garba dance is performed (above).

📷 **CLOSE-UP**

Technology Meets Tradition

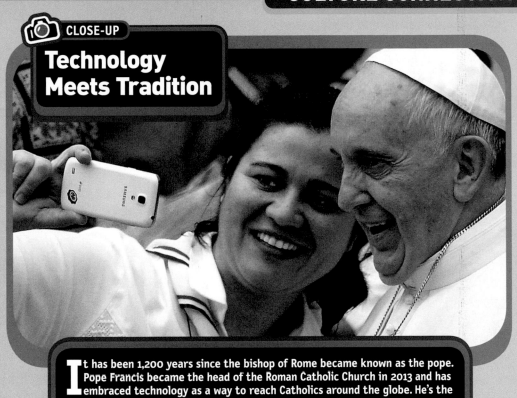

It has been 1,200 years since the bishop of Rome became known as the pope. Pope Francis became the head of the Roman Catholic Church in 2013 and has embraced technology as a way to reach Catholics around the globe. He's the first pope to pose for a selfie and has more than 22 million Twitter followers.

ISLAM

Muslims believe that the Koran, Islam's sacred book, records the words of Allah (God) as revealed to the Prophet Muhammad beginning around A.D. 610. Believers (above) circle the Kaaba in the Haram Mosque in Mecca, Saudi Arabia, the spiritual center of the faith.

JUDAISM

The traditions, laws, and beliefs of Judaism date back to Abraham (the Patriarch) and the Torah (the first five books of the Old Testament). Followers pray before the Western Wall (above), which stands below Islam's Dome of the Rock in Jerusalem.

QUIZ WHIZ

Take this quiz
to find out
how much you know
about the world
around you!

ANSWERS BELOW

① **True or false?** Beef tongue ice cream is a popular flavor in Tokyo, Japan.

② Wales is said to have more _____ per square mile than any other European country?
- a. sheep
- b. people
- c. castles
- d. whales

③ Why was the old London Stock Exchange nicknamed "Gorgonzola Hall?"
- a. It smelled like stinky Italian cheese.
- b. A cheese monger sold gorgonzola from the lobby of the building.
- c. Its marble resembled the cheese.
- d. It was owned by Mr. Alfred Gorgonzola.

④ Bricks of _____ were once used as currency in Siberia.
- a. tea leaves
- b. concrete
- c. clay
- d. gold

⑤ In Greek mythology, what was one cyclops's favorite snack?
- a. peaches
- b. humans
- c. snakes
- d. bubble gum

Not **STUMPED** yet? Check out the *NATIONAL GEOGRAPHIC KIDS QUIZ WHIZ* collection for more crazy **CULTURE** questions!

HOMEWORK HELP

Explore a New Culture

STAMPS OF
SOUTH AFRICA

CURRENCY
AND COINS OF
SOUTH AFRICA

THE FLAG OF
SOUTH AFRICA

You're a student, but you're also a citizen of the world. Writing a report on a foreign nation or your own country is a great way to better understand and appreciate how different people live. Pick the country of your ancestors, one that's been in the news, or one that you'd like to visit someday.

Passport to Success

A country report follows the format of an expository essay because you're "exposing" information about the country you choose.

Simple Steps

1. **RESEARCH** Gathering information is the most important step in writing a good country report. Look to Internet sources, encyclopedias, books, magazine and newspaper articles, and other sources to find important and interesting details about your subject.

2. **ORGANIZE YOUR NOTES** Put the information you gathered into a rough outline. For example, sort everything you found about the country's system of government, climate, etc.

3. **WRITE IT UP** Follow the basic structure of good writing: introduction, body, and conclusion. Remember that each paragraph should have a topic sentence that is then supported by facts and details. Incorporate the information from your notes, but make sure it's in your own words. And make your writing flow with good transitions and descriptive language.

4. **ADD VISUALS** Include maps, diagrams, photos, and other visual aids.

5. **PROOFREAD AND REVISE** Correct any mistakes, and polish your language. Do your best!

6. **CITE YOUR SOURCES** Be sure to keep a record of your sources.

Awesome Adventure

A mountaineer stands at the summit of Barrhorn in the Swiss Alps. At 11,844 feet (3,610 m), Barrhorn is one of the highest hiking mountains in Europe.

DARE to EXPLORE

Do you have what it takes to be a great explorer? Read these stories of four adventurers, and see how you can get started on the exploration path.

KENNETH SIMS
Geologist / geochemist

WANT TO BE A GEOLOGIST?
STUDY: Geology, math, and physics
WATCH: PBS's *The Volcano Watchers*
READ: *Endurance: Shackleton's Incredible Voyage* by Alfred Lansing

"Don't ever let fear of failure get in the way of your goals. There are no defeats, only setbacks."

A SWELTERING LAVA LAKE

SIMS REACHES A CRATER'S RIM.

"My job is to investigate something called radioactive isotopes. These are unstable atoms that are found in volcanic rock and lava. Researching them can give us clues about how volcanoes work and help us predict future eruptions.

"Collecting samples to study can be dangerous but exciting. I've climbed down ropes into the mouths of volcanoes, dived to volcanic vents on the ocean floor, and traveled to a frozen peak in Antarctica where molten lava bubbles within. To stare into an active volcano is like standing at the top of a football stadium filled with seething lava.

"Some of my experiences have been scary. But I try to stay unafraid. You do the best you can to keep safe while getting the job done. It's important to live life to its fullest."

EARTH HAS ABOUT 1,500 ACTIVE VOLCANOES.

LALY LICHTENFELD
Conservationist

WANT TO BE A CONSERVATIONIST?
STUDY: Biology, ecology, and history
WATCH: *Game of Lions,*
a National Geographic film

READ: *Facing the Lion* by
Joseph Lemasolai Lekuton

"Stay curious
and always try to
learn new things.
Being open to
new experiences
will lead to
amazing
opportunities."

BUILDING
A BOMA

"Sitting in my tent during an expedition into the wilderness of Tanzania, I was startled by a big, beautiful lioness ambling through our campsite. Lions usually try to avoid close encounters with humans. But this one padded right up to me. I sat very still, but my heart was pounding. Would she pounce or swipe at me? The animal just stood motionless for some time, looking into my eyes. Then she turned around and trotted off. It was a very special moment.

"My job is to protect big cats such as lions in Tanzania. Humans pose a big threat to these animals. That's because the big cats sometimes hunt cows and other livestock owned by people. When the humans try to stop them, the felines can get hurt—or worse. My team and I work to resolve conflicts between people and cats peacefully. For instance, we teach farmers how to build special fences called bomas around their livestock that keep lions out.

"Big cats around the world face threats. But there's so much we can do to help."

LIONS ARE THE ONLY CATS THAT LIVE IN GROUPS.

CORY RICHARDS
Adventure photographer

WANT TO BE A PHOTOGRAPHER?

STUDY: Photography, anthropology, and geology

WATCH: The documentary *Cave People of the Himalaya*

READ: *Banner in the Sky* by James Ramsey Ullman

"Don't let **obstacles** discourage you from reaching your **goals**. Anything is **possible** if you put your **heart** into it."

RICHARDS SCALES A PEAK IN THE ROCKY MOUNTAINS IN CANADA ON A PHOTO EXPEDITION.

RICHARDS' STUNNING PHOTOGRAPHY

CANADA

EUROPE'S CRIMEAN PENINSULA

"One time I was rappelling, or descending by rope, down a seaside cliff in Spain to photograph some climbers. Suddenly the rock that my rope was anchored to at the top of the cliff broke away. My stomach lurched as I went into a free fall, plummeting 50 feet (15 m) into the ocean. Once I hit the water, the heavy camera equipment strapped to my body dragged me under the waves. With my heart hammering, I freed myself from the gear and swam to the surface. My cameras were ruined, but I was alive.

"Working as a photographer can be a nonstop adventure. My career has taken me to every terrain imaginable, from icy peaks in Asia to the vast plains of Africa to coral reefs in the South Pacific Ocean. I've snapped pictures of people scaling mountains, diving, and skiing across Antarctica. I love using photography to show the incredible things humans are capable of doing.

"Getting the right shot involves creativity and sometimes danger. Stay open to new experiences, and you'll never be disappointed."

IN EXTREME COLD, CAMERAS CAN PACK UP WITH ICE.

MEAVE AND LOUISE LEAKEY

WANT TO BE A PALEONTOLOGIST?

STUDY: Geology, biology, and chemistry

WATCH: National Geographic's *Mysteries of Mankind*

READ: *The Skull in the Rock* by Lee R. Berger and Marc Aronson; *The Tree of Life: Charles Darwin* by Peter Sís

LOUISE

MEAVE

"Important lessons about **our existence** today can only be learned by **studying** the past."

LOUISE LEAKEY WORKING IN THE FIELD

"**S**earching for clues to our human ancestry is a lot like putting together complex, 3-D puzzles in which all the pieces are buried deep in the ground.

"One particular morning my mother and I had been out collecting fossils. Our bags were heavy, our water had run out, it was hot, and we still had a 20-minute walk to the car. But we stopped to look at the two final points on our list. We found the fossil of a piece of a skull barely visible on the surface and we dug out the large block of sandstone containing what we hoped was the entire fossil to carry back to camp. After several months of cleaning the fossil under a microscope, we realized what we'd discovered: the preserved, small skull of *Homo erectus*, one of the closest relatives to today's human beings.

"Paleontology requires patience and concentration, a love of the outdoors, and a deep curiosity about our past and what life was like before humans. In the field, you need to be comfortable with a rugged existence, away from all the comforts of home—and most important: You have to be a team player."

A 4.1-MILLION-YEAR-OLD JAW

A MORE THAN 3-MILLION-YEAR-OLD SKULL

SOME FOSSILS ARE 3.5 BILLION YEARS OLD.

National Geographic Emerging Explorer **Jessica Cramp** spends most of her time on the water in exotic locations tracking sharks. Here's a glimpse at all of the must-haves found inside her backpack.

1 LONG SARONG.
"I use it as a towel, drape it over my head and shoulders to act as a sunshade, and dip it in water to cool down. And it serves as a wrap when I get cold."

2 KEVLAR GLOVES.
"To avoid cuts from fishing line and hooks."

3 ZIPLOC BAGS.
"FLEXIBLE AND WATERPROOF, THEY'RE GOOD FOR KEEPING THINGS DRY ON BOATS, ESPECIALLY IF WE GET CAUGHT IN A RAINSTORM."

17 THINGS IN AN EXPLORER'S

4 TWO WATER BOTTLES.
"You have to stay hydrated out there."

5 BATHYMETRIC MAPS OF ISLANDS.
"TO NAVIGATE, TO MAKE CLEAR MARKS ON WHERE WE HAVE SURVEYED AND CAUGHT SHARKS, AND TO LOOK AT THE BOTTOM/REEF CONTOURS FOR AREAS THAT WOULD BE GOOD SHARK HABITAT."

6 MASK AND SNORKEL.
"I'm always prepared to get in!"

7 WATERPROOF NOTEBOOK AND PERMANENT MARKERS.
"FOR CAPTURING DATA. I ALWAYS BRING EXTRAS— SALT WATER IS NOT NICE TO MARKERS."

8 WATERPROOF BLUETOOTH SPEAKER.
"Long hours on boats are made easier with music or podcasts."

9
GOPRO AND EXTENDABLE POLE.
"THE CAMERA IS WATERPROOF, AND THE POLE ALLOWS ME TO EXTEND INTO THE WATER TO CAPTURE SHARK ACTIVITY."

10
BABY WIPES. "TO GET THE FISH SMELL OFF OF MY HANDS AFTER I'VE BEEN CHOPPING BAIT FOR HOURS. AND TO WIPE DRIED SALT OFF OF MY SKIN SO I CAN REAPPLY A FRESH COAT OF SUNSCREEN."

11

RAINCOAT AND EXTRA LAYERS.
"Getting soaking wet and then traveling long distances on boats gets you cold, quickly."

12
ANTIBIOTIC OINTMENT.
"If I do get cuts, I always have this on me to keep them from getting infected."

13
HEADLAMP.
"YOU NEVER KNOW WHEN YOU WILL BE STUCK PAST SUNSET."

BACKPACK

14

SUNSCREEN, HAT, AND SUNGLASSES.
"THE SUN IS SO STRONG ON THE WATER AND I DON'T WANT TO GET SKIN CANCER. I PROTECT MY SKIN, FACE, AND EYES AT ALL TIMES."

15
PHONE IN A WATERPROOF CASE.
"For photos and emergencies; also, it has a calculator and good quick note taking/ voice memo function."

16
PEPPERMINT AND COCONUT OIL.
"On hot days, I mix a few drops together and rub it on my chest and back to cool me down. Also, it acts as a natural mosquito repellent."

17
BANANAGRAMS. "WHEN I'M ON AN EXPEDITION, I LOVE TO HAVE A GAME AND THIS ONE IS COMPACT AND CAN BE USED TO LEARN NEW LANGUAGES, TOO."

BANANAGRAMS

RHIAN WALLER: KEEPING YOUR COOL!

Rhian's alarm went off again. Now they only had ten minutes of air left. Time was nearly up. She and her buddy would need to keep swimming toward the surface if they were going to make it back safely.

As they swam upward, they scanned their flashlights back and forth below them and to the side, trying to catch sight of their missing partner. But their beams of light were no match for the dark water.

Only five minutes remained on their timer. Rhian couldn't leave her missing buddy behind. But if she stayed much longer, both she and her remaining buddy would die.

Rhian gripped her buddy's hand tighter. They hadn't lost each other. But they hadn't found their teammate, either. They were getting close to the surface now. The timer was counting down. Suddenly, Rhian and her buddy broke through the top of the water.

The rain was still driving down. The winds were still kicking up waves. She frantically looked around. Then, she saw him. The missing diver was clinging to the wall just above the water's surface.

Rhian felt flooded with a sense of relief. She and the other diver swam to the wall. They joined their missing teammate. Before long, their boat captain had pulled the boat alongside them.

Rhian and her teammates dragged themselves onto the boat. They lay shivering and exhausted but ready for the long, choppy ride back. As they sped along, the missing teammate told Rhian his story.

When he reached the surface of the water, he didn't think he could

While diving to study cold-water corals off the coast of Chile, Rhian Waller is pushed to her limits. Check out this excerpt from **National Geographic Kids Chapters Diving With Sharks!**

Did You Know?

After a cold dive, it's important to replenish the nutrients in your body with a high-calorie meal. Rhian's favorite is a bacon sandwich and cookies!

risk swimming to the boat alone in the choppy waters. So he found something to hold on to. He had been searching for them, too. He had been just as worried and panicked as they were!

Rhian thought about the dive. It had certainly been dangerous. But during the worst moments, she and her teammates had remembered their training. They had looked out for one another and kept each other safe.

CHECK OUT THE BOOK!

NATIONAL GEOGRAPHIC KIDS · CHAPTERS

DIVING WITH SHARKS!

And More True Stories of Extreme Adventures!

CAVE of SECRETS

Explorers discover towering cliffs and **poisonous ooze** in the world's largest cave.

Hidden deep in the dense mountain jungle of Vietnam, a massive underworld waits to be explored. A team of scientists and cave experts boldly enters to explore the largest cave ever found, where they'll face dangerous drop-offs and freaky fungus.

No other cave comes close to Hang Son Doong in total size. Using precise laser measuring devices, the team determines that the 5.5-mile (8.9-km)-long cavern soars more than 600 feet (180 m) high and spreads almost 500 feet (150 m) wide in sections. An entire New York City block, complete with 40-story skyscrapers, could fit inside one of Hang Son Doong's vast chambers.

Near the entrance, the team members fight to keep their balance as they wade through a swift underground river. Then they make their way through a field of boulders—some the size of houses—and scramble around stalagmites and slippery rock formations. A wrong step can lead to a fall of over a hundred feet (30 m).

Deeper in the cavern the team slogs through a muddy trench a mile (1.6 km) long. A poisonous fungus lives in the mud that can cause the skin to fall off their feet. The team pushes on.

The other, larger sinkhole eventually brought some of the jungle down with it. A fantastic forest of 100-foot (30-m) trees rises from the rubble pile toward the bright sun. Monkeys, snakes, and birds inhabit the cave jungle.

JOURNEY'S END

The final hurdle is probably the toughest: climbing a slimy 200-foot (61-m) cliff made of solidified, waterborne minerals. Climbers drill in security anchors as they scale the cliff, which resembles a frozen, brown waterfall. After a two-day climb, they literally see light at the end of a tunnel as they reach the cave's exit. Satisfied with the expedition to explore, map, and photograph the world's largest cave, the team climbs out into the sunlight.

HIDDEN JUNGLE

The cavern's roof fell in at two places, creating spectacular natural skylights. The first, which features a mossy green rock mound at the bottom, is jokingly named "Watch Out for Dinosaurs." In the otherworldly setting, prehistoric reptiles seem likely to appear at any moment.

Getting the Shot

The cave passage becomes pitch black in areas—a big problem for a photographer who needs lots of light. Even the most powerful electric flashes can't do the job. "It was a nightmare for me to think about," photographer Carsten Peter says. His solution? Single-use flashbulbs (the kind you might see photographers popping in old movies) from the one company that still makes them.

All About Vietnam

Vietnam is located in Southeast Asia, bordered by China, Laos, and Cambodia.

About 40 percent of people in Vietnam have the last name Nguyen (NWEN).

The Tonkin snub-nosed monkey, one of the more endangered primates in the world, lives only in Vietnam.

Bet you didn't know

8 deep facts about caves

1 **Certain ice caves** in Iceland are filled with **hot springs.**

2 1,000-year-old **popcorn** was found in a **Utah cave.**

3 **Cave bears,** which are now extinct, weighed around **1,500** (680 kg) **pounds.**

5 **Caves** can be **formed by earthquakes.**

4 **A cave in American Fork Canyon** was used as a **dance hall** during **World War II.**

AN ICE CAVE INSIDE ICELAND'S LANGJÖKULL GLACIER

6 Many **cave-dwelling fish** don't have **eyes.**

7 **Ancient** cave paintings in **Australia** show an almost **8-foot-tall** (2.4-m) **bird.**

8 **Some** doctors in the **1800s** thought **cave air** could **cure illness.**

FROZEN IN TIME

ERNEST SHACKLETON'S PRESERVED HUT IN CAPE ROYDS, ANTARCTICA

ANTARCTIC EXPLORERS ERNEST SHACKLETON, ROBERT FALCON SCOTT, AND EDWARD WILSON, CIRCA 1903

NOW: Explorers eat a customized diet fine-tuned to give them enough calories to withstand the cold conditions and physical demands. On the menu? Porridge and cream for breakfast, energy bars, electrolyte drinks, and chicken curry for dinner.

THE SLEDS
THEN: Shackleton and Scott's teams hauled heavy loads in wooden sleds dragged by ponies and dogs.
NOW: Modern lightweight sleds are made of carbon fiber and are capable of carrying more equipment while still being sleek enough to smoothly travel over the ice.

THE CLOTHES
THEN: Early explorers wore wool, cotton, and animal fur. Gloves, boots, and sleeping bags were lined with reindeer fur.
NOW: High-tech mountaineering clothing is made from breathable fabrics that have been specially designed for the Antarctic's cold and dry environment.

Scientist at Base Orcadas in Antarctica

THE COMMUNICATION
THEN: Completely isolated in the Antarctic, explorers had no means of communicating with the outside world and could only write the details of their journey in notebooks.
NOW: Ultralight laptops connected to a mobile satellite hub help explorers stay connected, post pictures, and even watch movies.

When British adventurers Ernest Shackleton and Robert Falcon Scott explored Antarctica in the early 1900s, they set up camp in wooden huts, which they left behind in the icy environs once the expeditions were over.

One would think that over time, the huts would completely deteriorate in the harsh conditions of the coldest continent. But the structures remained upright, albeit damaged by water, wind, and snow over the years. Now, a team of conservationists have completely restored them, offering a time capsule into the explorers' lives a century ago.

So what's inside the huts? Thousands of artifacts, like clothes, scientific equipment, photographs, and even frozen butter. Here's a closer look at some of the items originally used—and how they compare to the gear used by today's Antarctic explorers.

THE FOOD
THEN: Scott's crew mostly munched on pemmican, a mixture of dried beef and fat plus water, and plenty of biscuits.

Meerkat Close Encounter

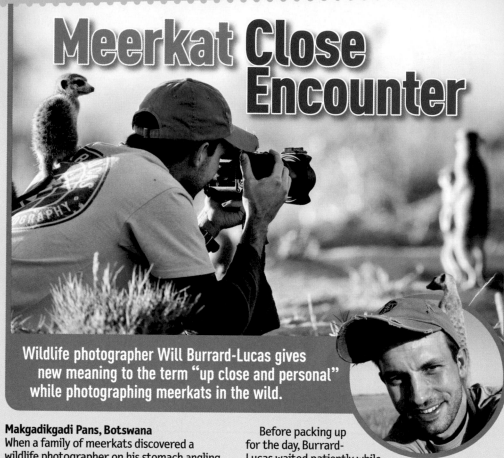

Wildlife photographer Will Burrard-Lucas gives new meaning to the term "up close and personal" while photographing meerkats in the wild.

Makgadikgadi Pans, Botswana

When a family of meerkats discovered a wildlife photographer on his stomach angling for a picture outside their burrow, they didn't hide. Instead they used him as a lookout rock!

Baby meerkat pups venturing aboveground for the first time took turns playing with photographer Will Burrard-Lucas's camera. One bold adult hoisted himself onto Burrard-Lucas's head and scaled to the top of the camera lens he was holding. "They were trying to get as high as they could to have a good look around," Burrard-Lucas says.

"For meerkats, the higher you get, the safer you are, because you can hopefully spot a predator before it spots you," says Kenton Kerns, a biologist at the Smithsonian's National Zoo in Washington, D.C. "If they can find a stable spot that's higher than their normal places, they'll do anything to get there—including climbing a human."

Before packing up for the day, Burrard-Lucas waited patiently while one curious meerkat peered through the lens of his camera on the ground. Another meerkat walked right in front of it. How's that for a close-up?

HOW TO
SURVIVE A
KILLER BEE ATTACK!

1 Buzz Off
Killer bees—or Africanized honey-bees—only attack when their hive is being threatened. If you see several bees buzzing near you, a hive is probably close by. Heed their "back off" attitude and slowly walk away.

2 Don't Join the Swat Team
Your first instinct might be to start swatting and slapping the bees. But that just makes the buzzers angry. Loud noises have the same effect, so don't start screaming, either. Just get away.

3 Don't Play Hide-and-Seek
Hives are often near water, but don't even think about outlasting the bees underwater. They'll hover and attack when you come up for air, even if you try to swim for it.

4 Make Like Speedy Gonzalez
Killer bees will chase you, but they'll give up when you're far enough away from the hive (usually about 200 yards [183 m]). Take off running and don't stop until the buzzing does.

5 Create a Cover-Up
Killer bees often go for the face and throat, which are the most dangerous places to be stung. While you're on the run, protect your face and neck with your hands, or pull your shirt over your head.

HOW TO SURVIVE A
BEE STING!

1. De-Sting Yourself
First, get inside or to a cool place. Then, remove the stinger by scraping a fingernail over the area, like you would to get a splinter out. Do not squeeze the stinger or use tweezers unless you absolutely can't get it out any other way because squeezing it may release more venom.

2. Put It on Ice
Wash the area with soap and water and apply a cool compress to reduce swelling. Continue icing the spot for 20 minutes every hour. Place a washcloth or towel between the ice and your skin.

3. Treat It Right
With a parent's permission, take an antihistamine and gently rub a hydrocortisone cream on the sting site.

4. Hands Off
Make sure you don't scratch the sting. You'll just increase the pain and swelling.

5. Recognize Danger
If you experience severe burning and itching, swelling of the throat and/or mouth, difficulty breathing, weakness, or nausea, or if you already know you are allergic to bees, get to an emergency room immediately.

137

GETTING the SHOT

Capturing good photographs of wild animals can be tough. To get amazing pictures of them, nature photographers often tap into their wild side, thinking and even acting like the creatures they're snapping. Whether tracking deadly snakes or swimming with penguins, the artists must be daring—but they also need to know when to keep their distance. Three amazing photographers tell NG KIDS the behind-the-scenes stories of how they got these incredible shots.

MY SHOT

EARN BADGES FOR YOUR CRITTER PICS.

ngkidsmyshot.com

FANG FOCUS

PHOTOGRAPHER: Mattias Klum
ANIMAL: Jameson's mamba
SHOOT SITE: Cameroon, Africa

"The Jameson's mamba is beautiful but dangerous. It produces highly toxic venom. My team searched for weeks for the reptile, asking locals about the best spots to see one. At last we came across a Jameson's mamba peeking out from tree leaves. Carefully, I inched closer. It's important to make this kind of snake think that you don't see it. Otherwise it might feel threatened and strike you. At about four and a half feet (1.4 m) away, I took the picture. Then I backed up and the snake slid off."

SECRETS FROM
AMAZING WILDLIFE PHOTOGRAPHERS

Usually solitary creatures, oceanic whitetip sharks have been observed swimming with pods of pilot whales.

SHARK TALE

PHOTOGRAPHER: Brian Skerry
ANIMAL: Oceanic whitetip shark
SHOOT SITE: The Bahamas

"I wanted to photograph an endangered oceanic whitetip shark. So I set sail with a group of scientists to an area where some had been sighted. Days later, the dorsal fin of a whitetip rose from the water near our boat. One scientist was lowered in a metal cage into the water to observe the fish. Then I dived in. Because I wasn't behind the protective bars, I had to be very careful. These nine-foot (2.7-m) sharks can be aggressive, but this one was just curious. She swam around us for two hours and allowed me to take pictures of her. She was the perfect model."

LEAPS and BOUNDS

PHOTOGRAPHER: Nick Nichols
ANIMAL: Bengal tiger
SHOOT SITE: Bandhavgarh National Park, India

"While following a tiger along a cliff, I saw him leap from the edge to his secret watering hole and take a drink. I wanted a close-up of the cat, but it wouldn't have been safe to approach him. Figuring he'd return to the spot, I set up a camera on the cliff that shoots off an infrared beam. Walking into the beam triggers the camera to click. The device was there for three months, but this was the only shot I got of the cat. Being near tigers makes the hair stand up on my arm. It was a gift to encounter such a magnificent creature."

Fewer than 2,500 Bengal tigers are left in the wild.

139

QUIZ WHIZ

Explore just how much you know about adventure with this quiz!
ANSWERS BELOW

① **What did the earliest Antarctic explorers eat during their expeditions?**
a. porridge
b. pemmican
c. blubber
d. energy bars

② **True or false?** The world's largest cave is hidden deep in a mountain jungle in Cambodia.

③ **1,000-year-old _____ was found in a Utah cave.**
a. animal dung
b. sausage
c. popcorn
d. butter

④ **Which of the following is a useful item for an ocean explorer?**
a. Ziploc bags
b. baby wipes
c. peppermint oil
d. all of the above

⑤ **How could you help your body recover after a cold dive?**
a. elevate your feet
b. replenish nutrients with a bacon sandwich
c. sunbathe
d. Read the *National Geographic Kids Almanac 2017*

Not **STUMPED** yet? Check out the *NATIONAL GEOGRAPHIC KIDS QUIZ WHIZ* collection for more crazy **ADVENTURE** questions!

ANSWERS: 1. b; 2. False. The largest cave is Hang Son Doong in Vietnam; 3. c; 4. d; 5. b

HOMEWORK HELP

How to Write a Perfect Essay

Need to write an essay? Does the assignment feel as big as climbing Mount Everest? Fear not. You're up to the challenge! The following step-by-step tips will help you with this monumental task.

1 **BRAINSTORM.** Sometimes the subject matter of your essay is assigned to you, sometimes it's not. Either way, you have to decide what you want to say. Start by brainstorming some ideas, writing down any thoughts you have about the subject. Then read over everything you've come up with and consider which idea you think is the strongest. Ask yourself what you want to write about the most. Keep in mind the goal of your essay. Can you achieve the goal of the assignment with this topic? If so, you're good to go.

2 **WRITE A TOPIC SENTENCE.** This is the main idea of your essay, a statement of your thoughts on the subject. Again, consider the goal of your essay. Think of the topic sentence as an introduction that tells your reader what the rest of your essay will be about.

3 **OUTLINE YOUR IDEAS.** Once you have a good topic sentence, you then need to support that main idea with more detailed information, facts, thoughts, and examples. These supporting points answer one question about your topic sentence—"Why?" This is where research and perhaps more brainstorming come in. Then organize these points in the way you think makes the most sense, probably in order of importance. Now you have an outline for your essay.

4 **ON YOUR MARK, GET SET, WRITE!** Follow your outline, using each of your supporting points as the topic sentence of its own paragraph. Use descriptive words to get your ideas across to the reader. Go into detail, using specific information to tell your story or make your point. Stay on track, making sure that everything you include is somehow related to the main idea of your essay. Use transitions to make your writing flow.

5 **WRAP IT UP.** Finish your essay with a conclusion that summarizes your entire essay and restates your main idea.

6 **PROOFREAD AND REVISE.** Check for errors in spelling, capitalization, punctuation, and grammar. Look for ways to make your writing clear, understandable, and interesting. Use descriptive verbs, adjectives, or adverbs when possible. It also helps to have someone else read your work to point out things you might have missed. Then make the necessary corrections and changes in a second draft. Repeat this revision process once more to make your final draft as good as you can.

FUN and GAMES

KNOCK, KNOCK.

Who's there?
Ben.
Ben who?
Ben ringing your doorbell for ten minutes!

EXPLORE!
NATIONAL GEOGRAPHIC KIDS'
virtual world online:
AnimalJam.com

Enter
the special code
NGKAJ17
for a bonus!

Find the HIDDEN ANIMALS

Animals often blend into their environments for protection. Find the animals listed below in the photographs. Write the letter of the correct photo next to each animal's name.

ANSWERS ON PAGE 338

1. sawblade shrimp
2. sand cat
3. black bear
4. flounder
5. white-tailed deer
6. white-tailed ptarmigan*

*Hint: A white-tailed ptarmigan is a type of bird that lives in mountain areas.

What in the World?

BIRD'S-EYE VIEW

These photos show views of how things look from up in the sky. Unscramble the letters to identify what's in each picture.

Bonus: Use the highlighted letters to solve the puzzle below. ANSWERS ON PAGE 338

NSDLIA

_____

ETSOFR

_____

THENEPAL DHRE

_____

OGNALMSFI

_____

LMSAEC

_____

ALOCR EFER

_____

WRFEOL LSEFDI

_____

GRIESEBC

_____

THO-IRA OLNBLOA

_____

HINT: What does the ground say to an earthquake?

ANSWER: Y _ _ U _ _ _ _ _ K _ _ U _ _ !

A-MAZE-ing Mind

START

EMOTION

TOUCH

TEMPERATURE

SMELL

HI! HOLA! BONJOUR!
LANGUAGE

SIGHT

HEARING

COORDINATION

BREATHING

END

Feeling brainy? Find the path through this maze that leads you from the top of the brain to the bottom without running into any obstacles. (Bonus! The illustrations show which functions each part of your brain is responsible for.) Ready, set, think!

ANSWER ON PAGE 338

Funny Fill-In

Here, Kitty!

Ask a friend to give you words to fill in the blanks in this story without showing it to him or her. Then read it out loud for a laugh.

We've been trekking through this forest so long, we need a break. So we sit _____ (adverb ending in –ly) on a(n) _____ (something soft). I suddenly get the feeling I'm being watched and turn around. There's a(n) _____ (adjective) huge wild cat with _____ (color) spots creeping up on us! "Don't worry, I've got this," _____ (friend's name) says _____ (adverb ending in –ly). _____ (same friend's name) unzips a suitcase and pulls out a tin of _____ (type of food, plural). He's/she's kind of _____ (adjective), but sometimes that's good. "Got anything else in there? Some _____ (noun, plural) or _____ (noun, plural)?" I ask. My friend just _____ (verb ending in –s) and tosses the tin to the wild cat, which is looking very hungry. It starts _____ (verb ending in –ing) and chomping _____ (adverb ending in –ly) on the tin. Then it starts _____ (verb ending in –ing) and _____ (verb ending in –ing) like a little kitten! We slowly back away. Nice kitty!

Noun Town

This city is full of nouns, or people, places, and things. But twelve compound nouns—nouns made up of two or more words, or two words combined to make one word—have been drawn exactly as they're named. Can you guess the compound nouns illustrated in each of the numbered scenes? Here's a hint: The answer to number 1 is "sleeping bag."

ANSWERS ON PAGE 338

Attention on Set

At least ten objects at the rehearsal for *Giant Squid Versus Aliens* have the word "ten" in their names—for example, the squid's *ten*tacles. Can you spot the rest?

ANSWERS ON PAGE 338

What in the World?

MELLOW YELLOW

These photos show close-up views of yellow things. Unscramble the letters to identify what's in each picture.
Bonus: Use the highlighted letters to solve the puzzle below. ANSWERS ON PAGE 338

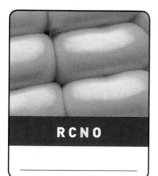

RCNO
_____

ENINST LABL
_____

LURFNOWSES
_____

ESANK
_____

YACNRA
_____

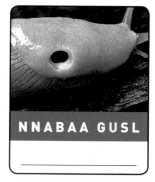

NNABAA GUSL
_____

TUBEYRFTL
_____

MOEYCNOBH
_____

ELONM
_____

HINT: What's the quickest way to make a banana split?

ANSWER: ___ ___ ___ **T** ___ ___ **I** ___ ___ ___ ___ ___ .

150

Red Panda

Just Joking

KNOCK, KNOCK.

Who's there?
Hugo
Hugo who?
Hugo-ing to let me in or not?

Two thieves robbing an apartment hear the owner coming home.

"Quick, jump out the window," says the first robber.

"Are you crazy? We're on the 13th floor!" says the second robber.

The first one replies, "This is no time to be superstitious!"

TONGUE TWISTER!

Say this fast three times:

Chimp chomps chips.

WANT MORE?

Check out the NG Kids book *Just Joking Cats* and the Just Joking app.

Q Why wouldn't they let the butterfly into the dance?

A Because it was a moth ball.

Q

What kind of insect eats brains?

A A zom-bee.

151

Riddle Me This

Answer these riddles! Read the questions at right, then find their corresponding punch lines illustrated and marked with yellow dots throughout this museum scene. The first one has been done for you.
ANSWERS ON PAGE 338

1. What kind of shoes do spies wear? *Sneak*-ers
2. What's black and white and pink all over? An embarrassed _ _ _ _ _
3. What has bark but no bite? A _ _ _ _
4. What comes down but never goes up? _ _ _ _
5. What's tall when it's young and short when it's old? A _ _ _ _ _ _
6. The more you take of these, the more you leave behind. _ _ _ _ _ _ _ _ _ _
7. What has a face and two hands but no arms or legs? A _ _ _ _ _
8. What can honk without a horn? A _ _ _ _ _
9. What has a neck but no head? A _ _ _ _ _
10. What invention lets you look right through a wall? A _ _ _ _ _ _

Laugh Out Loud

"I DON'T KNOW. I THINK THE BOW TIE MIGHT BE A BIT TOO MUCH!"

I NEED A GIFT FOR A FRIEND. WHAT DO YOU SUGGEST?

OH!

"DIDN'T I TELL YOU TO CLEAN OFF YOUR BELLY BEFORE DINNER?"

"HEY, EVERYBODY! IF YOU TURN YOUR HEAD THIS WAY, EVERYTHING LOOKS UPSIDE DOWN!"

Funny FILL-IN
Wild Ride

Ask a friend to give you words to fill in the blanks in this story without showing it to him or her. Then read it out loud for a laugh.

NEW RIDE

My friends and I were waiting to ride the _____ at the amusement park. But when
                                       noun, plural

we got to the front of the line, a park employee asked us if we would like to test a(n)

_____ new ride instead. As we climbed into a(n) _____ -shaped car, another park
adjective   noun

employee said, "Welcome to the _____ , the world's _____ roller coaster!"
                                noun   adjective ending in -est

Our car suddenly _____ . Then the car shot up _____ feet—we were so
                 past-tense verb   large number

high, I thought I could touch the _____ . The people below looked like
                                  something in the sky, plural

_____ . Next we did a barrel roll over the _____ teacups and flew over
animal, plural   verb ending in -ing

the _____ waterslide. Finally our car _____ backward as fast as
    mythical creature   past-tense verb

a(n) _____ before coming to a stop where we started. What a hair-raising experience!
     noun

My _____ felt a little _____ , but I still went on the ride again—twice.
   body part   adjective

THE SWOOPING SPACESHIP

CHECK OUT THE BOOK!

Funny FILL-IN
MY AMUSEMENT PARK ADVENTURE

Book Boggle

More than just books are at this book fair. Some of the stories have come to life—but the titles have become separated. Connect each numbered item with the other one it goes with to come up with the full titles of eight well-known books. For example, number 1 connects with number 11 for the answer *Treasure Island*.

ANSWERS ON PAGE 338

Just Joking

Zebra

KNOCK, KNOCK.
Who's there?
Spell.
Spell who?
Okay,
W-H-O.

What do you get if you cross a **chicken** with a **skunk?**
Q
A A fowl smell.

CUSTOMER: "There's a dead beetle in my soup."

WAITER: "Yes, sir, they're not very good swimmers."

TONGUE TWISTER!

Say this fast three times:

Bad money, mad bunny

What does a **vulture pack** for a **vacation?**
Q
A Carrion luggage.

WANT MORE?
Check out the NG Kids book *Just Joking Animal Riddles* and the Just Joking app.

Just Joking Animal Riddles
J. Patrick Lewis

Dog Daze

The eight snapshots above were taken at this dog park. Find the scene that appears in each picture. Hint: Some of the snapshots are upside down or sideways. ANSWERS ON PAGE 338

Just Joking

Snake

KNOCK, KNOCK.

Who's there?
Metaphors.
Metaphors who?
Mataphors be
with you.

Q What did one **math book** say to the other math book?

A I've got a lot of problems.

Q What **chews on trees** and **sings?**

A Justin Beaver.

CATHIE: Did your party guests enjoy the piñata?
DOUG: It was a huge hit!

You've **got** to be joking...

Q How do **turtles talk to** each other?

A On their shell phones.

CHECK OUT THE BOOK!

Just Joking 6

NATIONAL GEOGRAPHIC KIDS

300

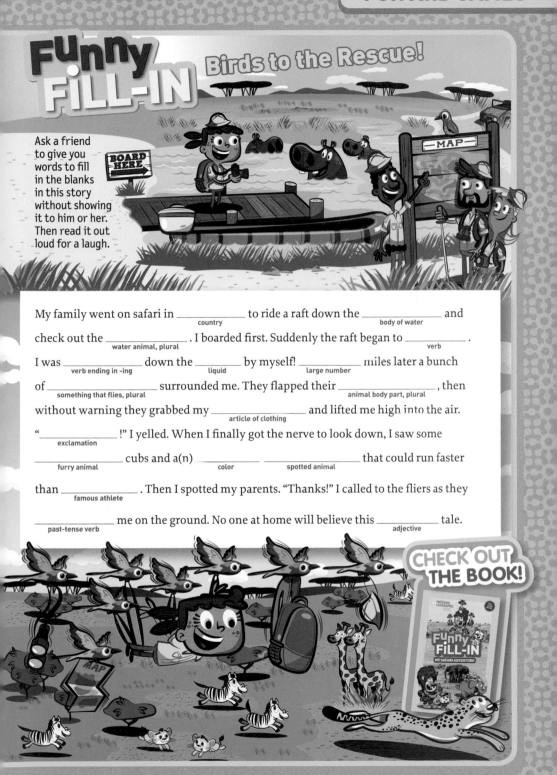

Funny Fill-in — Birds to the Rescue!

Ask a friend to give you words to fill in the blanks in this story without showing it to him or her. Then read it out loud for a laugh.

BOARD HERE

MAP

My family went on safari in _____ (country) to ride a raft down the _____ (body of water) and check out the _____ (water animal, plural). I boarded first. Suddenly the raft began to _____ (verb). I was _____ (verb ending in -ing) down the _____ (liquid) by myself! _____ (large number) miles later a bunch of _____ (something that flies, plural) surrounded me. They flapped their _____ (animal body part, plural), then without warning they grabbed my _____ (article of clothing) and lifted me high into the air. "_____ (exclamation)!" I yelled. When I finally got the nerve to look down, I saw some _____ (furry animal) cubs and a(n) _____ (color) _____ (spotted animal) that could run faster than _____ (famous athlete). Then I spotted my parents. "Thanks!" I called to the fliers as they _____ (past-tense verb) me on the ground. No one at home will believe this _____ (adjective) tale.

CHECK OUT THE BOOK!

Funny Fill-in
MY SAFARI ADVENTURE

Cosmonauts undergo weightlessness training in a pool in Moscow, Russia.

Super Science

1

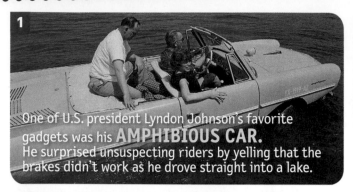

One of U.S. president Lyndon Johnson's favorite gadgets was his **AMPHIBIOUS CAR.** He surprised unsuspecting riders by yelling that the brakes didn't work as he drove straight into a lake.

2

THE RED SCHUMACHER MI3 IS THE FASTEST REMOTE-CONTROL CAR IN THE WORLD, ZOOMING AT A SPEED OF 161.76 MILES AN HOUR (260.32 KM/H).

3

LEARN TO PLAY GUITAR ON YOUR T-SHIRT. The electronic guitar T-shirt lets you play all major chords while the sound comes from a mini-amplifier attached to your belt.

4

Smartwatches let users read their email, check social media, monitor their health, and even pay for a cup of coffee.

17 FACTS ABOUT EXTREME

5

GOOGLE CARDBOARD

Pop your phone into a **GOOGLE CARDBOARD** headpiece, strap it on your face, and go anywhere in the world without taking a step, thanks to special virtual reality apps.

6

Shaped like a shark, dolphin, or orca whale, the Seabreacher watercraft jumps, dives, rolls, and speeds across the water at up to 55 miles an hour (89 km/h).

7

A company has developed **unmanned robotic helicopters** that can deliver food, medicine, mail, and more where roads don't go.

8

Ever played ANGRY BIRDS on water? The Displair is a touch screen made of mist that needs up to a half gallon (2 L) of water every hour to keep it going.

9

YOU CAN RIDE AROUND IN YOUR VERY OWN MONDO SPIDER, AN **8-legged,** (726-kg) **1,600-pound** ROBOT ARACHNID THAT MOVES AT 5 MILES AN HOUR (8 KM/H).

10

JetLev is a **water-propelled jetpack** that pumps 1,000 gallons (3,785 L) of water a minute through a backpack, launching the wearer 30 feet (9 m) into the air.

11 A company makes a **HARRY POTTER–LIKE WAND** that can learn up to 13 commands that will turn up the volume, change the channel, and do more on your TV.

12 A DISAPPEARING TELEVISION COULD SOON BE A REALITY. ONE CONCEPT IN DEVELOPMENT IS A SEE-THROUGH TV, WHICH USES TRANSPARENT LCD TECHNOLOGY TO LOOK LIKE GLASS WHEN TURNED OFF.

GADGETS

13 SMART LOCKS ARE CONTROLLED BY YOUR SMARTPHONE, NOT KEYS. SOME LOCKS CAN TELL WHO'S ENTERING YOUR HOUSE AND EVEN TAKE A PICTURE.

14 The HAPIfork aims to manage weight loss by measuring how often you raise your fork to your mouth and vibrating when you eat too quickly.

15 There's a basketball that records every dribble and shot you make, then transmits the data to your mobile device to help you achieve the perfect game.

16 A car company created **a self-driving model car called Shelley** that allows the company to test performance at speeds up to 155 miles an hour (249 km/h).

17 The BeBionic3—the world's MOST ADVANCED PROSTHETIC HAND—mimics real hand and wrist movements and is controlled by the wearer's actual muscles.

COOL inventions

CAR FOLDS UP

Pulling up to your favorite restaurant for dinner, you see that cars parked along the curb haven't left enough space for a regular auto to fit into. Luckily you have a CityCar. This prototype fold-up vehicle may help drivers get into tight spots and replace bigger cars that crowd cities. The electric two-seater features an oval pod for a driver and passenger. With the press of a button, the front and rear wheels slide toward each other, and the pod is pushed up vertically. Folded, the Transformer-like car is five feet (1.5 m) long. (Most other autos take up 16 feet [5 m].) With its tiny, flexible frame, the CityCar saves space, fuel—and your dinner plans.

PARKED

A PEN "DREW" THIS!

AND THIS!

3-D PEN

Doodles with a regular pen are, well, flat. But not when you use the 3Doodler. This cool electronic pen produces plastic to draw three-dimensional objects. As you sketch in the air, a string of heated plastic flows like ink. Use the flexible material to create shapes such as pyramids or boxes. You can also twirl the pen to make a coil. The plastic quickly hardens into whatever objects you've drawn. Artists have even made replicas of the Eiffel Tower (left) and model dinosaurs with the pen. Just pick a good spot to display your doodle masterpieces, because these drawings definitely won't fit on the pages of your notebook.

ACCIDENTS Happen

Hey, they happen. Sometimes accidents are totally embarrassing. But other times they lead to something awesome. Check out these fortunate mistakes.

BUT SOMETIMES THEY RESULT IN AMAZING DISCOVERIES.

THE INVENTION: ARTIFICIAL SWEETENER

THE MOMENT OF "OOPS": Dirty hands

THE DETAILS: In the late 1870s, Constantin Fahlberg was working in his lab when he tipped over a beaker of chemicals, spilling them all over his hands. Without pausing to wash, Fahlberg went on with his work. When he went home to eat, the chemical residue was still on his fingers. After biting into a piece of bread, he noticed that it tasted strangely sweet. It wasn't the bread—it was something on his hands.

Fahlberg rushed back to work and found that the substance in the beaker that had spilled was sweet—much sweeter than sugar. He named his discovery saccharin—the first artificial sweetener.

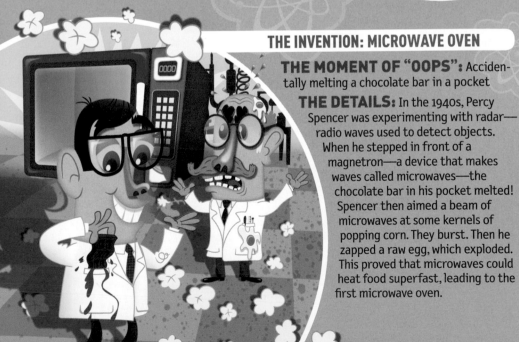

THE INVENTION: MICROWAVE OVEN

THE MOMENT OF "OOPS": Accidentally melting a chocolate bar in a pocket

THE DETAILS: In the 1940s, Percy Spencer was experimenting with radar—radio waves used to detect objects. When he stepped in front of a magnetron—a device that makes waves called microwaves—the chocolate bar in his pocket melted! Spencer then aimed a beam of microwaves at some kernels of popping corn. They burst. Then he zapped a raw egg, which exploded. This proved that microwaves could heat food superfast, leading to the first microwave oven.

WHAT IS LIFE?

This seems like such an easy question to answer. Everybody knows that singing birds are alive and rocks are not. But when we start studying bacteria and other microscopic creatures, things get more complicated.

SO WHAT EXACTLY IS LIFE?

Most scientists agree that something is alive if it can do the following: reproduce; grow in size to become more complex in structure; take in nutrients to survive; give off waste products; and respond to external stimuli, such as increased sunlight or changes in temperature.

KINDS OF LIFE

Biologists classify living organisms by how they get their energy. Organisms such as algae, green plants, and some bacteria use sunlight as an energy source. Animals (like humans), fungi, and some Archaea use chemicals to provide energy. When we eat food, chemical reactions within our digestive system turn our food into fuel.

Living things inhabit land, sea, and air. In fact, life also thrives deep beneath the oceans, embedded in rocks miles below the Earth's crust, in ice, and in other extreme environments. The life-forms that thrive in these challenging environments are called extremophiles. Some of these draw directly upon the chemicals surrounding them for energy. Since these are very different forms of life than what we're used to, we may not think of them as alive, but they are.

HOW IT ALL WORKS

To try and understand how a living organism works, it helps to look at one example of its simplest form—the single-celled bacterium called *Streptococcus*. There are many kinds of these tiny organisms, and some are responsible for human illnesses. What makes us sick or uncomfortable are the toxins the bacteria give off in our bodies.

A single *Streptococcus* bacterium is so small that at least 500 of them could fit on the dot above this letter *i*. These bacteria are some of the simplest forms of life we know. They have no moving parts, no lungs, no brain, no heart, no liver, and no leaves or fruit. Yet this life-form reproduces. It grows in size by producing long chain structures, takes in nutrients, and gives off waste products. This tiny life-form is alive, just as you are alive.

What makes something alive is a question scientists grapple with when they study viruses, such as the ones that cause the common cold and smallpox. They can grow and reproduce within host cells, such as those that make up your body. Because viruses lack cells and cannot metabolize nutrients for energy or reproduce without a host, scientists ask if they are indeed alive. And don't go looking for them without a strong microscope—viruses are a hundred times smaller than bacteria.

Scientists think life began on Earth some 3.9 to 4.1 billion years ago, but no fossils exist from that time. The earliest fossils ever found are from the primitive life that existed 3.6 billion years ago. Other life-forms, some of which are shown below, soon followed. Scientists continue to study how life evolved on Earth and whether it is possible that life exists on other planets.

MICROSCOPIC ORGANISMS*

Common soil *Bacillus*

Flu virus

Recently discovered primitive virus

Cyanobacteria

Diatom

Paramecium

E. coli bacteria

Streptococcus bacteria

*Organisms are not drawn to scale.

The Three Domains of Life

Biologists divide all living organisms into three domains: Bacteria, Archaea, and Eukarya. Archaean and Bacterial cells do not have nuclei; they are so different from each other that they belong to different domains. Since human cells have a nucleus, humans belong to the Eukarya domain.

1 BACTERIA

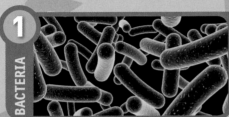

Domain Bacteria: These single-celled microorganisms are found almost everywhere in the world. Bacteria are small and do not have nuclei. They can be shaped like rods, spirals, or spheres. Some of them are helpful to humans, and some are harmful.

2 ARCHAEA

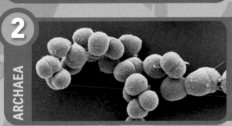

Domain Archaea: These single-celled micro-organisms are often found in extremely hostile environments. Like Bacteria, Archaea do not have nuclei, but they have some genes in common with Eukarya. For this reason, scientists think the Archaea living today most closely resemble the earliest forms of life on Earth.

3 EUKARYA

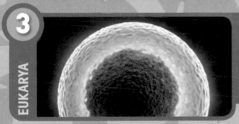

Domain Eukarya: This diverse group of life-forms is more complicated than Bacteria and Archaea, as Eukarya have one or more cells with nuclei. These are the tiny cells that make up your whole body. Eukarya are divided into four groups: fungi, protists, plants, and animals.

FYI

What is a domain? Scientifically speaking, a domain is a major taxonomic division into which natural objects are classified (see p. 30 for "What Is Taxonomy?").

FUNGI

Kingdom Fungi (about 100,000 species): Mainly multicellular organisms, fungi cannot make their own food. Mushrooms and yeast are fungi.

PROTISTS

Protists (about 250,000 species): Once considered a kingdom, this group is a "grab bag" that includes unicellular and multicellular organisms of great variety.

PLANTS

Kingdom Plantae (about 300,000 species): Plants are multicellular, and many can make their own food using photosynthesis (see p. 210 for "Photosynthesis").

ANIMALS

Kingdom Animalia (about 1,000,000 species): Most animals, which are multicellular, have their own organ systems. Animals do not make their own food.

YOU AND YOUR CELLS

Your body is made up of microscopically tiny structures called cells—many trillions of them!

Every living thing—from the tiniest bug to the biggest tree—is made up of cells, too. Cells are the smallest building blocks of life. Some living things, such as an amoeba, are made up of just one cell. Other living things contain many more. Estimates for an adult human, for example, range from 10 trillion to 100 trillion cells!

An animal cell is a bit like the world's tiniest water balloon. It's a jellylike blob surrounded by an oily "skin" called a cell membrane. The membrane works to let some chemicals into the cell and keep others out. The "jelly" on the inside is called cytoplasm. It's speckled with tiny cell parts, called organelles. Some organelles make energy. Others take apart and put together various chemicals, which become ingredients for different body functions such as growth and movement.

CHECK OUT THE BOOK!

ULTIMATE BODY-PEDIA

SEEING CELLS

The first microscope that clearly showed anything smaller than a flea was invented in the late 1500s. Later, people tinkered with microscopes and lenses to make them even more powerful. One of these people was the English scientist Robert Hooke.

Hooke designed a microscope of his own and drew detailed pictures of what he saw. In 1665, he published his illustrations in a book called *Micrographia*, which means

"little pictures." One picture shows boxy spaces in a slice of cork from a tree. Hooke called the spaces "cells" because they looked like little rooms. It would be another 200 years before scientists realized that cells make up all living things.

YOU HAVE A LOT OF NERVE!

Different parts of your brain control different activities, but how does your brain tell all the parts of your body what to do?

And, in return, how do your eyes, ears, and nose tell your brain what they see, hear, and smell? The answer is your nerves!

Nerves—thin, threadlike structures—carry messages between your brain and the rest of your body, in both directions. Nerves run down your spine and branch out all the way to your fingers and toes. This system of nerves controls your body, tells your muscles to move, and lets you experience the wonderful world around you. Nerves are part of your nervous system, which also includes your brain and spinal cord.

Your nerves are made of cells called neurons. Neurons send and receive messages between your brain and the other parts of your body by sending out alternating electrical and chemical signals.

Messages flash from neuron to neuron along your nerves and inside your brain. Signals from your eyes might tell the brain, "There's my school bus." The brain then sends signals that zoom from cell to cell making sense of the message. Then the brain sends signals back down to the nerves connected to your leg muscles to say, "Run to the bus stop!"

TOUR A NEURON

Neurons have four parts:

CELL BODY Contains the nucleus, which controls the activity of the cell and contains its DNA, or deoxyribonucleic acid

AXON Fiber that transmits impulses from the cell body to another nerve cell

DENDRITE Branchlike fiber extending from the cell body that receives signals from other neurons

MYELIN A fatty covering around the axons that insulate the axon, giving the white matter its characteristic color

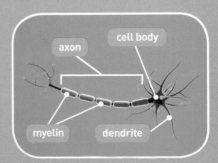

axon / cell body / myelin / dendrite

Your Amazing
brain

Inside your body's supercomputer

You carry around a three-pound (1.4-kg) mass of wrinkly material in your head that controls every single thing you will ever do. From enabling you to think, learn, create, and feel emotions to controlling every blink, breath, and heartbeat—this fantastic control center is your brain. It is a structure so amazing that a famous scientist once called it the "most complex thing we have yet discovered in our universe."

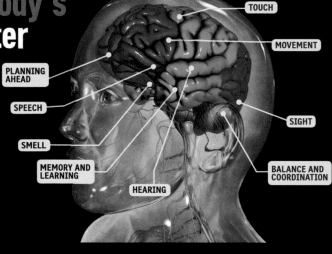

TOUCH

MOVEMENT

PLANNING AHEAD

SPEECH

SIGHT

SMELL

MEMORY AND LEARNING

BALANCE AND COORDINATION

HEARING

BRAIN MAP

■ FRONTAL LOBE
■ PARIETAL LOBE   CEREBRUM
■ OCCIPITAL LOBE
■ TEMPORAL LOBE

■ CEREBELLUM
■ BRAIN STEM

THE BIG QUESTION

WHAT TAKES UP TWO-THIRDS OF YOUR BRAIN'S WEIGHT AND ALLOWS YOU TO SWIM, EAT, AND SPEAK?

Answer: The huge hunk of your brain called the cerebrum. It's definitely the biggest part of the brain. The four lobes of the cerebrum house the centers for memory, the senses, movement, and emotion, among other things.

The cerebrum is made up of two hemispheres—the right and the left. Each side controls the muscles of the opposite side of the body.

CHECK YOUR MEMORY

How much can your brain remember? Put it to the test.

CHALLENGE

Take 30 seconds. Memorize as many of these pictures as you can. Cover the pictures. Now get a pencil and a piece of paper. Write down the pictures you remember. How many did you get right?

WHAT EXACTLY IS HAPPENING?

Looking at pictures actually helps your brain to remember better. Short-term memory, also called working memory, relies heavily on the visual cortex. Words that are read are processed very quickly by our brains. They don't stick around for very long. But recording a picture in your brain takes longer. The more time spent looking at the picture, the better the memory. Saying a word out loud does the same thing. It takes longer to speak a word than it does to read it. That's why you remember it better when you say it aloud. The lesson? When you are doing last-minute cramming for a test, look at pictures and speak things out loud. Your memory—and your test score—will thank you.

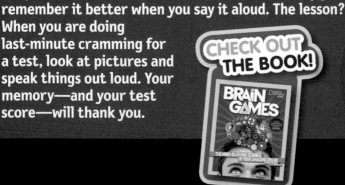

CHECK OUT THE BOOK!

BRAIN GAMES

National Geographic Kids

THE MIND-BLOWING SCIENCE OF YOUR AMAZING BRAIN

YOUR SHORT-TERM MEMORY CAN HOLD ONLY ABOUT SEVEN THINGS AT ONE TIME.

Your Amazing
Ears

OUTER EAR

INNER EAR

COCHLEA

Listen up!
Your ears are so
much more than
just two funny-
looking things
stuck to the side
of your head.
Here's an earful
on all that's cool
about these
awesome organs.

MIDDLE EAR

EAR DRUM

Your entire
inner ear can
fit inside the
tip of your
pinkie.

TRIPLE PLAY. The ears are made up of three sections: the outer ear, the middle ear, and the inner ear. Each part plays separate and equally important roles to keep your hearing sharp. Here's how sound travels through your ears.

OUTER EAR: The part you can see and feel, the outer ear consists of the pinna and the ear canal. Sound waves enter here and travel down the ear canal to the ear drum.

MIDDLE EAR: Sound waves create vibrations that strike the ear drum, causing the three tiny bones located here to move. The movement amplifies the sound and delivers it to the inner ear.

INNER EAR: Sound vibrations enter the cochlea, the small, snail-shaped, liquid-filled tube that's lined with tiny hairs. The vibrations make the tiny hairs wave back and forth and tickle the nerve cells. This causes the nerve cells to send messages to your brain that are interpreted as sound.

BETTER BALANCE. Your ears don't just let you hear—they keep you balanced, too. How? Above the cochlea in the inner ear is a set of three fluid-filled canals, called the semicircular canals. When you move your head, tiny hair cells in the canals move too, sending nerve impulses to the brain that tell you where you are. And that dizzy feeling you get when you've spun around in circles one too many times? That happens because the fluid in the semicircular canals continues to swish around even after you stop, confusing your brain into thinking that you're still spinning.

Some
people can
hear their own
eyeballs
move.

DRUM ROLL. Despite its name, the ear drum has nothing to do with percussion. Rather, this tiny piece of skin located between the outer and middle ear is called a "drum" because it's such a tightly stretched membrane. Bad ear infections or trauma can cause it to tear, or perforate, but the ear drum usually heals itself within a few months.

WAX ON. It's sticky, it's icky, and it can smell funky. So what's the point of ear wax, anyway? The yellowish brown stuff is packed with dead skin cells and chemicals that fight off infections. And it traps dirt and dust, too, keeping your middle and inner ears sparkly clean. So while it may be gunky, it keeps you healthy. And that's not just a ball of wax!

Bet you didn't know

7 popping facts to sound off about

1 Some **radio signals** coming from **Jupiter** make a sound like **popping popcorn.**

2 The **Parma wallaby** makes **coughing noises** to communicate with a **mate.**

3 The longest **recorded echo** lasted for nearly **2** minutes.

4 An orchestra in the Washington, D.C., area performs only music from **video games.**

5 Certain **sand dunes** occasionally **hum.**

6 Hot water and cold water make **different** sounds when poured.

7 The **western diamondback rattlesnake** can **vibrate** its **rattle** about **60** times a second.

175

That's GROSS!

WHO NEEDS SLOBBERING ZOMBIES AND SLIMY MONSTERS THIS HALLOWEEN? THE BACTERIA LIVING INSIDE YOUR BODY ARE ICKY ENOUGH.

Don't panic, but you're outnumbered by alien life-forms. They look like hairy hot dogs, spiky blobs, and oozing spirals, and they're crawling across—and deep inside—your body right this very minute. They're bacteria!

Your body is built of trillions of itty-bitty living blobs, called cells, that work together to do amazing things, such as hold in your organs or help beat your brother at *Clash of Clans*. But for every cell you call your own, about ten foreign bacteria are clustering around or near it. You can't see these hitchhikers, but you sure can smell a lot of them. Like any living thing, bacteria eat, reproduce, die, and create waste. A lot of this waste is the source of your body odor, bad breath, and torturous toots. In other words, some bacteria can make your life stink!

If the thought of being a human-shaped planet for microscopic inhabitants makes you queasy, relax. Most of your body's microbes have been harmlessly hanging out in your body for years and are essential for good health. And just like a fingerprint, your bacteria make you who you are, because no two people host the same mix of microorganisms. But that doesn't make things any less disgusting!

Little Monsters

Meet **four** famous bacteria that **call your body** "home sweet home..."

1 ACTINOMYCES VISCOSUS

When your dentist breaks out the power tools to jackhammer the brownish coat of slime known as plaque from your teeth, she's really attacking these mouth-dwelling bacteria.

4 BREVIBACTERIUM LINENS

This foul-smelling microbe thrives in the sweat simmering in your sneakers, unleashing an awful stink when you kick off your shoes. It's also used to ferment stinky Limburger cheese.

2 METHANOGENS

About half of all people have these supersimple microbes living in their guts. Methanogens produce methane, a greenhouse gas that animals—including humans—pass into the atmosphere when they, um, toot.

3 ESCHERICHIA COLI

This rod-shaped microbe lives deep in your guts, the body's busiest bacterial neighborhood. Helpful *E. coli* strains produce an important vitamin. Harmful ones make you vomit for days.

More Grossness

Your body's bacterial zoo begins when you're born, as you ingest bacteria from your mom's skin and milk. You also consume lots of harmless and helpful bacteria through food and water every day.

 Some bacteria are used by scientists to help produce new vaccines and other medicine.

Your body's bacteria eat everything from salt inside your intestines to chemicals in your sweat.

Belly-button lint—a mix of clothing fibers and dead skin cells—is a hot spot for bacteria. Scientists recently found more than 1,400 species of microbes living in people's navels.

THE UNIVERSE BEGAN WITH A BIG BANG

Clear your mind for a minute and try to imagine this: All the things you see in the universe today—all the stars, galaxies, and planets—are not yet out there. Everything that now exists is concentrated in a single, incredibly hot, dense state that scientists call a singularity. Then, suddenly, the basic elements that make up the universe flash into existence. Scientists say that actually happened about 13.8 billion years ago, in the moment we call the big bang.

For centuries scientists, religious scholars, poets, and philosophers have wondered how the universe came to be. Was it always there? Will it always be the same, or will it change? If it had a beginning, will it someday end, or will it go on forever?

These are huge questions. But today, because of recent observations of space and what it's made of, we think we may have some of the answers. Everything we can see or detect around us in the universe began with the big bang. We know the big bang created not only matter but also space itself. And scientists think that in the very distant future, stars will run out of fuel and burn out. Once again the universe will become dark.

POWERFUL PARTICLE

It's just one tiny particle, but without it the world as we know it would not exist. That's what scientists are saying after the recent discovery of the Higgs boson particle, a subatomic speck related to the Higgs field, which is thought to give mass to everything around us. Without the Higgs boson, all the atoms created in the big bang would have zipped around the cosmos too quickly to collect into stars and planets. So you can think of it as a building block of the universe—and of us!

EARLY LIFE ON EARTH

About 3.5 billion years ago Earth was covered by one gigantic reddish ocean. The color came from hydrocarbons.

The first life-forms on Earth were Archaea that could live without oxygen. They released large amounts of methane gas into an atmosphere that would have been poisonous to us.

About 3 billion years ago erupting volcanoes linked together to form larger landmasses. And a new form of life appeared—cyanobacteria, the first living things that used energy from the sun.

Some 2 billion years ago the cyanobacteria algae filled the air with oxygen, killing off the methane-producing Archaea. Colored pools of greenish brown plant life floated on the oceans. The oxygen revolution that would someday make human life possible was now under way.

About 530 million years ago the Cambrian explosion occurred. It's called an explosion because it's the time when most major animal groups first appeared in our fossil records. Back then, Earth was made up of swamps, seas, a few active volcanoes, and oceans teeming with strange life.

More than 450 million years ago life began moving from the oceans onto dry land. About 200 million years later dinosaurs began to appear. They would dominate life on Earth for more than 150 million years.

PLANETS

VENUS

MERCURY

EARTH

MARS

CERES

JUPITER

SUN

MERCURY
Average distance from the sun:
   35,980,000 miles (57,900,000 km)
Position from the sun in orbit: first
Equatorial diameter: 3,030 miles (4,878 km)
Length of day: 59 Earth days
Length of year: 88 Earth days
Surface temperatures: -300°F (-184°C)
   to 800°F (427°C)
Known moons: 0
Fun fact: Mercury has shrunk by about
   9 miles (14 km) in diameter since it
   was first formed billions of years ago.

VENUS
Average distance from the sun:
   67,230,000 miles (108,200,000 km)
Position from the sun in orbit: second
Equatorial diameter: 7,520 miles (12,100 km)
Length of day: 243 Earth days
Length of year: 224.7 Earth days
Average surface temperature: 864°F (462°C)
Known moons: 0
Fun fact: There's a mountain on Venus that's
   1.25 times taller than Mount Everest.

EARTH
Average distance from the sun:
   93,000,000 miles (149,600,000 km)
Position from the sun in orbit: third
Equatorial diameter: 7,900 miles (12,750 km)
Length of day: 24 hours
Length of year: 365 days
Surface temperatures: -126°F (-88°C)
   to 136°F (58°C)
Known moons: 1
Fun fact: 40,000 tons (36,300 t) of cosmic
   dust falls on Earth every year.

MARS
Average distance from the sun:
   141,633,000 miles (227,936,000 km)
Position from the sun in orbit: fourth
Equatorial diameter: 4,221 miles (6,794 km)
Length of day: 25 Earth hours
Length of year: 1.9 Earth years
Surface temperatures: -270°F (-168°C)
   to 80°F (27°C)
Known moons: 2
Fun fact: In 2015, scientists confirmed
   evidence of liquid water on Mars.

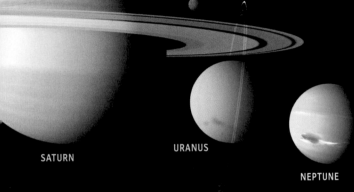

This artwork shows the 13 planets and dwarf planets. The relative sizes and positions of the planets are shown but not the relative distances between them.

SATURN

URANUS

NEPTUNE

PLUTO

HAUMEA

MAKEMAKE

ERIS

JUPITER
Average distance from the sun:
   483,682,000 miles (778,412,000 km)
Position from the sun in orbit: sixth
Equatorial diameter: 88,840 miles (142,980 km)
Length of day: 9.9 Earth hours
Length of year: 11.9 Earth years
Average surface temperature: -235°F (-148°C)
Known moons: 67*
Fun fact: Droplets of neon dissolved in helium
   fall like rain on the planet Jupiter.

SATURN
Average distance from the sun:
   890,800,000 miles (1,433,500,000 km)
Position from the sun in orbit: seventh
Equatorial diameter: 74,900 miles (120,540 km)
Length of day: 10.7 Earth hours
Length of year: 29.5 Earth years
Average surface temperature: -218°F (-139°C)
Known moons: 62*
Fun fact: Saturn's outermost ring is roughly
   7,000 times larger than the planet itself.

*Includes provisional moons, which await confirmation
   and naming from the International Astronomical Union.

URANUS
Average distance from the sun:
   1,784,000,000 miles (2,870,970,000 km)
Position from the sun in orbit: eighth
Equatorial diameter: 31,760 miles (51,120 km)
Length of day: 17.2 Earth hours
Length of year: 84 Earth years
Average surface temperature: -323°F (-197°C)
Known moons: 27
Fun fact: Some methane storms on Uranus
   are so big and bright, you can see them
   from telescopes on Earth.

NEPTUNE
Average distance from the sun:
   2,795,000,000 miles (4,498,250,000 km)
Position from the sun in orbit: ninth
Equatorial diameter: 30,775 miles (49,528 km)
Length of day: 16 Earth hours
Length of year: 164.8 Earth years
Average surface temperature: -353°F (-214°C)
Known moons: 14*
Fun fact: Neptune experiences the strongest
   sustained winds of any planet in the solar
   system.

For information about dwarf planets—Ceres,
Pluto, Haumea, Makemake, and Eris—see p. 183.

By the Numbers

SOLAR SYSTEM

Check out **how long** it would take **for the planets** in our solar system **to race around the sun** if they were runners **on a track.**

Psst! Did you notice that the planets seem too close to the sun—and to each other? You're right! To help show how long it takes each planet to fully orbit the sun, we fudged a little and illustrated the planets as if they were running a race—instead of showing their correct distances. To find out their *real* distances from the sun and each other, go online to check out a video and get even more scoop on our solar system.

natgeo.com/kids/solar-system

CHECK OUT THE BOOK!

By The Numbers

A season on Uranus lasts roughly 21 years.

NEPTUNE
164.8 YEARS

URANUS
84 YEARS

JUPITER
11.9 YEARS

SATURN
29.5 YEARS

Earth orbits the sun almost 165 times before Neptune orbits it once.

MARS
1.9 YEARS

EARTH
1 YEAR

VENUS
224.7 DAYS

MERCURY
88 DAYS

Temperatures on Mercury can range from about minus 280°F (-173°C) at night to 800°F (427°C) during the day.

DWARF PLANETS

Haumea

Eris

Pluto

Thanks to advanced technology, astronomers have been spotting many never-before-seen celestial bodies with their telescopes. One new discovery? A population of icy objects orbiting the sun beyond Pluto. The largest, like Pluto itself, are classified as dwarf planets. Smaller than the moon but still massive enough to pull themselves into a ball, dwarf planets nevertheless lack the gravitational "oomph" to clear their neighborhood of other sizable objects. So, while larger, more massive planets pretty much have their orbits to themselves, dwarf planets orbit the sun in swarms that include other dwarf planets as well as smaller chunks of rock or ice.

So far, astronomers have identified five dwarf planets: Ceres (which circles the sun in the asteroid belt between Mars and Jupiter), Pluto, Haumea, Makemake, and Eris. Astronomers are studying hundreds of newly found objects in the frigid outer solar system, trying to figure out just how big they are. As time and technology advance, the family of known dwarf planets will surely continue to grow.

CERES
Position from the sun in orbit: fifth
Length of day: 9.1 Earth hours
Length of year: 4.6 Earth years
Known moons: 0

PLUTO
Position from the sun in orbit: tenth
Length of day: 6.4 Earth days
Length of year: 248 Earth years
Known moons: 5

HAUMEA
Position from the sun in orbit: eleventh
Length of day: 3.9 Earth hours
Length of year: 282 Earth years
Known moons: 2

MAKEMAKE
Position from the sun in orbit: twelfth
Length of day: 22.5 Earth hours
Length of year: 305 Earth years
Known moons: 0

ERIS
Position from the sun in orbit: thirteenth
Length of day: 25.9 Earth hours
Length of year: 561 Earth years
Known moons: 1

DESTINATION SPACE

ALIEN SEA

Orange haze blurs the view outside your spaceship's window. You're descending to Titan, the largest of Saturn's 62 moons and 1.5 times bigger than Earth's moon. The smog beneath you thins, and you gasp in amazement: On the alien surface below, rivers flow through canyons. Waves crash in oceans. But Titan is no place like home.

Your special spacecraft splashes down in Kraken Mare, Titan's largest sea. The pumpkin-orange coastline is lined by craggy cliffs. Rocks dot the shore. But because it's a frigid minus 290°F (179°C) here, the rocks are made of solid ice.

Rain begins to fall. It isn't water—it's methane and ethane. On Earth these are polluting gases. On Titan they form clouds and fall as rain that fills the rivers and oceans. You scoop up a sample of ocean liquid for a closer look: Scientists think there's a chance that Titan's seas might be home to alien life.

It'd be very strange if something did live here. On Earth everything living is partly made of water. Since there's no liquid water on Titan's surface, creatures here would be formed of methane or ethane. And because it's so cold, they'd move in slow motion.

Before you can get a good look at your sample, you hear a rumble. It's an ice volcano, thousands of feet tall. It shoots out a slurry of ice and ammonia (a chemical used as a cleaning product on Earth). You'd better get away before the icy blasts sink your boat!

Destination
Titan

Location
Orbiting the planet Saturn

Distance
886 million miles
(1.43 billion km)
from Earth

Time to reach
3 years

Weather
minus 290°F (-179°C),
with scattered methane
rainstorms

THE MOON
TITAN

At minus 290°F (-179°C), Titan seems way too cold for alien life. But it might not be. Even on Earth, creatures called **cryophiles thrive in below-freezing** temperatures. *Brr!*

SEE PHOTOS
TAKEN BY
Hubble!
natgeo.com
/kids/hubble

Sky Calendar
2017

Jupiter

Leonid meteor shower

Partial solar eclipse

January 3–4 Quadrantids Meteor Shower Peak. Featuring up to 40 meteors and hour, this shower is best viewed when the moon sets after midnight.

April 1 Mercury at Greatest Eastern Elongation. Visible low in the western sky just after sunset, Mercury will be at its highest point on the horizon.

April 7 Jupiter at Opposition. The giant planet is at its closest approach to Earth.

May 6–7 Eta Aquarids Meteor Shower Peak. View about 30 to 60 meteors an hour.

June 15 Saturn at Opposition. The best time to view the ringed planet. It makes its closest approach to Earth.

August 12–13 Perseid Meteor Shower Peak. One of the best! Up to 60 meteors an hour. Best viewing is in the direction of the constellation Perseus.

August 21 Total Solar Eclipse. Beginning at the Pacific Ocean then moving through the central United States, the eclipse can be viewed in parts of Oregon, Idaho, Wyoming, Nebraska, Missouri, Kentucky, Tennessee, North Carolina, and South Carolina. A partial eclipse may be visible in most of North America and some of northern South America.

October 21–22 Orionid Meteor Shower Peak. View up to 20 meteors an hour. Look toward the constellation Orion for the best show.

November 13 Conjunction of Venus and Jupiter. These two bright planets will appear very close together in the eastern sky just before sunrise.

November 17–18 Leonid Meteor Shower Peak. View up to 15 meteors an hour.

December 3 Supermoon, Full Moon. The moon will be full and at its closest approach to Earth, likely appearing bigger and brighter than usual.

December 13–14 Geminid Meteor Shower Peak. A spectacular show! Up to 120 multicolored meteors an hour.

Various dates throughout 2017
View the International Space Station. Visit spotthestation.nasa.gov to find out when the ISS will be flying over your neighborhood.

Dates may vary slightly depending on your location. Check with a local planetarium for the best viewing time in your area.

CONSTELLATIONS

Nothing to do on a clear night? Look up! There's so much to see in that starry sky. The constellations you can see among the stars vary with the season. As the following maps show, some are more visible in the winter and spring, while others can be spotted in the summer and fall.

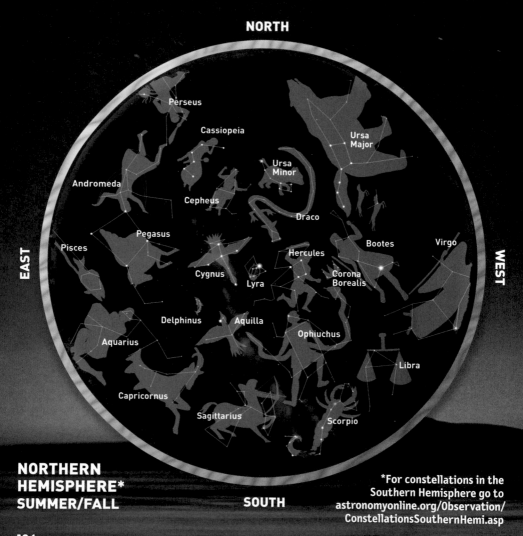

NORTH

Perseus

Cassiopeia

Ursa Major

Ursa Minor

Andromeda

Cepheus

Draco

Pegasus

Bootes

Virgo

Pisces

Hercules

EAST

Cygnus

Corona Borealis

WEST

Lyra

Delphinus

Aquilla

Aquarius

Ophiuchus

Libra

Capricornus

Sagittarius

Scorpio

NORTHERN HEMISPHERE* SUMMER/FALL

SOUTH

*For constellations in the Southern Hemisphere go to astronomyonline.org/Observation/ConstellationsSouthernHemi.asp

Planet or Star?

On a clear night, you'll see a sky filled with glittering lights. But not every bright spot is a star—you may be peeking at a planet instead. How do you tell a star from a planet? While stars twinkle, planets shine more steadily and tend to be the brightest objects in the sky, other than the moon. Planets also move slowly across the sky from night to night. If you think you've spotted one, keep checking on it as the week goes by. If it has moved closer or farther from the moon, then it's probably a planet.

WANT TO SPOT A SATELLITE? Look for an **OBJECT** that travels quickly and steadily among **THE STARS.**

NORTH

EAST

WEST

SOUTH

Cepheus
Draco
Cassiopea
Ursa Minor
Bootes
Andromeda
Perseus
Ursa Major
Auriga
Aries
Virgo
Gemini
Leo
Cancer
Taurus
Crater
Canis Minor
Orion
Hydra
Canis Major

NORTHERN HEMISPHERE *
WINTER/SPRING

Continents on the Move

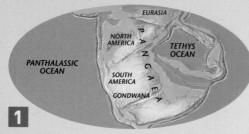

1 **PANGAEA** About 240 million years ago, Earth's landmasses were joined together in one super-continent that extended from Pole to Pole.

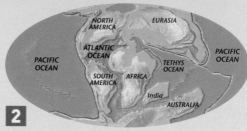

2 **BREAKUP** By 94 million years ago, Pangaea had broken apart into landmasses that would become today's continents. Dinosaurs roamed Earth during a period of warmer climates.

3 **EXTINCTION** About 65 million years ago, an asteroid smashed into Earth, creating the Gulf of Mexico. Scientists think this impact resulted in the extinction of half the world's species, including the dinosaurs. This was one of several mass extinctions.

4 **ICE AGE** By 18,000 years ago, the continents had drifted close to their present positions, but most far northern and far southern lands were buried beneath huge glaciers.

A LOOK INSIDE

The distance from Earth's surface to its center is 3,963 miles (6,378 km) at the Equator. There are four layers: a thin, rigid crust; the rocky mantle; the outer core, which is a layer of molten iron; and finally the inner core, which is believed to be solid iron.

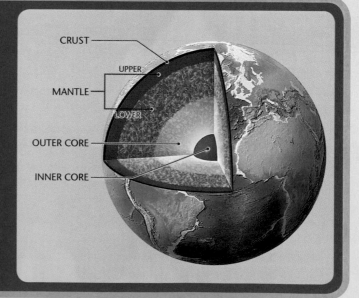

CRUST
UPPER
MANTLE
LOWER
OUTER CORE
INNER CORE

ROCK STARS

The world is full of rocks—some big, some small, some formed deep beneath the Earth, and some formed at the surface. While they may look similar, not all rocks are created equal. Look closely, and you'll see differences between every boulder, stone, and pebble. Here's more about the three top varieties of rocks.

Igneous

Named for the Greek word meaning "from fire," igneous rocks form when hot, molten liquid called magma cools. Pools of magma form deep underground and slowly work their way to the Earth's surface. If they make it all the way, the liquid rock erupts and is called lava. As the layers of lava build up they form a mountain called a volcano. Typical igneous rocks include obsidian, basalt, and pumice, which is so chock-full of gas bubbles that it actually floats in water.

OBSIDIAN   PUMICE

Metamorphic

Metamorphic rocks are the masters of change! These rocks were once igneous or sedimentary, but thanks to intense heat and pressure deep within the Earth, they have undergone a total transformation from their original form. These rocks never truly melt; instead, the heat twists and bends them until their shapes substantially change. Metamorphic rocks include slate as well as marble, which is used for buildings, monuments, and sculptures.

MARBLE   SLATE

Sedimentary

When wind, water, and ice constantly wear away and weather rocks, smaller pieces called sediment are left behind. These are sedimentary rocks, also known as gravel, sand, silt, and clay. As water flows downhill it carries the sedimentary grains into lakes and oceans, where they get deposited. As the loose sediment piles up, the grains eventually get compacted or cemented back together again. The result is new sedimentary rock. Sandstone, gypsum, limestone, and shale are sedimentary rocks that have formed this way.

SANDSTONE   GYPSUM

Name That ROCK

Whether you're kicking one down the road or climbing on top of one at the park, rocks are all around you. But what kind of rocks are they? Can you identify the variety of rocks on this page?

Answers are at the bottom of page 191.

A This is the stuff of hopscotch and tic-tac-toe. It was formed with the skeletons of microorganisms.

B This volcanic rock forms after lava has cooled quickly, and it is the only rock that floats!

CHECK OUT THE BOOK!

GET OUTSIDE GUIDE

C This rock formed in a similar way to granite, but you can see large crystals in it.

D This rock is so soft it can break up in water.

fun fact

Diamonds are the hardest rocks on Earth. They come in a variety of colors, including yellow, red, and even green.

E Some of the oldest fossils found on Earth are preserved in this soft sedimentary rock.

F The most common volcanic rock on Earth, it formed by cooling quickly, but it has fine grains on the surface.

G A seated Abraham Lincoln and Michelangelo's "David" were both carved out of this white, metamorphic rock.

A. Chalk, B. Pumice; C. Gabbro; D. Mudstone; E. Shale; F. Basalt; G. Marble

Volcano!

Fiery hot lava flows down a Hawaiian mountainside like dark, thick syrup. **When it reaches the sea, it hisses and explodes** in scalding jets of steam.

> Lava flowing from a volcano can be hotter than **2100°F** (1149°C).

Farther up the slope, volcanologist Ken Hon picks his way slowly across the rough surface. The hot lava is slippery to walk on. "It's like walking on ice," Hon says. "But the bottom part of your boots starts to melt a little. If you fall, you'll get burned."

Hon plants his feet carefully and slowly. He is collecting data on the lava flowing out of Kilauea (kee-luh-WAY-uh, shown here), a volcano that has been erupting since 1983. Knowing the lava's movements can save lives on the slopes below. But Hon must be careful. New waves of lava are flowing down toward him. Every few minutes he looks up to see where the streams are and makes sure the moving lava hasn't cut off his escape route.

"It's searing hot out there—like the heat from an oven," Hon says. "Up close, you have to wear firefighters' gear so the clothes you're wearing don't catch on fire or melt."

SLOW FLOW

Earth's interior is so hot that rock softens and flows. Volcanoes form at certain places where liquid rock, or magma, pushes through cracks to the Earth's surface. The cracks eject lava, which is what magma is called when it reaches the surface. Ash that forms volcanic mountains also explodes from the crater. Some volcanoes, such as Kilauea, typically erupt gently. But they can pour out rivers of lava that engulf everything in their path.

LAVA ON ROAD

"Back in 1990, lava entered the town of Kalapana," Hon says. "We had to evacuate people from about 150 homes. The lava inched forward and consumed all of the houses." Everyone escaped. But today Kalapana is buried under 30 feet (9.1 m) of lava.

In 2014, about 20 families in Pahoa, Hawaii, were evacuated as Kīlauea's lava once again threatened homes.

Volcanoes aren't scary to Hon. They're fascinating and exciting. Still, Hon knows how to keep safe—and knows when the lava is too close. But the danger is worth it, because the more Hon and other scientists can learn about volcanoes, the safer they can keep the people who live around these powerful forces of nature.

Hawaii's Mauna Loa is the world's largest active volcano.

More than **1,500** volcanoes on Earth are active.

DOOMED HOUSE

LAVA LAMPS

FOUR WAYS VOLCANOES ERUPT

1. FIERY FLOW
Lava sprays through cracks in the Earth and flows down the slopes.

2. SHORT BURST
The pressure in the gas inside stickier magma increases, causing small but frequent bursts of lava.

3. ROCKY RUSH
Stickier magma forms a dome in the volcano's opening. The dome collapses and then explodes, sending ash and rock down the volcano's sides.

4. HUGE *KABOOM!*
The stickiest magma traps large amounts of gas and produces great pressure in the magma chamber. The gas blows the magma into pieces, shooting ash and rock miles into the air.

Get Out of the Way!

As magma moves upward inside a volcano, the volcano becomes more likely to erupt. Here are signs that it might be happening.

- Many small or moderate earthquakes
- Bulges and other deformations in the volcano's surface
- Major changes in the release of gases from cracks and other openings

HOT SPOT

FOUNTAINS OF SUPERHEATED WATER CREATE A WEIRD LANDMARK.

A bizarre blob of steaming fountains bursts with water and color from the barren landscape. It may look like a scene from another planet, but the surreal Fly Geyser unexpectedly gushes up from the Nevada, U.S.A., desert. The mounds stand 12 feet (3.7 m) tall, spouting scalding water 5 feet (1.5 m) higher. At first glance, Fly Geyser seems to be a natural wonder, but it's not quite natural. It's technically not a geyser either. It's an accident.

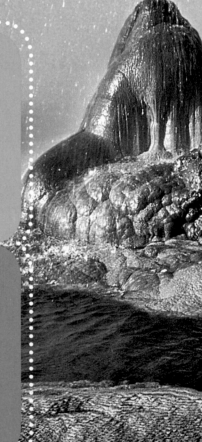

BIRTH OF FLY GEYSER Although Fly Geyser is powered by nature, it got a kick start from humans. The fountains spew water that continuously flows from a single underground hole, which was drilled by workers about 50 years ago. They had hoped to strike water that was so hot it could power an electrical plant with geothermal energy. The boiling water spurting from the Fly Geyser originates deep below the surface, where it is heated by shallow magma—hot, liquid rock. This wet zone is covered by a hard layer of rock, which traps the hot water. Because it can't escape as steam, the pressurized water's temperature rises far above the normal boiling point. The artificial, drilled hole gives the water a way out, like the opening of a soda bottle.

IT'S ALIVE! Even though the water spewing from Fly Geyser tops 200°F (93°C), the temperature turned out to be too low for a geothermal plant. The hole was plugged, but the hot water eventually forced its way up. Minerals that dissolved in the exiting water gradually built the mounds and surrounding terraces.

Fly Geyser's mounds and terraces aren't only alive with color—they're literally alive. The brilliant reds, yellows, and greens are caused by organisms called thermophiles, or "heat lovers." They are the only life-forms that can survive in such high, deadly temperatures. Different colors of thermophiles live in water at different temperatures, creating Fly Geyser's changing colors.

THEY'RE GONNA BLOW!

Natural geysers are more complicated than Fly Geyser. The world's most famous geyser, Wyoming's Old Faithful in Yellowstone National Park, doesn't spray continuously like Fly Geyser. Instead, it erupts about 16 times a day, shooting a steamy torrent of water more than 130 feet (40 m) into the air. What makes Old Faithful and other natural geysers different from Fly Geyser is their complex plumbing systems. The hot water's path to the surface becomes constricted, and the pressure builds. The heated water begins to bubble, and then explodes up and out. "It's like a volcano," explains U.S. Geological Survey researcher Shaul Hurwitz. "Once it starts erupting, all the stored water is released rapidly."

HOT PURSUIT Fly Geyser wasn't hot enough to support a geothermal plant, but it was a necessary step in a hit-or-miss process. Other heat-seeking holes in the area tapped into hotter water and were put to use. That water makes steam that cranks big machines to create electricity. Most power plants use steam, but geothermal ones don't burn coal or gas to make it, so they're much cleaner.

QUIZ WHIZ

Discover your science smarts by taking this quiz!
ANSWERS BELOW

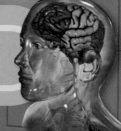

1 **True or false?** Your short-term memory can hold about twelve things at a time.

2 _____ is/are the hardest type of rock on earth.
a. Diamonds
b. Pumice
c. Marble
d. Sandstone

3 Ceres is a _____.
a. mineral
b. volcano
c. dwarf planet
d. smart phone feature

4 Adult humans have up to _____ cells in their body.
a. 100
b. 1,000
c. 1 million
d. 100 trillion

5 What falls like rain on Jupiter?
a. hydrogen combined with oxygen
b. neon dissolved in helium
c. methane
d. cats and dogs

Not **STUMPED** yet? Check out the *NATIONAL GEOGRAPHIC KIDS QUIZ WHIZ* collection for more crazy **SCIENCE** questions!

Research Like a Pro

There is so much information on the Internet. How do you find what you need and make sure it's accurate?

Be Specific

To come up with the most effective keywords—words that describe what you want to know more about—write down what you're looking for in the form of a question, and then circle the most important words in that sentence. Those are the keywords to use in your search. And for best results, use words that are specific rather than general.

Research

Research on the Internet involves "looking up" information using a search engine (see list below). Type one or two keywords, and the search engine will provide a list of websites that contain information related to your topic.

Use Trustworthy Sources

When conducting Internet research, be sure the website you use is reliable and the information it provides can be trusted. Sites produced by well-known, established organizations, companies, publications, educational institutions, or the government are your best bets.

Don't Copy

Avoid Internet plagiarism. Take careful notes and cite the websites you use to conduct research.

HELPFUL AND SAFE SEARCH ENGINES FOR KIDS

Google Safe Search
squirrelnet.com/search/Google_SafeSearch.asp

GoGooligans
gogooligans.com

AOL Kids
kids.aol.com

Flowering namaqua daisies create a spectacular display at the Goegap Nature Reserve in Namaqualand, South Africa.

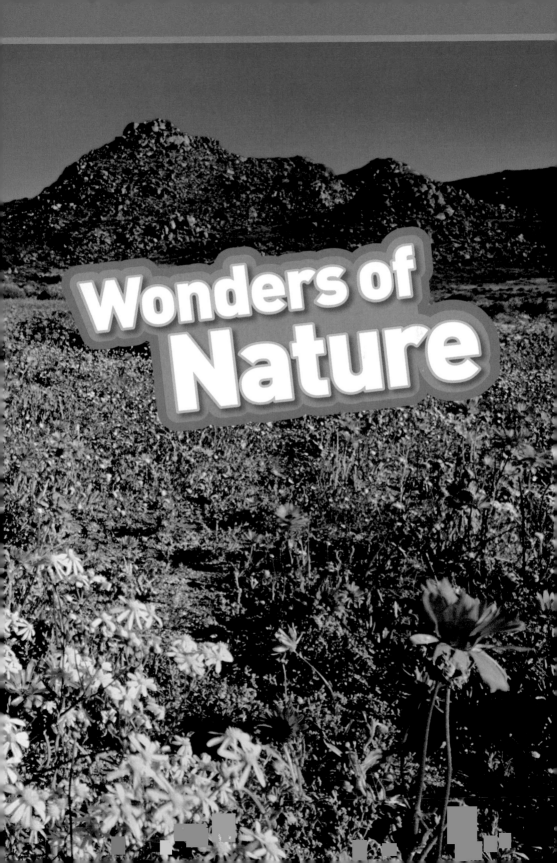

Wonders of Nature

1 A HEAT WAVE CAN MAKE TRAIN TRACKS BEND.

2 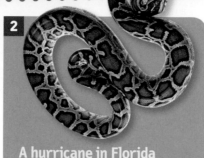 A hurricane in Florida caused **900 captive** pythons to escape.

3 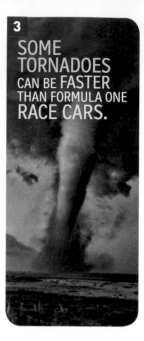 SOME TORNADOES CAN BE FASTER THAN FORMULA ONE RACE CARS.

17

4 You can tell the TEMPERATURE by COUNTING a cricket's CHIRPS.

FREAKY FACTS ABOUT

5  A 2003 heat wave turned grapes to raisins before they were picked from the vine.

6 SANDSTORMS CAN SWALLOW UP ENTIRE CITIES.

7  A MUDSLIDE CAN CARRY ROCKS, TREES, VEHICLES, AND ENTIRE BUILDINGS.

8 A spiderweb **INSIDE** your **HOUSE** may be a **SIGN** that **COLDER WEATHER** is coming.

9 CATS AND DOGS HAVE BEEN KNOWN TO SENSE WHEN A TORNADO IS APPROACHING.

10

In ANTARCTICA, SNOW can fall so hard YOU CAN'T SEE your hand IN FRONT OF YOUR FACE.

11 In 525 B.C., a **SANDSTORM BURIED** hundreds of **SOLDIERS** in an **EGYPTIAN DESERT.**

12

Lava from volcanoes can start wildfires.

13 About **2,000** thunderstorms rain down on Earth **every minute.**

WEATHER

14 Worms CRAWL UP from UNDERGROUND when a FLOOD IS COMING.

15

Some frogs get noisier just before it rains.

16 RAINDROPS can be the SIZE OF A HOUSEFLY and fall at roughly 20 miles an hour (32 km/h).

17

WILDFIRES SOMETIMES CREATE FLAME-THROWING TORNADOES CALLED FIRE WHIRLS.

Weather and Climate

Weather is the condition of the atmosphere—temperature, wind, humidity, and precipitation—at a given place at a given time. Climate, however, is the average weather for a particular place over a long period of time. Different places on Earth have different climates, but climate is not a random occurrence. It is a pattern that is controlled by factors such as latitude, elevation, prevailing winds, the temperature of ocean currents, and location on land relative to water. Climate is generally constant, but evidence indicates that human activity is causing a change in the patterns of climate.

WEATHER EXTREMES

BIGGEST SNOWFLAKE: The biggest snowflake ever recorded was 15 inches (38.1 cm) wide.

LIGHTNING HOT: Temperatures in the air around a lightning bolt can hit 50,000°F (27,760°C)

RAINIEST DAY: 72 inches (183 cm) of rain was recorded in a 24-hour period in 1966 on Reunion Island, a French island in the Indian Ocean, during Tropical Cyclone Denise.

GLOBAL CLIMATE ZONES

Climatologists, people who study climate, have created different systems for classifying climates. One often-used system is called the Köppen system, which classifies climate zones according to precipitation, temperature, and vegetation. It has five major categories—Tropical, Dry, Temperate, Cold, and Polar—with a sixth category for locations where high elevations override other factors.

ARCTIC OCEAN
ARCTIC CIRCLE
TROPIC OF CANCER
ATLANTIC OCEAN
PACIFIC OCEAN
EQUATOR
PACIFIC OCEAN
INDIAN OCEAN
TROPIC OF CAPRICORN
ANTARCTIC CIRCLE

Climate
■ Tropical ■ Dry ■ Humid temperate ■ Humid cold ■ Polar

WATER CYCLE

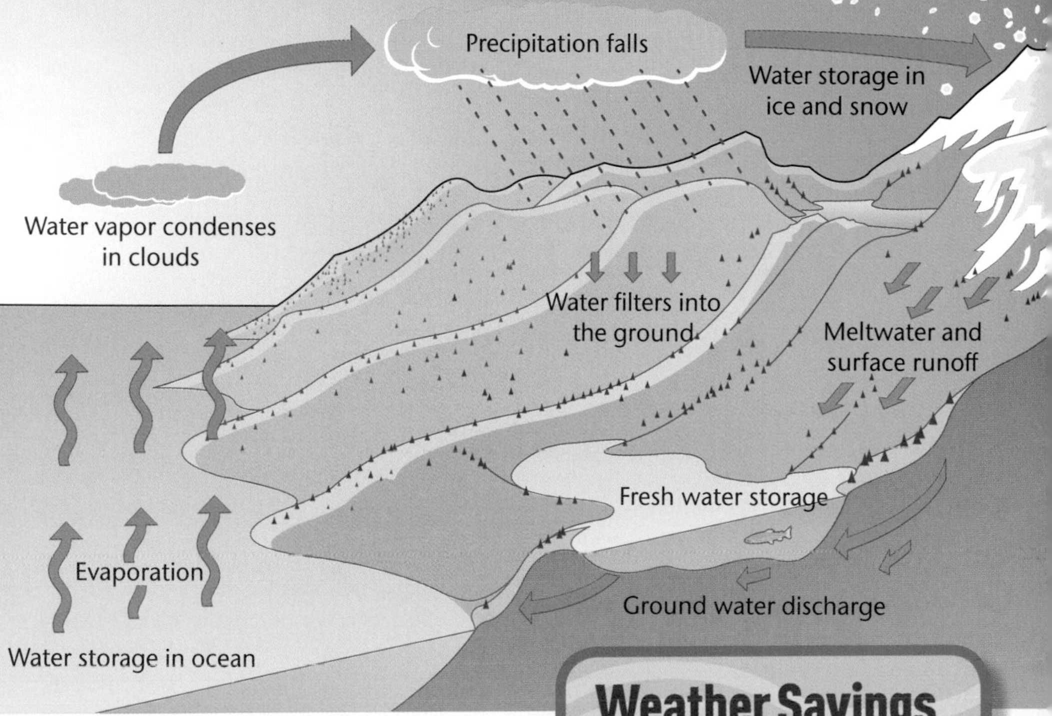

Precipitation falls

Water storage in ice and snow

Water vapor condenses in clouds

Water filters into the ground

Meltwater and surface runoff

Fresh water storage

Evaporation

Ground water discharge

Water storage in ocean

The amount of water on Earth is more or less constant—

only the form changes. As the sun warms Earth's surface, liquid water is changed to water vapor in a process called **evaporation.** Water on the surface of plants' leaves turn into water vapor in a process called **transpiration.** As water vapor rises into the air, it cools and changes form again. This time it becomes clouds in a process called **condensation.** Water droplets fall from the clouds as **precipitation,** which then travels as groundwater or runoff back to the lakes, rivers, and oceans, where the cycle (shown above) starts all over again.

To a meteorologist— a person who studies the weather— a "light rain" is less than 1/48 of an inch (0.5 mm). A "heavy rain" is more than 1/6 of an inch (4 mm).

Weather Sayings

These words of weather wisdom have been passed down for generations. But they're not always accurate—be sure to check the forecast!

- Red sky in the morning, sailors take warning. Red sky at night, sailors' delight.

- Clear nights mean cold days.

- If a circle forms 'round the moon, then it will rain very soon.

- Rain before seven stops by eleven.

- In a green sky, the cows will fly.

Types of Clouds

If you want a clue about the weather, look up at the clouds. They'll tell a lot about the condition of the air and what weather might be on the way. Clouds are made of both air and water. On fair days, warm air currents rise up and push against the water in clouds, keeping it from falling. But as the raindrops in a cloud get bigger, it's time to set them free. The bigger raindrops become too heavy for the air currents to hold up, and they fall to the ground.

How Much Does a Cloud Weigh?

A light, fluffy, cumulus cloud typically weighs about 216,000 pounds (97,975 kg). That's about the weight of 18 elephants. A rain-soaked cumulonimbus cloud typically weighs 105.8 million pounds (48,000,000 kg), or about 9,000 elephants.

1 STRATUS These clouds make the sky look like a bowl of thick gray porridge. They hang low in the sky, blanketing the day in dreary darkness. Stratus clouds form when cold, moist air close to the ground moves over a region.

2 CIRRUS These wispy tufts of clouds are thin and hang high up in the atmosphere where the air is extremely cold. Cirrus clouds are made of tiny ice crystals.

3 CUMULONIMBUS These are the monster clouds. Rising air currents force fluffy cumulus clouds to swell and shoot upward, as much as 70,000 feet (21,000 m). When these clouds bump against the top of the troposphere, or the tropopause, they flatten out on top like tabletops.

4 CUMULUS These white, fluffy clouds make people sing, "Oh, what a beautiful morning!" They form low in the atmosphere and look like marshmallows. They often mix with large patches of blue sky. Formed when hot air rises, cumulus clouds usually disappear when the air cools at night.

Make a Barometer

ARE YOU FASCINATED BY WEATHER? Then you should make your own barometer to track the weather where you live!

SUPPLY LIST

- Ruler
- Tall glass
- Drinking straw
- Bubble gum
- Tape
- Water and blue food coloring

STEPS

1. Tape a clear drinking straw to a ruler. The bottom of the straw should line up with the ½-inch (12–13 mm) mark on the ruler.

2. Stand the ruler up in a tall glass and tape it to the inside of the glass so it stays straight. Fill the glass ¾ full with water.

3. Here's the fun part: Chew on a piece of gum for a while, then stick it to the top of the straw.

4. Pour out ¼ of the water so that the water in the straw is higher than the water in the cup.

5. Keep an eye on your barometer. When atmospheric pressure increases, the water level in your straw will rise (which usually means fair weather). When atmospheric pressure decreases, the water level will fall (and can mean clouds or rain are on the way). Record your findings in your meteorologist notebook!

> Barometers were invented in Italy in the early 1600s by Evangelista Torricelli.

Time: about 10 minutes

KEEP A WEATHER JOURNAL

Recording the daily temperature, rainfall, and barometric changes will help you track patterns in the weather. Try to take a measurement every day and record it in a journal. Set up a chart for each component of your weather station. After a few weeks, you might start to see some patterns, and soon you'll be making predictions—like a regular meteorologist!

TOP OF STRAW

Natural Disasters

Every world region has its share of natural disasters—the mix just varies from place to place. And the names of similar storms may vary as well. Take, for example, cyclones, typhoons, and hurricanes. The only difference among these disasters is where in the world they strike. In the Atlantic and the Northeast Pacific, they're hurricanes; in the Northwest Pacific near Asia they're typhoons; and in the South Pacific and Indian Oceans, they're cyclones.

Despite their distinct titles, these natural disasters are each classified by violent winds, massive waves, torrential rain, and floods. The only obvious variation among these storms? They spin in the opposite direction if they're south of the Equator.

TYPHOON!

HURRICANES IN 2017

HELLO, MY NAME IS . . .

Hurricane names come from six official international lists. The names alternate between male and female.

When a storm becomes a hurricane, a name from the list is used, in alphabetical order. Each list is reused every six years. A name "retires" if that hurricane caused a lot of damage or many deaths.

Arlene
Bret
Cindy
Don
Emily
Franklin
Gert
Harvey
Irma
Jose
Katia
Lee
Maria
Nate
Ophelia
Philippe
Rina
Sean
Tammy
Vince
Whitney

A monster storm with gusts of 235 miles an hour (380 km/h) barrels down onto a cluster of islands in the heart of the Philippines in November 2013. Howling winds whip debris into the street as palm trees bend nearly in half, and seawater rises as high as a two-story building. This is Super Typhoon Haiyan, and it's about as dangerous as they come.

When does a typhoon become a super-typhoon? According to the U.S. National Oceanic and Atmospheric Administration (NOAA), winds must sustain speeds of over 150 miles an hour (240 km/h) for at least a minute. And not only is Haiyan powerful, it's also gigantic: The storm's clouds cover at least two-thirds of the Philippines, which is roughly the size of Arizona, U.S.A.

The word "typhoon" comes from the Greek *typhon*, meaning "whirlwind." These superstrong storms form when tropical winds suck up moisture as they pass over warm water. Increasing in speed and strength as they near the coast, typhoons can topple homes and cause massive flooding once they hit land.

The Philippines endures an average of eight or nine tropical storms every year. But none have been as disastrous as Haiyan. Resulting in over 6,300 casualties, affecting 16 million people, and racking up millions of dollars in damage, the storm was one of the strongest typhoons to ever hit land anywhere in the world.

Scale of Hurricane Intensity

CATEGORY	ONE	TWO	THREE	FOUR	FIVE
DAMAGE	Minimal	Moderate	Extensive	Extreme	Catastrophic
WINDS	74–95 mph (119–153 kph)	96–110 mph (154–177 kph)	111–129 mph (178–208 kph)	130–156 mph (209–251 kph)	157 mph or higher (252+ kph)
(DAMAGE refers to wind and water damage combined.)					

EARTHQUAKE!

It was a force strong enough to move Mount Everest. When a 7.8-magnitude earthquake rocked Nepal in April 2015 the world's tallest mountain actually shifted more than an inch (3 cm) southwest.

The damage below the mountain was much more significant, however. The earthquake was the worst to hit the Himalayan nation in nearly a century. More than 8,500 died and scores more were injured in the aftermath of the earthquake and its aftershocks. Villages were reduced to rubble, and more than half a million homes around the country were seriously damaged. The earthquake and its aftershocks also triggered landslides and a deadly avalanche on Mount Everest, causing even more damage and taking the lives of dozens of villagers and trekkers aiming to reach the peak.

No doubt, Nepal was devastated by the earthquake. But the resilient nation reopened schools within five weeks, and humanitarian efforts are helping to rebuild homes and businesses—and resume life as normal in Nepal.

BLIZZARD!

Buffalo, New York, U.S.A., is no stranger to snow. In fact, the town typically receives an average of about seven feet (2.1 m) per year. But no one was quite prepared for the massive snowstorm that hit the region in November 2014, burying parts of Buffalo in more than five feet (1.5 m) of heavy snow. With freezing winds whipping off of nearby Lake Erie, bands of heavy snow fell at a rate of up to five inches (12.7 cm) per hour at times. The snow trapped people in their homes, stranding cars on the highway, closing schools for a week, and stalling almost all activity in the town and surrounding areas. All told, 13 people died during the blizzard.

And once the snow stopped? Massive loads of snow—estimated to match the weight of two cars—caused rooftops to buckle, forcing people to evacuate from apartment buildings and homes. It took thousands of truckloads to remove the snow from city streets before unseasonably warm temperatures that hit the region just one week later melted the rest away.

What is a *tornado?*

TORNADOES, ALSO KNOWN AS TWISTERS, are funnels of rapidly rotating air that are created during a thunderstorm. With wind speeds of up to 300 miles an hour (483 km/h), tornadoes have the power to pick up and destroy everything in their path.

Supercell

A massive rotating thunderstorm that generates the most destructive of all tornadoes. A series of supercells in the southern United States caused an outbreak of 92 tornadoes in ten states over a 15-hour period in 2008.

Weather Alert

TORNADOES HAVE OCCURRED IN ALL 50 U.S. STATES AND ON EVERY CONTINENT EXCEPT ANTARCTICA.

Funnel cloud

This rotating funnel of air formed in a cumulus or cumulonimbus cloud becomes a tornado if it touches the ground.

Fire whirls

These tornadoes made of wind and fire occur during a wildfire. Their flaming towers can be five to ten stories tall and can last for more than an hour. They are also called fire devils.

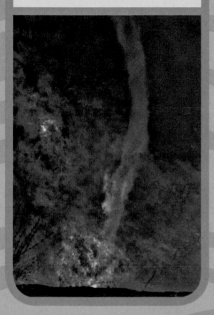

THE ENHANCED FUJITA SCALE

The Enhanced Fujita (EF) Scale, named after tornado expert T. Theodore Fujita, classifies tornadoes based on wind speed and the intensity of damage that they cause.

EF0
65–85 mph winds
(105–137 kph)
Slight damage

EF1
86–110 mph winds
(138–177 kph)
Moderate damage

EF2
111–135 mph winds
(178–217 kph)
Substantial damage

EF3
136–165 mph winds
(218–266 kph)
Severe damage

EF4
166–200 mph winds
(267–322 kph)
Massive damage

EF5
More than
200 mph winds
(322+ kph)
Catastrophic damage

Waterspout

This funnel-shaped column forms over water and is usually weaker than a land tornado.

HOW DOES YOUR GARDEN GROW?

Three characteristics make plants distinct:

1. Most have chlorophyll (a green pigment that makes photosynthesis work and turns sunlight into energy), while some are parasitic.

2. They cannot change their location on their own.

3. Their cell walls are made from a stiff material called cellulose.

The plant kingdom is more than 300,000 species strong, growing all over the world: on top of mountains, in the sea, in frigid temperatures—everywhere. Without plants, life on Earth would not be able to survive. Plants provide food and oxygen for animals and humans.

Photosynthesis

Plants are lucky—they don't have to hunt or shop for food. Most use the sun to produce their own food. In a process called photosynthesis, the plant's chloroplast (the part of the plant where the chemical chlorophyll is located) captures the sun's energy and combines it with carbon dioxide from the air and nutrient-rich water from the ground to produce a sugar called glucose. Plants burn the glucose for energy to help them grow. As a waste product, plants emit oxygen, which humans and other animals need to breathe. When we breathe, we exhale carbon dioxide, which the plants then use for more photosynthesis—it's all a big, finely tuned system. So the next time you pass a lonely houseplant, give it thanks for helping you live.

Bet you didn't know

6 facts about plants that will grow on you

1 Medicine made with certain passion-flowers is used to help people sleep.

2 Leaves of a species of mimosa plant curl when touched.

3 Attenborough's pitcher plant secretes nectar to lure bugs and rodents into its "mouth."

4 A common sunflower's main head consists of up to 4,000 tiny flowers.

5 The seed pods of some snap-dragon plants can look like human skulls.

6 One kind of eucalyptus tree can have rainbow-colored bark.

CARNIVOROUS Plants

Most plants get their nutrients from soil. But many carnivorous plants grow in places where the soil is poor, so they eat insects instead. Here's more about these meat-eaters!

Sarracenia

Sarracenia is a genus of plants that trap bugs with their pitchers, or pitcher-shaped leaves, but that's not all. Some species contain a chemical-laced nectar that dazes their prey. After a few sips, a woozy insect becomes less steady on its feet, leaving it little chance to fend off an inevitable—and untimely—death.

sundew

The "dew" on this plant is inviting to insects. But those droplets—made of a thick, sticky substance attached to the tips of the plant's hairs—are deadly. After landing on the plant's narrow leaves to suck up moisture, the insect gets stuck in the hairs and eventually suffocates or dies from exhaustion. Digestive enzymes in the droplets break down the insect, completing the meal.

cobra lily

This plant picks up its ferocious name from its pitcher, which is formed from a modified leaf that looks like a cobra ready to strike. Instead of using fangs to attack its prey, the cobra lily draws insects into its sunny pitcher, thanks to transparent windows on top of its trap that work like a skylight. The insects are drawn to the light, but once they're trapped inside, it's, uh, lights out.

butterwort

The shiny leaves on this plant may look inviting to a thirsty insect, but watch out! Things are not what they seem. The butterwort's leaves are covered with short hairs that are topped with a gluey fluid that acts as a trap. The fluid also contains enzymes that slowly digest the victim.

monkey cup

These plants, native to Southeast Asia, typically trap insects. But they've also been known to eat much bigger species, including small mammals like mice, rats, and occasionally even birds that come to sip at its pitcher. At least the monkeys who are said to drink rainwater out of the plant's pitcher manage to stay out of harm's way!

pitcher plant

Bugs beware! There are many kinds of pitcher plants, but they're all dangerous places to dine. A bug is attracted to the plant's delicious nectar, but if a hungry insect crawls too close to the edge, it slips down the plant's slick insides and becomes trapped at the bottom of the pitcher.

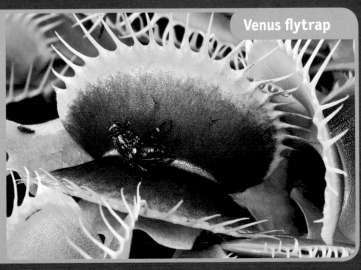

Venus flytrap

No wonder this plant shares a name with a planet—it's truly out of this world! Its leaves are like trapdoors, drawing small insects in with sweet-smelling nectar. If tiny hairs on the surface of the trap are brushed twice in quick succession, the leaves snap shut in the blink of an eye. This sophisticated system ensures that the plant won't waste energy on nonfood items.

Biomes

A BIOME, OFTEN CALLED A MAJOR LIFE ZONE, is one of the natural world's major communities where plants and animals adapt to their specific surroundings. Biomes are classified depending on the predominant vegetation, climate, and geography of a region. They can be divided into six major types: forest, freshwater, marine, desert, grassland, and tundra. Each biome consists of many ecosystems.

Biomes are extremely important. Balanced ecological relationships among biomes help to maintain the environment and life on Earth as we know it. For example, an increase in one species of plant, such as an invasive one, can cause a ripple effect throughout the whole biome.

FOREST

Forests occupy about one-third of Earth's land area. There are three major types of forests: tropical, temperate, and boreal (taiga). Forests are home to a diversity of plants, some of which may hold medicinal qualities for humans, as well as thousands of animal species, some still undiscovered. Forests can also absorb carbon dioxide, a greenhouse gas, and give off oxygen.

The rabbit-size royal antelope lives in West Africa's dense forests.

FRESHWATER

Most water on Earth is salty, but freshwater ecosystems—including lakes, ponds, wetlands, rivers, and streams—usually contain water with less than one percent salt concentration. The countless animal and plant species that live in a freshwater biome vary from continent to continent, but they include algae, frogs, turtles, fish, and the larvae of many insects.

The place where fresh and salt water meet is called an estuary.

MARINE

The marine biome covers almost three-fourths of Earth's surface, making it the largest habitat on our planet. Oceans make up the majority of the saltwater marine biome. Coral reefs are considered to be the most biodiverse of any of the biome habitats. The marine biome is home to more than one million plant and animal species.

> Estimated to be up to 100,000 years old, sea grass growing in the Mediterranean Sea may be the oldest living thing on Earth.

DESERT

Covering about one-fifth of Earth's surface, deserts are places where precipitation is less than ten inches (25 cm) per year. Although most deserts are hot, there are other kinds as well. The four major kinds of deserts are hot, semiarid, coastal, and cold. Far from being barren wastelands, deserts are biologically rich habitats.

> Some sand dunes in the Sahara are tall enough to bury a 50-story building.

GRASSLAND

Biomes called grasslands are characterized by having grasses instead of large shrubs or trees. Grasslands generally have precipitation for only about half to three-fourths of the year. If it were more, they would become forests. Grasslands can be divided into two types: tropical (savannas) and temperate. Some of the world's largest land animals, such as elephants, live there.

> Grasslands in North America are called prairies; in South America, they're called pampas.

TUNDRA

The coldest of all biomes, a tundra is characterized by an extremely cold climate, simple vegetation, little precipitation, poor nutrients, and a short growing season. There are two types of tundra: arctic and alpine. A tundra is home to few kinds of vegetation. Surprisingly, though, there are quite a few animal species that can survive the tundra's extremes, such as wolves, caribou, and even mosquitoes.

> Formed 10,000 years ago, the arctic tundra is the world's youngest biome.

THE OC

PACIFIC OCEAN

STATS

Surface area
65,436,200 sq mi (169,479,000 sq km)

Portion of Earth's water area
47 percent

Greatest depth
Challenger Deep
(in the Mariana Trench)
-36,070 ft (-10,994 m)

Surface temperatures
Summer high: 90°F (32°C)
Winter low: 28°F (-2°C)

Tides
Highest: 30 ft (9 m) near Korean peninsula
Lowest: 1 ft (0.3 m) near Midway Islands

Cool creatures: giant Pacific octopus,
bottlenose whale, clownfish, great
white shark

ATLANTIC OCEAN

STATS

Surface area
35,338,500 sq mi (91,526,300 sq km)

Portion of Earth's water area
25 percent

Greatest depth
Puerto Rico Trench
-28,232 ft (-8,605 m)

Surface temperatures
Summer high: 90°F (32°C)
Winter low: 28°F (-2°C)

Tides
Highest: 52 ft (16 m)
Bay of Fundy, Canada
Lowest: 1.5 ft (0.5 m)
Gulf of Mexico and Mediterranean Sea

Cool creatures: blue whale, Atlantic spotted
dolphin, sea turtle

GREAT WHITE SHARK

GREEN SEA TURTLE

EANS

INDIAN OCEAN

STATS

Surface area
28,839,800 sq mi (74,694,800 sq km)

Portion of Earth's water area
21 percent

Greatest depth
Java Trench
-23,376 ft (-7,125 m)

Surface temperatures
Summer high: 93°F (34°C)
Winter low: 28°F (-2°C)

Tides
Highest: 36 ft (11 m)
Lowest: 2 ft (0.6 m)
Both along Australia's west coast

Cool creatures: humpback whale, Portuguese man-of-war, dugong (sea cow)

DUGONG

ARCTIC OCEAN

STATS

Surface area
5,390,000 sq mi (13,960,100 sq km)

Portion of Earth's water area
4 percent

Greatest depth
Molloy Deep
-18,599 ft (-5,669 m)

Surface temperatures
Summer high: 41°F (5°C)
Winter low: 28°F (-2°C)

Tides
Less than 1 ft (0.3 m) variation throughout the ocean

Cool creatures: beluga whale, orca, harp seal, narwhal

ORCA

To see the major oceans and bays in relation to landmasses, look at the map on pages 258 and 259.

PRISTINE SEAS

Explorers work to protect the last truly wild places in the ocean.

Around the world, only one percent of the ocean is fully protected from fishing.

A YELLOW-EDGED LYRETAIL PROWLS CORAL NEAR PITCAIRN ISLAND.

DR. ENRIC SALA

KEEPING OUR OCEANS PRISTINE

Oceans cover more than 70 percent of Earth's surface. Even with all of that water, only a tiny percentage is not impacted by human activity—but conservationists are working to change that. The National Geographic Pristine Seas team, led by National Geographic Explorer-in-Residence Enric Sala, travels to some of the most remote parts of the oceans to explore life underwater and create protected areas. One such location? The Pitcairn Islands in the South Pacific, where the Pristine Seas squad created the world's largest marine reserve, setting aside a swath of sea bigger than the entire state of California, U.S.A., for special protection. That means that there is no fishing or seafloor mining allowed in the reserve, a move meant to keep the thousands of fish, plants, and coral living there healthy and thriving.

PITCAIRN ISLAND

More than 102 million tons (92.6 million t) of wild fish and shellfish are caught in the oceans every year.

A DIVER EXPLORES BOUNTY BAY NEAR PITCAIRN ISLAND.

GREY REEF SHARK

Ninety percent of the large predators in the ocean, like sharks and tuna, are gone.

SAVING THE SHARKS

The Pristine Seas expedition has also made its mark on the uninhabited Southern Line Islands, an archipelago deep in the South Pacific. Dozens of grey reef sharks swirl around these islands, feeding on the fish around the coral reefs. But they face constant danger. Sought out by humans for their fins—considered a delicacy in some parts of Asia—these sharks are vulnerable to overfishing, which is when people catch them at too fast a rate for the species to replace themselves. But by working with the local government, Sala and his crew have established a 12-nautical-mile fishing exclusion zone around each island. It's a step in the right direction for protecting the ecology of the island and, ultimately, boosting the shark's dwindling population.

QUIZ WHIZ

Quiz yourself to find out if you're a natural when it comes to nature knowledge!

ANSWERS BELOW

1 **True or false?** You can tell the temperature by counting a cricket's chirps.

2 A light, fluffy cumulus cloud can weigh as much as what?
a. a feather
b. 18 elephants
c. 5 trucks
d. 9,000 rhinos

3 Monkey cups, butterworts, and sundews are all types of what?
a. flowers
b. mushrooms
c. carnivorous plants
d. cookies

4 A tornado made of wind and fire is also known as a _____.

5 _____ percent of the large predators in the ocean are gone.
a. 90
b. 10
c. 5
d. 50

Not **STUMPED** yet? Check out the *NATIONAL GEOGRAPHIC KIDS QUIZ WHIZ* collection for more crazy **NATURE** questions!

ANSWERS:
1. True; 2. b; 3. c; 4. fire whirl; 5. a

HOMEWORK HELP

SPEAK NATURALLY

Oral Reports Made Easy

Does the thought of public speaking start your stomach churning like a tornado? Would you rather get caught in an avalanche than give a speech?

Giving an oral report does not have to be a natural disaster. The basic format is very similar to that of a written essay. There are two main elements that make up a good oral report—the writing and the presentation. As you write your oral report, remember that your audience will be hearing the information as opposed to reading it. Follow the guidelines below, and there will be clear skies ahead.

TIP:
Make sure you practice your presentation a few times. Stand in front of a mirror or have a parent record you so you can see if you need to work on anything, such as eye contact.

Writing Your Material

Follow the steps in the "How to Write a Perfect Essay" section on p. 141, but prepare your report to be spoken rather than written. Try to keep your sentences short and simple. Long, complex sentences are harder to follow. Limit yourself to just a few key points. You don't want to overwhelm your audience with too much information. To be most effective, hit your key points in the introduction, elaborate on them in the body, and then repeat them once again in your conclusion.

An oral report has three basic parts:

- **Introduction**—This is your chance to engage your audience and really capture their interest in the subject you are presenting. Use a funny personal experience or a dramatic story, or start with an intriguing question.

- **Body**—This is the longest part of your report. Here you elaborate on the facts and ideas you want to convey. Give information that supports your main idea, and expand on it with specific examples or details. In other words, structure your oral report in the same way you would a written essay so that your thoughts are presented in a clear and organized manner.

- **Conclusion**—This is the time to summarize the information and emphasize your most important points to the audience one last time.

Preparing Your Delivery

1 Practice makes perfect.
Practice! Practice! Practice! Confidence, enthusiasm, and energy are key to delivering an effective oral report, and they can best be achieved through rehearsal. Ask family and friends to be your practice audience and give you feedback when you're done. Were they able to follow your ideas? Did you seem knowledgeable and confident? Did you speak too slowly or too fast, too softly or too loudly? The more times you practice giving your report, the more you'll master the material. Then you won't have to rely so heavily on your notes or papers, and you will be able to give your report in a relaxed and confident manner.

2 Present with everything you've got.
Be as creative as you can. Incorporate videos, sound clips, slide presentations, charts, diagrams, and photos. Visual aids help stimulate your audience's senses and keep them intrigued and engaged. They can also help to reinforce your key points. And remember that when you're giving an oral report, you're a performer. Take charge of the spotlight and be as animated and entertaining as you can. Have fun with it.

3 Keep your nerves under control.
Everyone gets a little nervous when speaking in front of a group. That's normal. But the more preparation you've done—meaning plenty of researching, organizing, and rehearsing—the more confident you'll be. Preparation is the key. And if you make a mistake or stumble over your words, just regroup and keep going. Nobody's perfect, and nobody expects you to be.

2017 marks the 20th anniversary of the Hong Kong handover. On July 1, 1997, the United Kingdom returned the city to China after more than 150 years of British control.

History
Happens

Jungle of Secrets

Scientists uncover a hidden city near a temple called ANGKOR WAT

I n the midst of Cambodia's steamy jungle looms a majestic medieval temple. Called Angkor Wat, the nearly 900-year-old structure was built in the capital of the Khmer Empire, a powerful civilization in Southeast Asia. But until recently, few were aware of something tucked in the forest beyond the temple—a hidden city.

MISSING METROPOLIS
The Khmer Empire thrived between the 9th and 15th centuries. Many people worshipped at the temple of Angkor Wat in the capital city of Angkor, which was about the size (area) of New York City. Scientists believe that in the 14th and 15th centuries, droughts and other extreme natural disasters caused many people to abandon the region and move south. Eventually, thick

> In this nation, it's considered an insult to touch someone's head.

forests grew over much of the area.

Built in the 12th century to honor a god, Angkor Wat was in continual use even after the capital city was abandoned. When a French explorer came across the temple in the 1800s, he spread word of its beauty, drawing visitors and archaeologists to the area.

Scientists suspected that another, older city from the Khmer Empire called Mahendraparvata was hidden in the jungle around the temple. According to writings found in old texts, the city was built in A.D. 802 and served as the Khmer Empire's capital before it moved to Angkor.

AIRBORNE DETECTIVES
In 2012 a team of scientists wanted to investigate the region in search of the remains of Mahendraparvata. A thick tangle of trees

Angkor Wat appears on Cambodia's flag (left).

TREE ROOTS GROW OVER RUINS IN A JUNGLE NEAR ANGKOR WAT.

ASIA
PACIFIC OCEAN
CAMBODIA
INDIAN OCEAN

THAILAND
LAOS
Angkor Wat
Tonle Sap
CAMBODIA
Phnom Penh ★
VIETNAM
Gulf of Thailand
South China Sea

covering the land made exploring on foot difficult. So instead the team took to the skies.

Crisscrossing over forest canopies in a helicopter, archaeologist Damian Evans used an instrument called LIDAR to scan the ground. LIDAR works by rapidly firing off pulses of laser light. A sensor on the instrument measures how long it takes for each pulse to bounce back from the ground. If a set of laser beams has a shorter return time than the previous pulses sent, it could mean the beams have hit something elevated, such as a building. A longer return time could mean that the beams are bouncing off of a low valley or deep riverbed. Using GPS technology, cartographers then combined all of the measurements to create a map of the terrain.

As the scientists analyzed the map, they noticed an area with a network of roads and canals built into a mountain. It appeared to

match the description of Mahendraparvata found in the old texts. Evans and his team knew this had to be the hidden city.

IT'S A JUNGLE OUT THERE

The archaeologists started their expedition north of Angkor Wat under the heat of a sizzling sun. They cut away tree leaves blocking their path with machetes, waded knee-deep in bogs, and dodged dangerous land mines that had been left in the jungle after a war.

Finally they stumbled upon dozens of crumbled temples and evidence of roads and canals, all organized into city blocks. They had reached their destination, and it was indeed Mahendraparvata.

In the coming years, Evans and his team will continue to investigate the area. But the scientists will have their work cut out for them. After all, this jungle is very good at keeping secrets.

225

Knight Life

Protector of the Castle

It started with a childhood full of boring chores and ended at age 21 with a ceremonial smack to the head that knocked some men on their tails. The road to knighthood was long and rough, but the journey was often worth the trouble. Successful knights found fortune and glory.

In times of war and peace, knights led a dangerous life. These professional warriors were charged with protecting the lord's land from invaders, leading the castle's men-at-arms during sieges, and fighting on behalf of the church. Between battles, they competed in deadly games called tournaments to sharpen their skills.

In exchange for military service, knights were granted their own lands—along with peasants to farm it—and noble titles. The mightiest knights rose to rival lords in power and property. Sir Ulrich von Liechtenstein, one of the 13th century's most famous knights, owned three castles.

Not just anyone could become a knight. Armor, weapons, and warhorses cost more than a typical peasant might earn in a lifetime, so knights often hailed from noble families. They started their training early in life—at the age most kids today begin first grade.

Lord Lore
England's royal family still grants knighthood to actors, scientists, and other accomplished citizens.

How to Become a Knight

1. Serve as a Page

A boy destined for knighthood left home at age seven to become a servant in a great lord's castle. The page learned courtly manners, received a basic education, and played rough with other pages.

2. Squire for a Knight

Once he turned 14, a page became a squire for a knight. He learned about armor by cleaning his master's suit and helping him dress for battle. He practiced fighting with swords, shields, and other weaponry. Most important of all, he learned to attack from the saddle of a huge warhorse—the type of mounted combat knights were famous for.

3. Get Dubbed

By age 21, a squire was ready for his dubbing ceremony. He knelt before his lord or lady and received a hard slap to help him remember his oath. (This brutal blow later evolved into a friendlier sword tap on the shoulders.) The newly dubbed knight was given the title "sir" and could seek service at a lord's castle.

Knightly Numbers

55 pounds (25 kg) of armor weighed down a knight on the battlefield.

45 years was the life expectancy of the average knight.

45 days per year was the typical term of service a knight owed his lord.

Good knights acted chivalrously, which meant they protected the weak, treated women with respect, served the church, and were generous and humble.

Must-See SIGHTS

WHAT: HERCULANEUM
WHERE: Ercolano, Italy

WHY IT'S COOL: Buried by ash and lava from the eruption of Mount Vesuvius in A.D. 79, this port town is said to be better preserved than its neighbor Pompeii. Some ruins here stand up to two stories high.

WHAT: THE GREAT BUDDHA
WHERE: Kamakura, Japan

WHY IT'S COOL: More than 760 years old, this giant bronze statue has stayed standing through a lot—even surviving a giant tsunami. At 44 feet (13.35 m) tall, it's one of Japan's most famous icons.

WHAT: U.S.S. *ARIZONA* MEMORIAL
WHERE: Honolulu, Hawaii, U.S.A.

WHY IT'S COOL: This site, which can be reached by ferry from the visitor's center, marks the memory of Japan's attack on the United States on December 7, 1941.

When you visit these historical landmarks around the world, you'll step into places almost untouched by time.

WHAT: PETRA
WHERE: Jordan

WHY IT'S COOL: You have to walk in the desert to reach this more than 2,000-year-old ancient city. But the trek is worth it as it reveals awe-inspiring buildings carved into cliffs.

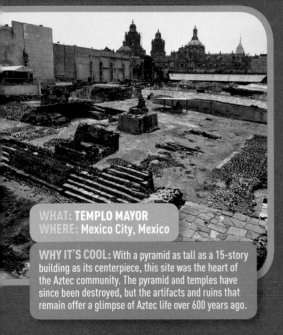

WHAT: TEMPLO MAYOR
WHERE: Mexico City, Mexico

WHY IT'S COOL: With a pyramid as tall as a 15-story building as its centerpiece, this site was the heart of the Aztec community. The pyramid and temples have since been destroyed, but the artifacts and ruins that remain offer a glimpse of Aztec life over 600 years ago.

WHAT: ST. BASIL'S CATHEDRAL
WHERE: Moscow, Russia

WHY IT'S COOL: This colorful cathedral was commissioned by Ivan the Terrible in 1552 to celebrate a military victory. Today, it remains a stunning symbol of classic Russian architecture.

229

1

BLACKBEARD put **BURNING FUSES** on the ends of his beard to scare his enemies.

2

HARDTACK BISCUITS were a staple on pirate ships, but pirates had to be careful when taking a bite. The biscuits were often infested with **GRUBBY MAGGOTS.**

3

THE GOLDEN AGE OF PIRACY HAPPENED BETWEEN 1660 AND 1730. PIRATES WOULD ATTACK SHIPS CARRYING TREASURE FROM THE AMERICAS TO EUROPE.

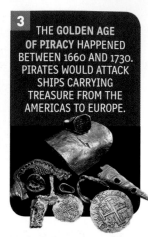

4

To a pirate, a ship's medicine cabinet was just as valuable as money or jewels. Disease, injuries, food poisoning, and flea or rat bites were common.

ARRRGH! 17 FACTS ABOUT

5

Two women pirates—*ANNE BONNY AND MARY READ*—sailed with Captain John "Calico Jack" Rackham in the early 1700s. Dressed like men, they fought alongside the rest of the crew.

6

THE PRIVATEER **FRANCIS DRAKE** BROUGHT MUCH WEALTH TO ENGLAND'S QUEEN ELIZABETH I BY RAIDING SPANISH SHIPS. THE QUEEN KNIGHTED HIM IN 1581, CALLING HIM "MY PIRATE."

7

Some of the first flags on pirate ships were **RED,** not black.

8

The city of **Port Royal, Jamaica,** was a thriving town for pirates until 1692 when it was **destroyed** by a combination *EARTHQUAKE AND TSUNAMI.*

9 Cutlasses are the short, sharp swords pirates used to fight with.

10

The Welshman **BARTHOLOMEW ROBERTS** was captured by pirates who forced him to join them. As the pirate **BLACK BART,** he captured more than 400 ships.

11 Pirates who broke ship rules were **OFTEN LEFT ON DESERTED ISLANDS** with no food or water. Sometimes they were given a **PISTOL WITH 1 BULLET.**

12 In battles, pirates used *pistols* that fired *only 1 shot* before they had to be reloaded.

13 **PIRATES DRANK GROG,** a mixture of **rum, lime juice, and water.** Vitamin C from the lime helped prevent scurvy, a disease that can cause swelling, bleeding, and tooth loss.

PIRATES

14

THERE IS NO DOCUMENTED RECORD OF PIRATES HAVING TO **"walk the plank"** TO THEIR DEATH.

15 The nickname "JOLLY ROGER" for pirate flags likely comes from the French words *jolie rouge*, which means "PRETTY RED."

16 The skull and crossbones on many pirate flags was a **SYMBOL OF DEATH.** Today, it is used to warn of poison or danger.

17 "Barbarossa," which means "red beard," was the name of two fearsome pirate brothers who operated along North Africa's Barbary Coast in the 16th century.

HORUSCE und HAREIADEN BARBAROSSA

MYSTERY OF THE STONE GIANTS

WHO PLACED THE STATUES ON EASTER ISLAND? SCIENTISTS WEIGH IN.

MOAI HEAD

A strange army of jumbo-size stones carved to look like humans have "guarded" the coast of Easter Island in the Pacific Ocean for centuries. But not even the island's inhabitants are sure how they got there.

Scientists think islanders began creating the *moai*—which can weigh more than 90 tons (81,647 kg) and stand as tall as a three-story building—some 800 years ago to honor their ancestors. Inland, archaeologists unearthed ancient tools used to carve figures from volcanic rock. But that was about 11 miles (18 km) from where most of the statues now stand. And back then, the islanders didn't have wheels, cranes, or animals to move the rock giants.

Wondering if the islanders could have transported the statues upright with just rope and muscle power, one group of archaeologists attempted to move a ten-foot (3-m)-tall moai replica by wrapping three cords around the statue's forehead.

TINY TOURIST!

ROW OF MOAI

Easter Island's first inhabitants arrived between 800 and 1,200 years ago. They canoed from other Pacific islands for more than 1,000 miles (1,600 km).

With a team of people pulling each rope they were able to "walk" the moai a short distance by rocking it side to side. Another team laid an actual moai onto a giant log and pulled the log forward. But these techniques might have worked only over short distances and on flat land, or would have damaged the moai. Some researchers suggest the statues were laid on wooden sleds, which were dragged across log tracks. But the truth may never be revealed. Today the only remaining witnesses to the event are the moai themselves. And their stone lips are sealed.

CAN AN ISLAND PARADISE DISAPPEAR IN A DAY? THAT'S WHAT ONE ANCIENT LEGEND SAYS ABOUT THE EMPIRE OF ATLANTIS. TODAY, SCIENTISTS CONTINUE TO TRY TO LOCATE THE LOST ISLAND.

MYSTERY OF
ATLANTIS

Plato, an ancient Greek philosopher, described Atlantis as a wealthy city with palaces, a silver-and-gold temple, abundant fruit trees, and elephants roaming the land. But the good times didn't last. Plato wrote that sudden earthquakes jolted Atlantis and whipped up waves that sank the island within a day.

Was Plato's story true? Recently, researchers in Spain used underground radar in search of buried buildings. Results showed something like a crumbled wall in the soil 40 feet (12.1 m) below, but because there was water beneath the site, a dig seemed improbable.

Other explorers think Atlantis is in the Mediterranean Sea, where images supposedly show remains of canals and walls. Others are skeptical about the story entirely. Such an advanced city, they say, couldn't have been built in the Stone Age, when Plato's story was set.

So, was Atlantis real, fake, or something in between? The search continues.

TREASURE!

Check out these stories of lost treasures found!

SUNKEN GOLD

In the summer of 2013, Rick Schmitt was scuba diving off the coast of eastern Florida when he discovered $300,000 worth of gold chains, coins, and jewelry on the ocean floor. The riches date back to the 1700s, when Spanish ships called galleons often ferried treasure from North and South America to Europe. In July 1715 a hurricane sank 11 galleons near Florida's coast, scattering valuables along the seafloor. Nearly 300 years later, Schmitt found only a portion of this loot. Many more riches still linger at the bottom of the ocean.

MAYA RICHES

During a 2012 expedition to the jungles of northern Guatemala, a team of archaeologists discovered a tomb filled with precious stones and ancient bones dating back to the seventh century. Maya hieroglyphics on a jar in the burial chamber revealed that the bones may have belonged to a warrior queen. The exact worth of the treasure hasn't been calculated—but most people agree that this find is priceless.

PALACE PRIZE

In 2011, workers renovating Hanuman Dhoka, a palace that once housed Nepal's royal family, came upon three safes and a tank filled with gold jewelry, bows with silver arrows, and gold masks. The loot was thought to be at least 500-year-old offerings made to Hindu gods and goddesses, and no one knows for sure why it was placed here. But with the treasure soon on exhibit, the renovated palace museum won't just be spruced up— it'll be blinged out!

THE SECRETS OF
STONEHENGE

Could a new discovery help solve this ancient puzzle?

Dazzling rays from the sun burst through a strange ring of stones set on a grassy field. This huge monument, called Stonehenge, has towered above England's Salisbury Plain for thousands of years—but it's still one of the world's biggest mysteries.

THE UNEXPLAINED
For centuries people have tried to unlock Stonehenge's secrets.

Some theories have suggested that migrants from continental Europe built the site as an astronomical observatory or as a temple to the sun and moon gods. No theories have been proven. But a new discovery may provide more information about the builders of Stonehenge and could help explain why the monument was constructed in this region.

HUNTING FOR CLUES
While digging around a spring about a mile and a half (2.4 km) from Stonehenge, archaeologist David Jacques and his team uncovered hundreds of bones belonging to aurochs—a species of cattle twice the size of a modern-day bull that thrived in ancient times. In fact the site held the largest collection of auroch bones ever found in Europe. That suggests that the spring was a pit stop along an auroch migration route where the animals drank water.

The team also unearthed 31,000 flints, a stone tool used for hunting. "We started to wonder if the area was also a hunting ground and feasting site for ancient people," Jacques says. "Just one auroch could've fed a hundred people, so the place would've been a big draw."

The animal bones and tools date back to 7500 B.C. The age of the artifacts caused Jacques to conclude that people moved to the region around 9,500 years ago to hunt auroch. And he thinks descendants of these settlers assembled the mysterious stone ring.

UNITED KINGDOM

ATLANTIC OCEAN

EUROPE

ATLANTIC OCEAN

AFRICA

SCOTLAND

NORTHERN IRELAND

UNITED KINGDOM

North Sea

Irish Sea

IRELAND

ENGLAND

WALES

London

Celtic Sea

Stonehenge

English Channel

FRANCE

WAR!

Since the beginning of time, different countries, territories, and cultures have feuded with each other over land, power, and politics. Major military conflicts include the following wars:

1095–1291 THE CRUSADES
Starting late in the 11th century, these wars over religion were fought in the Middle East for nearly 200 years.

1337–1453 HUNDRED YEARS' WAR
France and England battled over rights to land for more than a century before the French eventually drove the English out in 1453.

1754–1763 FRENCH AND INDIAN WAR (part of Europe's Seven Years' War)
A nine-year war between the British and French for control of North America.

1775–1783 AMERICAN REVOLUTION
Thirteen British colonies in America united to reject the rule of the British government and to form the United States of America.

1861–1865 AMERICAN CIVIL WAR
Occurred when the northern states (the Union) went to war with the southern states, which had seceded, or withdrawn, to form the Confederate States of America. Slavery was one of the key issues in the Civil War.

1910–1920 MEXICAN REVOLUTION
The people of Mexico revolted against the rule of dictator President Porfirio Díaz, leading to his eventual defeat and to a democratic government.

1914–1918 WORLD WAR I
The assassination of Austria's Archduke Ferdinand by a Serbian nationalist sparked this wide-spreading war. The U.S. entered after Germany sunk the British ship *Lusitania,* killing more than 120 Americans.

1918–1920 RUSSIAN CIVIL WAR
Following the 1917 Russian Revolution, this conflict pitted the Communist Red Army against the foreign-backed White Army. The Red Army won, leading to the establishment of the Union of Soviet Socialist Republics (U.S.S.R.) in 1922.

1936–1939 SPANISH CIVIL WAR
Aid from Italy and Germany helped the Nationalists gain victory over the Communist-supported Republicans. The war resulted in the loss of more than 300,000 lives and increased tension in Europe leading up to World War II.

1939–1945 WORLD WAR II
This massive conflict in Europe, Asia, and North Africa involved many countries that aligned with the two sides: the Allies and the Axis. After the bombing of Pearl Harbor in Hawaii in 1941, the U.S. entered the war on the side of the Allies. More than 50 million people died during the war.

1946–1949 CHINESE CIVIL WAR
Also known as the "War of Liberation," this pitted the Communist and Nationalist parties in China against each other. The Communists won.

1950–1953 KOREAN WAR
Kicked off when the Communist forces of North Korea, with backing from the Soviet Union, invaded their democratic neighbor to the south. A coalition of 16 countries from the United Nations stepped in to support South Korea.

CRACKING THE CODE

1950s–1975 VIETNAM WAR

Fought between the Communist North, supported by allies including China, and the government of South Vietnam, supported by the United States and other anticommunist nations.

1967 SIX-DAY WAR

A battle for land between Israel and the states of Egypt, Jordan, and Syria. The outcome resulted in Israel's gaining control of coveted territory, including the Gaza Strip and the West Bank.

1991–PRESENT SOMALI CIVIL WAR

Began when Somalia's last president, a dictator named Mohamed Siad Barre, was overthrown. The war has led to years of fighting and anarchy.

2001–2014 WAR IN AFGHANISTAN

After attacks in the U.S. by the terrorist group al Qaeda, a coalition that eventually included more than 40 countries invaded Afghanistan to find Osama bin Laden and other al Qaeda members and to dismantle the Taliban. Bin Laden was killed in a U.S. covert operation in 2011. The North Atlantic Treaty Organization (NATO) took control of the coalition's combat mission in 2003. That combat mission officially ended in 2014.

2003–2011 WAR IN IRAQ

A coalition led by the U.S., and including Britain, Australia, and Spain, invaded Iraq over suspicions that Iraq had weapons of mass destruction.

S eeking to gain an edge over the Allied forces during World War II, Germany employed the Enigma machine to send out information to its forces. The machine allowed its operator to type a message, and then scramble it using a letter substitution system, and it was capable of creating several billion encrypted combinations. The Germans—who used the machine for battlefield, naval, and diplomatic communications—believed that the Enigma's code was impossible to break.

But little did they know that a British team was hard at work trying to crack the code. There was even a top-secret school set up for just that mission at Bletchley Park in Buckinghamshire, England. In 1940, a team of mathematicians and intelligence experts, led by code breaker Alan Turing, developed the Bombe machine (shown above), a complex electronic device that was able to rapidly decode the Enigma's messages, allowing Allied forces to respond to German threats within hours instead of weeks. Standing seven feet (2 m) tall and wider than a king-size bed, the Bombe heralded the start of the computer age.

Once the Enigma machine was cracked, the British built more than 200 Bombe machines to decipher some 3,000 messages a day, giving the Allies key intelligence about German positions and strategy. It's believed that the work of the British code breakers played a huge role in the Allied victory against Germany, saving millions of lives in the process.

The Constitution & the Bill of Rights

The United States Constitution was written in 1787 by a group of political leaders from the 13 states that made up the U.S. at the time. Thirty-nine men, including Benjamin Franklin and James Madison, signed the document to create a national government. While some feared the creation of a strong federal government, all 13 states eventually ratified, or approved, the Constitution, making it the law of the land. The Constitution has three major parts: the preamble, the articles, and the amendments.

Here's a summary of what topics are covered in each part of the Constitution. Check out the Constitution online or at your local library for the full text.

THE PREAMBLE outlines the basic purposes of the government: *We the People of the United States, in order to form a more perfect Union, establish justice, insure domestic tranquility, provide for the common defense, promote the general welfare, and secure the blessings of liberty to ourselves and our posterity, do ordain and establish this Constitution for the United States of America.*

SEVEN ARTICLES outline the powers of Congress, the president, and the court system:

Article I outlines the legislative branch—the Senate and the House of Representatives—and its powers and responsibilities.

Article II outlines the executive branch—the Presidency—and its powers and responsibilities.

Article III outlines the judicial branch—the court system—and its powers and responsibilities.

Article IV describes the individual states' rights and powers.

Article V outlines the amendment process.

Article VI establishes the Constitution as the law of the land.

Article VII gives the requirements for the Constitution to be approved.

THE AMENDMENTS, or additions to the Constitution, were put in later as needed. In 1791, the first ten amendments, known as the **Bill of Rights**, were added. Since then another seventeen amendments have been added. This is the Bill of Rights:

1st Amendment: guarantees freedom of religion, speech, and the press, and the right to assemble and petition. The U.S. may not have a national religion.

2nd Amendment: discusses the militia and the right of people to bear arms

3rd Amendment: prohibits the military or troops from using private homes without consent

4th Amendment: protects people and their homes from search, arrest, or seizure without probable cause or a warrant

5th Amendment: grants people the right to have a trial and prevents punishment before prosecution; protects private property from being taken without compensation

6th Amendment: guarantees the right to a speedy and public trial

7th Amendment: guarantees a trial by jury in certain cases

8th Amendment: forbids "cruel and unusual punishments"

9th Amendment: states that the Constitution is not all-encompassing and does not deny people other, unspecified rights

10th Amendment: grants the powers not covered by the Constitution to the states and the people

Read the full text version of the United States Constitution at constitutioncenter.org/constitution/full-text

238

Branches of Government

The **UNITED STATES GOVERNMENT** is divided into three branches: **executive, legislative**, and **judicial**. The system of checks and balances is a way to control power and to make sure one branch can't take the reins of government. For example, most of the president's actions require the approval of Congress. Likewise, the laws passed in Congress must be signed by the president before they can take effect.

White House

Executive Branch

The Constitution lists the central powers of the president: to serve as Commander in Chief of the armed forces; make treaties with other nations; grant pardons; inform Congress on the state of the union; and appoint ambassadors, officials, and judges. The executive branch includes the president and the 15 governmental departments.

Legislative Branch

This branch is made up of Congress—the Senate and the House of Representatives. The Constitution grants Congress the power to make laws. Congress is made up of elected representatives from each state. Each state has two representatives in the Senate, while the number of representatives in the House is determined by the size of the state's population. Washington, D.C., and the territories elect nonvoting representatives to the House of Representatives. The Founding Fathers set up this system as a compromise between big states—which wanted representation based on population—and small states—which wanted all states to have equal representation rights.

The U.S. Capitol in Washington, D.C.

Judicial Branch

The judicial branch is composed of the federal court system—the U.S. Supreme Court, the courts of appeals, and the district courts. The Supreme Court is the most powerful court. Its motto is "Equal Justice Under Law." This influential court is responsible for interpreting the Constitution and applying it to the cases that it hears. The decisions of the Supreme Court are absolute—they are the final word on any legal question.

There are nine justices on the Supreme Court. They are appointed by the president of the United States and confirmed by the Senate.

The U.S. Supreme Court Building in Washington, D.C.

The Indian Experience

American Indians are indigenous to North and South America—they are the people who were here before Columbus and other European explorers came to these lands. They lived in nations, tribes, and bands across both continents. For decades following the arrival of Europeans in 1492, American Indians clashed with the newcomers who had ruptured the Indians' way of living.

Tribal Land

During the 19th century, both United States legislation and military action restricted the movement of American Indians, forcing them to live on reservations and attempting to dismantle tribal structures. For centuries Indians were displaced or killed, or became assimilated into the general U.S. population. In 1924 the Indian Citizenship Act granted citizenship to all American Indians. Unfortunately, this was not enough to end the social discrimination and mistreatment that many Indians have faced. Today, American Indians living in the U.S. still face many challenges.

Healing the Past

Many members of the 560-plus recognized tribes in the United States live primarily on reservations. Some tribes have more than one reservation, while others have none. Together these reservations make up less than 3 percent of the nation's land area. The tribal governments on reservations have the right to form their own governments and to enforce laws, similar to individual states. Many feel that this sovereignty is still not enough to right the wrongs of the past: They hope for a change in the U.S. government's relationship with American Indians.

> Some American Indians used cranberry juice to dye clothing, rugs, and blankets.

> Fewer than 4,000 people speak Blackfoot, a language native to North America.

Top: A Blackfoot man dances at a pow-wow.
Middle: A Salish woman in traditional dress in Montana
Bottom: Little Shell men in traditional costume

The president of the United States is the chief of the executive branch, the Commander in Chief of the U.S. armed forces, and head of the federal government. Elected every four years, the president is the highest policy-maker in the nation. The 22nd Amendment (1951) says that no person may be elected to the office of president more than twice. There have been 44 presidencies and 43 presidents.

JAMES MADISON

4th President of the United States ★ 1809–1817

BORN March 16, 1751, at Belle Grove, Port Conway, VA

POLITICAL PARTY Democratic-Republican

NO. OF TERMS two

VICE PRESIDENTS 1st term: George Clinton
2nd term: Elbridge Gerry

DIED June 28, 1836, at Montpelier, Orange County, VA

GEORGE WASHINGTON

1st President of the United States ★ 1789–1797

BORN Feb. 22, 1732, in Pope's Creek, Westmoreland County, VA

POLITICAL PARTY Federalist

NO. OF TERMS two

VICE PRESIDENT John Adams

DIED Dec. 14, 1799, at Mount Vernon, VA

JAMES MONROE

5th President of the United States ★ 1817–1825

BORN April 28, 1758, in Westmoreland County, VA

POLITICAL PARTY Democratic-Republican

NO. OF TERMS two

VICE PRESIDENT Daniel D. Tompkins

DIED July 4, 1831, in New York, NY

Every U.S. president has a favorite food. **GEORGE WASHINGTON'S WAS ICE CREAM.**

JOHN QUINCY ADAMS

6th President of the United States ★ 1825–1829

BORN July 11, 1767, in Braintree (now Quincy), MA

POLITICAL PARTY Democratic-Republican

NO. OF TERMS one

VICE PRESIDENT John Caldwell Calhoun

DIED Feb. 23, 1848, at the U.S. Capitol, Washington, DC

JOHN ADAMS

2nd President of the United States ★ 1797–1801

BORN Oct. 30, 1735, in Braintree (now Quincy), MA

POLITICAL PARTY Federalist

NO. OF TERMS one

VICE PRESIDENT Thomas Jefferson

DIED July 4, 1826, in Quincy, MA

ANDREW JACKSON

7th President of the United States ★ 1829–1837

BORN March 15, 1767, in the Waxhaw region, NC and SC

POLITICAL PARTY Democrat

NO. OF TERMS two

VICE PRESIDENTS 1st term: John Caldwell Calhoun
2nd term: Martin Van Buren

DIED June 8, 1845, in Nashville, TN

THOMAS JEFFERSON

3rd President of the United States ★ 1801–1809

BORN April 13, 1743, at Shadwell, Goochland (now Albemarle) County, VA

POLITICAL PARTY Democratic-Republican

NO. OF TERMS two

VICE PRESIDENTS 1st term: Aaron Burr
2nd term: George Clinton

DIED July 4, 1826, at Monticello, Charlottesville, VA

MARTIN VAN BUREN

8th President of the United States ★ 1837–1841

BORN Dec. 5, 1782, in Kinderhook, NY

POLITICAL PARTY Democrat

NO. OF TERMS one

VICE PRESIDENT Richard M. Johnson

DIED July 24, 1862, in Kinderhook, NY

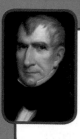

WILLIAM HENRY HARRISON
9th President of the United States ★ 1841
BORN Feb. 9, 1773, in Charles City County, VA
POLITICAL PARTY Whig
NO. OF TERMS one (cut short by death)
VICE PRESIDENT John Tyler
DIED April 4, 1841, in the White House, Washington, DC

JOHN TYLER
10th President of the United States ★ 1841–1845
BORN March 29, 1790, in Charles City County, VA
POLITICAL PARTY Whig
NO. OF TERMS one (partial)
VICE PRESIDENT none
DIED Jan. 18, 1862, in Richmond, VA

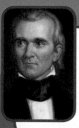

JAMES K. POLK
11th President of the United States ★ 1845–1849
BORN Nov. 2, 1795, near Pineville, Mecklenburg County, NC
POLITICAL PARTY Democrat
NO. OF TERMS one
VICE PRESIDENT George Mifflin Dallas
DIED June 15, 1849, in Nashville, TN

ZACHARY TAYLOR
12th President of the United States ★ 1849–1850
BORN Nov. 24, 1784, in Orange County, VA
POLITICAL PARTY Whig
NO. OF TERMS one (cut short by death)
VICE PRESIDENT Millard Fillmore
DIED July 9, 1850, in the White House, Washington, DC

MILLARD FILLMORE
13th President of the United States ★ 1850–1853
BORN Jan. 7, 1800, in Cayuga County, NY
POLITICAL PARTY Whig
NO. OF TERMS one (partial)
VICE PRESIDENT none
DIED March 8, 1874, in Buffalo, NY

FRANKLIN PIERCE
14th President of the United States ★ 1853–1857
BORN Nov. 23, 1804, in Hillsborough (now Hillsboro), NH
POLITICAL PARTY Democrat
NO. OF TERMS one
VICE PRESIDENT William Rufus De Vane King
DIED Oct. 8, 1869, in Concord, NH

JAMES BUCHANAN
15th President of the United States ★ 1857–1861
BORN April 23, 1791, in Cove Gap, PA
POLITICAL PARTY Democrat
NO. OF TERMS one
VICE PRESIDENT John Cabell Breckinridge
DIED June 1, 1868, in Lancaster, PA

James Buchanan was the first president to receive a **TELEGRAM** from overseas.

TELEGRAM

ABRAHAM LINCOLN
16th President of the United States ★ 1861–1865
BORN Feb. 12, 1809, near Hodgenville, KY
POLITICAL PARTY Republican (formerly Whig)
NO. OF TERMS two (assassinated)
VICE PRESIDENTS 1st term: Hannibal Hamlin
2nd term: Andrew Johnson
DIED April 15, 1865, in Washington, DC

ANDREW JOHNSON
17th President of the United States ★ 1865–1869
BORN Dec. 29, 1808, in Raleigh, NC
POLITICAL PARTY Democrat
NO. OF TERMS one (partial)
VICE PRESIDENT none
DIED July 31, 1875, in Carter's Station, TN

ULYSSES S. GRANT

18th President of the United States ★ *1869–1877*

BORN April 27, 1822, in Point Pleasant, OH

POLITICAL PARTY Republican

NO. OF TERMS two

VICE PRESIDENTS 1st term: Schuyler Colfax
2nd term: Henry Wilson

DIED July 23, 1885, in Mount McGregor, NY

GROVER CLEVELAND

22nd and 24th President of the United States
1885–1889 ★ *1893–1897*

BORN March 18, 1837, in Caldwell, NJ

POLITICAL PARTY Democrat

NO. OF TERMS two (nonconsecutive)

VICE PRESIDENTS 1st administration:
Thomas Andrews Hendricks
2nd administration:
Adlai Ewing Stevenson

DIED June 24, 1908, in Princeton, NJ

RUTHERFORD B. HAYES

19th President of the United States ★ *1877–1881*

BORN Oct. 4, 1822, in Delaware, OH

POLITICAL PARTY Republican

NO. OF TERMS one

VICE PRESIDENT William Almon Wheeler

DIED Jan. 17, 1893, in Fremont, OH

BENJAMIN HARRISON

23rd President of the United States ★ *1889–1893*

BORN Aug. 20, 1833, in North Bend, OH

POLITICAL PARTY Republican

NO. OF TERMS one

VICE PRESIDENT Levi Parsons Morton

DIED March 13, 1901, in Indianapolis, IN

President Rutherford B. Hayes's wife, Lucy, loved pets. The couple owned the **FIRST SIAMESE CAT** in the country.

WILLIAM MCKINLEY

25th President of the United States ★ *1897–1901*

BORN Jan. 29, 1843, in Niles, OH

POLITICAL PARTY Republican

NO. OF TERMS two (assassinated)

VICE PRESIDENTS 1st term:
Garret Augustus Hobart
2nd term:
Theodore Roosevelt

DIED Sept. 14, 1901, in Buffalo, NY

JAMES A. GARFIELD

20th President of the United States ★ *1881*

BORN Nov. 19, 1831, near Orange, OH

POLITICAL PARTY Republican

NO. OF TERMS one (assassinated)

VICE PRESIDENT Chester A. Arthur

DIED Sept. 19, 1881, in Elberon, NJ

THEODORE ROOSEVELT

26th President of the United States ★ *1901–1909*

BORN Oct. 27, 1858, in New York, NY

POLITICAL PARTY Republican

NO. OF TERMS one, plus balance of McKinley's term

VICE PRESIDENTS 1st term: none
2nd term: Charles Warren Fairbanks

DIED Jan. 6, 1919, in Oyster Bay, NY

CHESTER A. ARTHUR

21st President of the United States ★ *1881–1885*

BORN Oct. 5, 1829, in Fairfield, VT

POLITICAL PARTY Republican

NO. OF TERMS one (partial)

VICE PRESIDENT none

DIED Nov. 18, 1886, in New York, NY

WILLIAM HOWARD TAFT

27th President of the United States ★ *1909–1913*

BORN Sept. 15, 1857, in Cincinnati, OH

POLITICAL PARTY Republican

NO. OF TERMS one

VICE PRESIDENT James Schoolcraft Sherman

DIED March 8, 1930, in Washington, DC

WOODROW WILSON
28th President of the United States ★ 1913–1921
BORN Dec. 29, 1856, in Staunton, VA
POLITICAL PARTY Democrat
NO. OF TERMS two
VICE PRESIDENT Thomas Riley Marshall
DIED Feb. 3, 1924, in Washington, DC

WARREN G. HARDING
29th President of the United States ★ 1921–1923
BORN Nov. 2, 1865, in Caledonia
(now Blooming Grove), OH
POLITICAL PARTY Republican
NO. OF TERMS one (died while in office)
VICE PRESIDENT Calvin Coolidge
DIED Aug. 2, 1923, in San Francisco, CA

CALVIN COOLIDGE
30th President of the United States ★ 1923–1929
BORN July 4, 1872, in Plymouth, VT
POLITICAL PARTY Republican
NO. OF TERMS one, plus balance of
Harding's term
VICE PRESIDENTS 1st term: none
2nd term:
Charles Gates Dawes
DIED Jan. 5, 1933, in Northampton, MA

HERBERT HOOVER
31st President of the United States ★ 1929–1933
BORN Aug. 10, 1874,
in West Branch, IA
POLITICAL PARTY Republican
NO. OF TERMS one
VICE PRESIDENT Charles Curtis
DIED Oct. 20, 1964, in New York, NY

FRANKLIN D. ROOSEVELT
32nd President of the United States ★ 1933–1945
BORN Jan. 30, 1882, in Hyde Park, NY
POLITICAL PARTY Democrat
NO. OF TERMS four (died while in office)
VICE PRESIDENTS 1st & 2nd terms: John
Nance Garner; 3rd term:
Henry Agard Wallace;
4th term: Harry S. Truman
DIED April 12, 1945,
in Warm Springs, GA

HARRY S. TRUMAN
33rd President of the United States ★ 1945–1953
BORN May 8, 1884, in Lamar, MO
POLITICAL PARTY Democrat
NO. OF TERMS one, plus balance of
Franklin D. Roosevelt's term
VICE PRESIDENTS 1st term: none
2nd term:
Alben William Barkley
DIED Dec. 26, 1972, in Independence, MO

DWIGHT D. EISENHOWER
34th President of the United States ★ 1953–1961
BORN Oct. 14, 1890, in Denison, TX
POLITICAL PARTY Republican
NO. OF TERMS two
VICE PRESIDENT Richard M. Nixon
DIED March 28, 1969,
in Washington, DC

Dwight D. Eisenhower
carried
THREE LUCKY COINS
in his pocket:
a silver dollar, a five-guinea
gold piece, and a French franc.

JOHN F. KENNEDY
35th President of the United States ★ 1961–1963
BORN May 29, 1917, in Brookline, MA
POLITICAL PARTY Democrat
NO. OF TERMS one (assassinated)
VICE PRESIDENT Lyndon B. Johnson
DIED Nov. 22, 1963, in Dallas, TX

LYNDON B. JOHNSON
36th President of the United States ★ 1963–1969
BORN Aug. 27, 1908, near Stonewall, TX
POLITICAL PARTY Democrat
NO. OF TERMS one, plus balance of
Kennedy's term
VICE PRESIDENTS 1st term: none
2nd term: Hubert
Horatio Humphrey
DIED Jan. 22, 1973, near San Antonio, TX

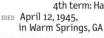

RICHARD NIXON

37th President of the United States ★ *1969–1974*

BORN Jan. 9, 1913, in Yorba Linda, CA

POLITICAL PARTY Republican

NO. OF TERMS two (resigned)

VICE PRESIDENTS 1st term & 2nd term (partial): Spiro Theodore Agnew; 2nd term (balance): Gerald R. Ford

DIED April 22, 1994, in New York, NY

GERALD R. FORD

38th President of the United States ★ *1974–1977*

BORN July 14, 1913, in Omaha, NE

POLITICAL PARTY Republican

NO. OF TERMS one (partial)

VICE PRESIDENT Nelson Aldrich Rockefeller

DIED Dec. 26, 2006, in Rancho Mirage, CA

JIMMY CARTER

39th President of the United States ★ *1977–1981*

BORN Oct. 1, 1924, in Plains, GA

POLITICAL PARTY Democrat

NO. OF TERMS one

VICE PRESIDENT Walter Frederick (Fritz) Mondale

RONALD REAGAN

40th President of the United States ★ *1981–1989*

BORN Feb. 6, 1911, in Tampico, IL

POLITICAL PARTY Republican

NO. OF TERMS two

VICE PRESIDENT George H. W. Bush

DIED June 5, 2004, in Los Angeles, CA

GEORGE H.W. BUSH

41st President of the United States ★ *1989–1993*

BORN June 12, 1924, in Milton, MA

POLITICAL PARTY Republican

NO. OF TERMS one

VICE PRESIDENT James Danforth (Dan) Quayle III

WILLIAM J. CLINTON

42nd President of the United States ★ *1993–2001*

BORN Aug. 19, 1946, in Hope, AR

POLITICAL PARTY Democrat

NO. OF TERMS two

VICE PRESIDENT Albert Gore, Jr.

GEORGE W. BUSH

43rd President of the United States ★ *2001–2009*

BORN July 6, 1946, in New Haven, CT

POLITICAL PARTY Republican

NO. OF TERMS two

VICE PRESIDENT Richard Bruce Cheney

BARACK OBAMA

44th President of the United States ★ *2009–2017*

BORN Aug. 4, 1961, in Honolulu, HI

POLITICAL PARTY Democrat

NO. OF TERMS two

VICE PRESIDENT Joseph Biden

Ronald Reagan, who died at **AGE 93**, lived longer than any other elected president.

The 45th President of the United States takes office January 20, 2017.

Who will win?

Cool Things About AIR FORCE ONE

The president of the United States takes a lot of work trips as part of the job. But the commander in chief doesn't fly business class on a regular plane—he or she takes a private jet, *Air Force One*. Here are five reasons why *Air Force One* is the coolest plane in the air.

President Barack Obama flew OVER ONE MILLION MILES (1.6 million km) on more than 940 FLIGHTS aboard *Air Force One*.

1 JUMBO JET
Most private planes are small. *Air Force One* is definitely *not*. The customized 747 airliner, designed to carry up to 102 passengers, has three levels, stands as tall as a six-story building, and is longer than five school buses. With a full load *Air Force One* can weigh up to a whopping 416 tons (377 t), which is the equivalent of more than 80 big elephants. In the air it's nimble enough to cruise at more than 600 miles an hour (966 km/h).

2 SUPER FIRST-CLASS
The president doesn't just get a big seat on *Air Force One*—there's a whole apartment. Located in the nose of the plane under the cockpit, the presidential suite includes a bedroom, a private bathroom with a shower, and enough space to exercise. The first family even has its own entrance to the plane. The president also has a private office, which explains one of the plane's nicknames, "the Flying White House."

3 DOCTOR ON BOARD
Air Force One doesn't have to make an emergency landing if there's a medical issue, because a doctor is on every flight. The clinic has an office with a small pharmacy, blood supplies, and an emergency operating table.

It costs about $180,000 AN HOUR to fly *Air Force One*.

President Obama visited MORE THAN 45 COUNTRIES during his presidency.

④ AIRPLANE FOOD

Unlike most midair meals, food on *Air Force One* is fine dining. Among the 26 crew members are cooks and several flight attendants who can serve 100 meals at a time from the airplane's two kitchens. The commander in chief can place orders 24/7 for whatever he or she wants—or doesn't want. (President George H.W. Bush banned broccoli from his flights on *Air Force One*.)

⑤ LIFT TO THE AIRPORT

The president doesn't have to fight traffic on the way to the airport. He or she takes a personal helicopter from the White House. Called *Marine One* because it's operated by the Marine Corps, the chopper lands on the White House lawn and ferries everyone over to the plane.

CIVIL RIGHTS

The Little Rock Nine study during the weeks when they were blocked from school.

Although the Constitution protects the civil rights of American citizens, it has not always been able to protect all Americans from persecution or discrimination. During the first half of the 20th century, many Americans, particularly African Americans, were subjected to widespread discrimination and racism. By the mid-1950s, many people were eager to end the bonds of racism and bring freedom to all men and women.

The civil rights movement of the 1950s and 1960s sought to end the racial discrimination against African Americans, especially in the southern states. The movement wanted to restore the fundamentals of economic and social equality to those who had been oppressed.

The Little Rock Nine

September 4, 1957, marked the first day of school at Little Rock Central High in Little Rock, Arkansas. But this was no ordinary back-to-school scene: Armed soldiers surrounded the entrance, awaiting the arrival of Central's first ever African-American students. The welcome was not warm, however, as the students—now known as the Little Rock Nine—were refused entry into the school by the soldiers and a group of protesters, angry about the potential integration. This did not deter the students, who gained the support of President Dwight D. Eisenhower to eventually earn their right to go to an integrated school. Today, the Little Rock Nine are still considered civil rights icons for challenging a racist system—and winning!

Key Events in the Civil Rights Movement

1954	The Supreme Court case *Brown* v. *Board of Education* declares school segregation illegal.
1955	Rosa Parks refuses to give up her bus seat to a white passenger and spurs a bus boycott.
1957	The Little Rock Nine help to integrate schools.
1960	Four black college students begin sit-ins at a restaurant in Greensboro, North Carolina.
1961	Freedom Rides to southern states begin as a way to protest segregation in transportation.
1963	Martin Luther King, Jr., leads the famous March on Washington.
1964	The Civil Rights Act, signed by President Lyndon B. Johnson, prohibits discrimination based on race, color, religion, sex, and national origin.
1967	Thurgood Marshall becomes the first African American to be named to the Supreme Court.
1968	President Lyndon B. Johnson signs the Civil Rights Act of 1968, which prohibits discrimination in the sale, rental, and financing of housing.

STONE OF HOPE:
THE LEGACY OF MARTIN LUTHER KING, JR.

Dr. Martin Luther King, Jr., born in Atlanta, Georgia, in 1929, never backed down in his stand against racism. He dedicated his life to achieving equality and justice for Americans of all colors. King experienced racial prejudice early in life. As an adult fighting for civil rights, his speeches, marches, and mere presence motivated people to fight for justice for all. His March on Washington in 1963 was one of the largest activist gatherings in our nation's history.

Sadly, King was assassinated by James Earl Ray on April 4, 1968. But his spirit lives on through a memorial on the National Mall in Washington, D.C. Built in 2011, 48 years after Dr. King's famous "I Have a Dream" speech, the memorial features a 30-foot (9-m) statue of Dr. King carved into a granite boulder named the "Stone of Hope."

Each year, thousands of visitors pay tribute to this inspirational figure, who will forever be remembered as one of the most prominent leaders of the civil rights movement.

EQUAL in '63 RIGHTS

"The time is always right to do what is right."

Martin Luther King, Jr. Memorial in Washington, D.C.

In 1964, at the age of 35, Martin Luther King, Jr., became the youngest person ever to win the Nobel Peace Prize.

Dr. King's "I Have a Dream" speech drew 250,000 people to the National Mall in Washington, D.C., in 1963.

8 Daring Women in U.S. History!

Who: Dolley Madison
Lived: 1768–1849
Why she's daring: As the nation's First Lady from 1809 to 1817, she single-handedly saved a famous—and valuable—portrait of George Washington when it faced almost certain destruction during the War of 1812. As British troops approached the White House, Madison refused to leave until the painting was taken to safety.

Who: Nellie Tayloe Ross
Lived: 1876–1977
Why she's daring: In 1925, Ross became the nation's first woman governor after boldly campaigning for the Wyoming seat left vacant when her husband suddenly passed away. She went on to run the U.S. Mint from 1933 to 1953.

Who: Bessie Coleman
Lived: 1892–1926
Why she's daring: When U.S. flight schools denied her entry, Coleman traveled to France to earn her pilot's license and became the first African-American female aviator. Later, her high-flying, daredevil stunts in air shows earned her the nickname "Queen Bess."

Who: Sacagawea
Lived: c. 1788–1812
Why she's daring: As the only woman to accompany Lewis and Clark into the American West, Sacagawea's calm presence and smarts saved the expedition many times. She served as a Shoshone interpreter for the explorers, found edible plants to feed the crew, and even saved important documents and supplies from a capsizing boat.

Who: Brenda Berkman
Lived: 1951–
Why she's daring: Berkman is one of the first female firefighters hired by the FDNY in New York City. But the path to become one of the "bravest" was not easy: After facing gender discrimination, Berkman won a landmark lawsuit that forced the FDNY to revise its physical exam and eventually hire dozens more female firefighters. Before retiring as a captain in 2006, Berkman became a leader among women firefighters.

Who: Kathrine Switzer
Lived: 1947–
Why she's daring: After being told that no woman could ever run the Boston Marathon, a then 19-year-old Switzer made it her mission to do just that. She completed the 26.2-mile event in 1967, despite being famously attacked by the enraged race manager who tried to pull her off the course as she ran. By breaking the gender barrier in an area once dominated by men, Switzer's triumph revolutionized the sports world.

Who: Dolores Huerta
Lived: 1930–
Why she's daring: As a teacher who saw many of her students living in poverty, Huerta rallied to raise awareness for the poor, especially among farmworkers, immigrants, and women. Later, she encouraged Hispanic women to enter politics, helping to increase in the number of women holding offices at the local, state, and federal levels. She received the Presidential Medal of Freedom in 2012.

Who: Lucille Ball
Lived: 1911–1989
Why she's daring: Famous for playing an iconic funny girl in the hit show *I Love Lucy*, Ball worked even more magic behind the screen. A pioneer in the entertainment industry, Ball was the first woman to head a major television studio. At the same time, she made 72 movies, cementing her position as one of the most legendary actresses and comediennes in the world.

QUIZ WHIZ

Go back in time to seek the answers to this history quiz!
ANSWERS BELOW

1 What was the life expectancy of the average medieval knight?

a. 45 years
b. 100 years
c. 30 years
d. 78 years

2 **True or false?** In Cambodia, it's considered an insult to touch someone's head.

3 Japan's 760-year-old Great Buddha statue once withstood which kind of natural disaster?

a. an earthquake
b. a blizzard
c. a tsunami
d. a tornado

4 **Fill in the blank.** Some of the first flags on pirate ships were _____, not black.

5 What's the name of the jumbo-size stone statues lining the coast of Easter Island?

a. Stone Guardians
b. Moai
c. Rock Stars
d. Easter Bunnies

Not **STUMPED** yet? Check out the *NATIONAL GEOGRAPHIC KIDS QUIZ WHIZ* collection for more crazy **HISTORY** questions!

ANSWERS:
1. a; 2. True; 3. c; 4. red; 5. b

Brilliant Biographies

A biography is the story of a person's life. It can be a brief summary or a long book. Biographers—those who write biographies—use many different sources to learn about their subjects. You can write your own biography of a famous person whom you find inspiring.

How to Get Started

Choose a subject you find interesting. If you think Cleopatra is cool, you have a good chance of getting your reader interested, too. If you're bored by ancient Egypt, your reader will be snoring after your first paragraph.

Your subject can be almost anyone: an author, an inventor, a celebrity, a politician, or a member of your family. To find someone to write about, ask yourself these simple questions:

1. Whom do I want to know more about?
2. What did this person do that was special?
3. How did this person change the world?

Do Your Research

- Find out as much about your subject as possible. Read books, news articles, and encyclopedia entries. Watch video clips and movies, and search the Internet. Conduct interviews, if possible.
- Take notes, writing down important facts and interesting stories about your subject.

Write the Biography

- Come up with a title. Include the person's name.
- Write an introduction. Consider asking a probing question about your subject.
- Include information about the person's child-hood. When was this person born? Where did he or she grow up? Whom did he or she admire?
- Highlight the person's talents, accomplishments, and personal attributes.
- Describe the specific events that helped to shape this person's life. Did this person ever have a problem and overcome it?
- Write a conclusion. Include your thoughts about why it is important to learn about this person.
- Once you have finished your first draft, revise and then proofread your work.

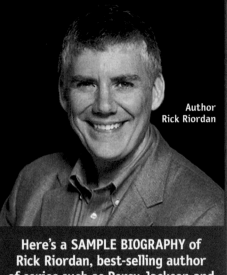

Author
Rick Riordan

Here's a SAMPLE BIOGRAPHY of Rick Riordan, best-selling author of series such as Percy Jackson and the Olympians and Magnus Chase and the Gods of Asgard.
Of course, there is so much more for you to discover, and write about on your own!

Rick Riordan—Author

Rick Riordan was born on June 5, 1964, in San Antonio, Texas, U.S.A. Born into a creative family—his mom was a musician and artist and his dad was a ceramicist—Riordan began writing in middle school, and he published his first short stories while attending college.

After graduating from University of Texas at Austin, Riordan went on to teach English to middle schoolers, spending his summers as a music director at a summer camp. Writing adult mysteries on the side, Riordan soon discovered his knack for writing for younger readers and published *The Lightning Thief*, the first book in the Percy Jackson series, in 2005. *The Sea of Monsters* soon followed. Before long, Riordan quit his teaching job to become a full-time writer.

Today Riordan has penned dozens of books, firmly establishing himself as one of the most accomplished and well-known authors of our time. When he's not writing, Riordan likes to read, swim, play guitar, and travel with his wife, Becky, and their sons Haley and Patrick.

Sunrise illuminates terraced rice fields in Longsheng, Guangxi Province, China.

Geography
Rocks

THE POLITICAL WORLD

Earth's land area is made up of seven continents, but people have divided much of the land into smaller political units called countries. Australia is a continent made up of a single country, and Antarctica is used for scientific research. But the other five continents include almost 200 independent countries. The political map shown here depicts boundaries—imaginary lines created by treaties—that separate countries. Some boundaries, such as the one between the United States and Canada, are very stable and have been recognized for many years.

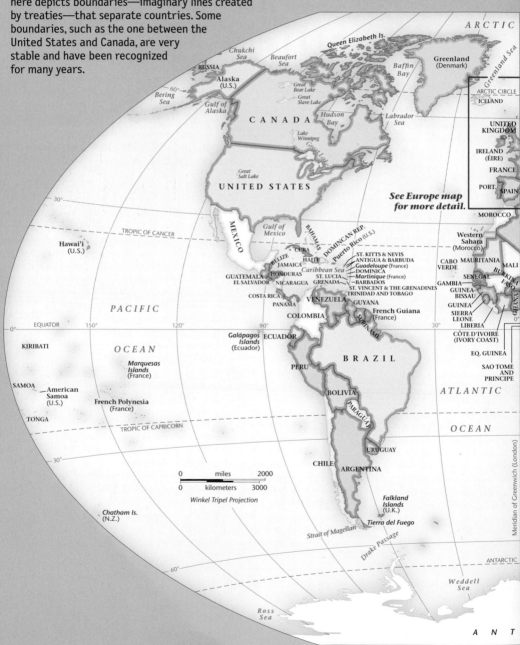

See Europe map for more detail.

miles 2000
kilometers 3000

Winkel Tripel Projection

Other boundaries, such as the one between Sudan and South Sudan in northeast Africa, are relatively new and still disputed. Countries come in all shapes and sizes. Russia and Canada are giants; others, such as El Salvador and Qatar, are small. Some countries are long and skinny—look at Chile in South America! Still other countries—such as Indonesia and Japan in Asia—are made up of groups of islands. The political map is a clue to the diversity that makes Earth so fascinating.

OCEAN

Barents Sea
Svalbard (Norway)
Novaya Zemlya
North Land
Kara Sea
New Siberian Islands
Laptev Sea
East Siberian Sea

NORWAY
SWEDEN
FINLAND
DEN.
GERMANY
EST.
LATV.
LITH.
POLAND
BELARUS

R U S S I A

Bering Sea
Sea of Okhotsk

Lake Baikal

UKRAINE
MOLD.
ROMANIA
BULGARIA
ITALY
ALBANIA
GREECE
TURKEY
GEORGIA
ARM.
AZERB.
Caspian Sea
UZBEK.
TURKMEN.
TAJIKISTAN

KAZAKHSTAN

KYRGYZSTAN

MONGOLIA

C H I N A

NORTH KOREA
SOUTH KOREA
JAPAN

TUNISIA
Mediterranean Sea
CYPRUS
SYRIA
LEBANON
ISRAEL
IRAQ
JORDAN
AFGHAN.

TAIWAN
The People's Republic of China claims Taiwan as its 23rd province. Taiwan's government (Republic of China) maintains that there are two political entities.

ALGERIA
LIBYA
EGYPT
Red Sea
SAUDI ARABIA
BAHRAIN
QATAR
U.A.E.
OMAN
IRAN
KUWAIT
PAKISTAN
NEPAL
BHUTAN
BANGLADESH

Taiwan

Northern Mariana Islands (U.S.)

PACIFIC

NIGER
CHAD
SUDAN
ERITREA
YEMEN
DJIBOUTI
Arabian Sea
INDIA
MYANMAR (BURMA)
THAILAND
LAOS
VIETNAM
South China Sea
Philippine Sea
PHILIPPINES
Guam (U.S.)

MARSHALL ISLANDS

OCEAN

BENIN
NIGERIA
CAMEROON
C.A.R.
SOUTH SUDAN
ETHIOPIA
SOMALIA
Bay of Bengal
SRI LANKA
CAMBODIA
BRUNEI
PALAU
FEDERATED STATES OF MICRONESIA

TOGO
GABON
CONGO
DEM. REP. OF THE CONGO
RWANDA
BURUNDI
UGANDA
KENYA
TANZANIA
MALDIVES
MALAYSIA
SINGAPORE
INDONESIA
New Guinea
PAPUA NEW GUINEA
NAURU
KIRIBATI
EQUATOR

Cabinda (Angola)
ANGOLA
ZAMBIA
MALAWI
SEYCHELLES
COMOROS
MADAGASCAR

I N D I A N

TIMOR-LESTE (EAST TIMOR)
SOLOMON ISLANDS
TUVALU

NAMIBIA
ZIMBABWE
BOTSWANA
MOZAMBIQUE
MAURITIUS
Réunion (France)

O C E A N

Coral Sea
VANUATU
New Caledonia (France)
FIJI

SOUTH AFRICA
SWAZILAND
LESOTHO

A U S T R A L I A

Great Australian Bight
Tasman Sea
North Island
NEW ZEALAND
South Island

Kerguelen Islands (France)

Tasmania

Ross Sea

A R C T I C A

CIRCLE

257

THE PHYSICAL WORLD

Earth is dominated by large landmasses called continents—seven in all—and by an interconnected global ocean that is divided into four parts by the continents. More than 70 percent of Earth's surface is covered by oceans, and the rest is made up of land areas.

Different landforms give variety to the surface of the continents. The Rocky Mountains divide North America, the Andes mark the western edge of South America, and the Himalaya tower above South Asia. The Plateau of Tibet forms the rugged core of Asia, while

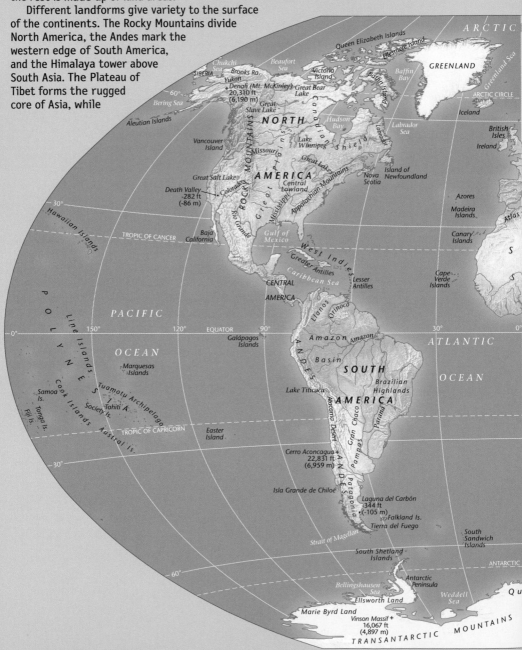

the Northern European Plain extends from the North Sea to the Ural Mountains. Much of Africa is a plateau, and dry plains cover large areas of Australia. Mountains rise more than 16,000 feet (4,877 m) above Antarctica's massive ice sheets. Mountains and trenches make the ocean floors as varied as any continent. A mountain chain called the Mid-Atlantic Ridge runs the length of the Atlantic Ocean. In the western Pacific, trenches drop deep into the ocean floor.

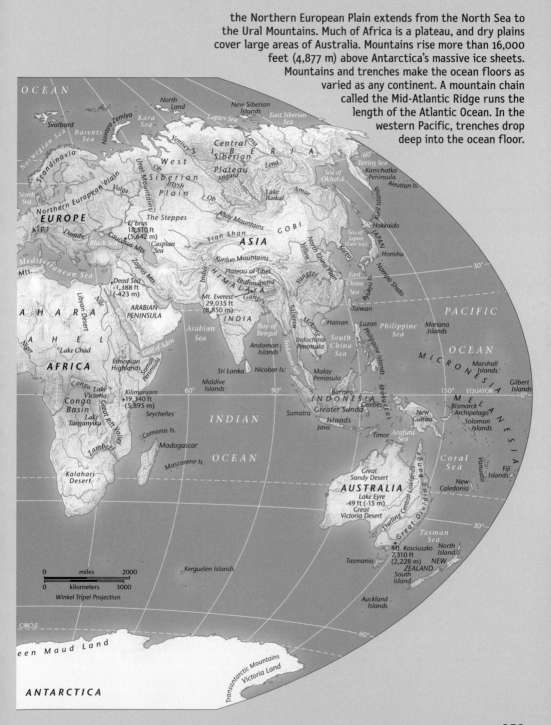

OCEAN

North Land
New Siberian Islands
Svalbard
Kara Sea
Laptev Sea
East Siberian Sea
Novaya Zemlya
Barents Sea
Yenisey
Central Siberian Plateau
S I B E R I A
Norwegian Sea
Scandinavia
West Siberian Plain
Ob
Lena
Lena
Angara
60°
Bering Sea
Kamchatka Peninsula
Aleutian Is.
Ural Mountains
Irtysh
Sea of Okhotsk
North Sea
Northern European Plain
Volga
Ob
Lake Baikal
Amur
Kuril Islands
EUROPE
Alps
Danube
El'brus 18,510 ft (5,642 m)
The Steppes
Altay Mountains
GOBI
Hokkaido
Caucasus Mts.
Caspian Sea
Tian Shan
ASIA
Sea of Japan (East Sea)
JAPAN
Honshu
Black Sea
Zagros Mts.
Kunlun Mountains
North China Plain
Yellow
Korea
Nampo Shoto
30°
Mediterranean Sea
Dead Sea -1,388 ft (-423 m)
Plateau of Tibet
Brahmaputra
Yangtze
East China Sea
Mts.
ARABIAN PENINSULA
H I M A L A Y A
Ganges
Taiwan
PACIFIC
S A H A R A
Libyan Desert
Nile
Arabian Sea
Mt. Everest 29,035 ft (8,850 m)
Salween
Mekong
Hainan
Luzon
Philippine Sea
Mariana Islands
S A H E L
Niger
Lake Chad
Gulf of Aden
Ethiopian Highlands
Somali Peninsula
INDIA
Bay of Bengal
Andaman Islands
Indochina Peninsula
South China Sea
Philippine Islands
OCEAN
M I C R O N E S I A
Marshall Islands
AFRICA
Sri Lanka
Nicobar Is.
Malay Peninsula
Andaman Sea
Gilbert Islands
Congo Basin
Lake Victoria
Kilimanjaro +19,340 ft (5,895 m)
Maldive Islands
60°
90°
Borneo
INDONESIA
Celebes
Moluccas
150°
EQUATOR
0°
Bismarck Archipelago
MELANESIA
Congo
Great Rift Valley
Lake Tanganyika
Seychelles
INDIAN
Sumatra
Greater Sunda Islands
New Guinea
Solomon Islands
Zambezi
Comoros Is.
Madagascar
Java
Timor
Arafura Sea
Coral Sea
New Caledonia
Vanuatu
Fiji Islands
Kalahari Desert
Mascarene Is.
OCEAN
Great Sandy Desert
AUSTRALIA
Lake Eyre -49 ft (-15 m)
Great Victoria Desert
Great Dividing Range
Darling
Central Lowlands
Tasman Sea
30°
Kerguelen Islands
Mt. Kosciuszko 7,310 ft (2,228 m)
Tasmania
North Island
NEW ZEALAND
South Island
0 miles 2000
0 kilometers 3000
Winkel Tripel Projection
Auckland Islands
CIRCLE
60°
een Maud Land
Transantarctic Mountains
Victoria Land
ANTARCTICA

KINDS OF MAPS

Maps are special tools that geographers use to tell a story about Earth. Maps can be used to show just about anything related to places. Some maps show physical features, such as mountains or vegetation. Maps can also show climates or natural hazards and other things we cannot easily see. Other maps illustrate different features on Earth—political boundaries, urban centers, and economic systems.

AN IMPERFECT TOOL

Maps are not perfect. A globe is a scale model of Earth with accurate relative sizes and locations. Because maps are flat, they involve distortions of size, shape, and direction. Also, cartographers—people who create maps—make choices about what information to include. Because of this, it is important to study many different types of maps to learn the complete story of Earth. Three commonly found kinds of maps are shown on this page.

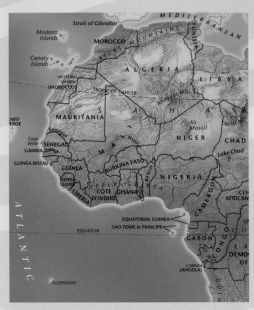

PHYSICAL MAPS. Earth's natural features—landforms, water bodies, and vegetation—are shown on physical maps. The map above uses color and shading to illustrate mountains, lakes, rivers, and deserts of western Africa. Country names and borders are added for reference, but they are not natural features.

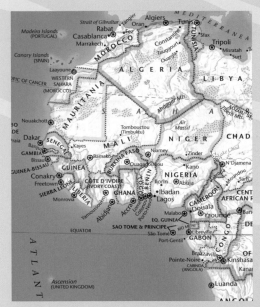

POLITICAL MAPS. These maps represent characteristics of the landscape created by humans, such as boundaries, cities, and place-names. Natural features are added only for reference. On the map above, capital cities are represented with a star inside a circle, while other cities are shown with black dots.

THEMATIC MAPS. Patterns related to a particular topic or theme, such as population distribution, appear on these maps. The map above displays the region's climate zones, which range from tropical wet (bright green) to tropical wet and dry (light green) to semiarid (dark yellow) to arid or desert (light yellow).

MAKING MAPS

Long ago, cartographers worked with pen and ink, carefully handcrafting maps based on explorers' observations and diaries. Today, mapmaking is a high-tech business. Cartographers use Earth data stored in "layers" in a Geographic Information System (GIS) and special computer programs to create maps that can be easily updated as new information becomes available. The cartographers at right are changing country labels on a map of the Balkans.

Satellites in orbit around Earth act as eyes in the sky, recording data about the planet's land and ocean areas. The data is converted to numbers that are transmitted back to computers that are specially programmed to interpret the data. They record it in a form that cartographers can use to create maps.

MAP PROJECTIONS

To create a map, cartographers transfer an image of the round Earth to a flat surface, a process called projection. All projections involve distortion. For example, an interrupted projection (bottom map) shows accurate shapes and relative sizes of land areas, but oceans have gaps. Other types of projections are cylindrical, conic, or azimuthal—each with certain advantages, but all with some distortion.

GEOGRAPHIC FEATURES

From roaring rivers to parched deserts, from underwater canyons to jagged mountains, Earth is covered with beautiful and diverse environments. Here are examples of the most common types of geographic features found around the world.

DESERT

Deserts are land features created by climate, specifically by a lack of water. Here, a camel caravan crosses the Sahara in North Africa.

VALLEY

Valleys, cut by running water or moving ice, may be broad and flat or narrow and steep, such as the Indus River Valley in Ladakh, India (above).

RIVER

As a river moves through flatlands, it twists and turns. Above, the Rio Los Amigos winds through a rain forest in Peru.

MOUNTAIN

Mountains are Earth's tallest landforms, and Mount Everest (above) rises highest of all, at 29,035 feet (8,850 m) above sea level.

GLACIER

Glaciers—"rivers" of ice— such as Alaska's Hubbard Glacier (above) move slowly from mountains to the sea. Global warming is shrinking them.

CANYON

Steep-sided valleys called canyons are created mainly by running water. Buckskin Gulch in Utah (above) is the deepest "slot" canyon in the American Southwest.

WATERFALL

Waterfalls form when a river reaches an abrupt change in elevation. Above, Kaieteur Falls, in Guyana, has a sheer drop of 741 feet (226 m).

Bet you didn't know

7 extreme facts about Earth

1 You can find **pink lakes** in western Australia.

2 There is **3 times more air** at sea level than at the **top of Mt. Everest.**

3 About 12,000 years ago, the **Sahara** had a **wetter climate** and was covered with forests.

4 Finland has more than **185,000 lakes.**

5 Indonesia is home to more than **78 active volcanoes.**

6 Canada's Mt. Thor has a **4,100-ft. (1,250-m) vertical drop** that is considered the world's **tallest and steepest cliff.**

7 Parts of Chile's Atacama Desert **have gone hundreds of years without rain.**

SPOTLIGHT ON
AFRICA

Elephants
can sleep both
standing up and
lying down.

Zanzibar, an
island off Africa's
east coast, is
made up entirely
of coral.

African elephants
in Zambia

The massive continent of Africa, where humankind began millions of years ago, is second to only Asia in size. Stretching nearly as far from west to east as it does from north to south, Africa is home to both the longest river in the world (the Nile) and the largest hot desert on Earth (Sahara).

Namibian woman in traditional dress

Speedy Species

Some of the world's fastest animals live in Africa, such as cheetahs, pronghorn antelopes, wildebeests, and lions. Each of these species can reach speeds topping 50 miles an hour (80 km/h).

Cheetah

Fast Growth

Thanks to better quality health care and more access to medicine, Africa's population is expected to more than double to at least 2.4 billion people by 2050.

Star Struck

The force is strong in Tunisia, where the parts of the original Star Wars movies were filmed. The sandy scenes were created in various desert locations in the North African nation.

Sea Life

Africa may have one of the shortest coastlines of all the continents, but its coastal waters are packed with wildlife that includes sea turtles, dolphins, humpback whales, and whale sharks.

Whale shark

Protecting the Environment

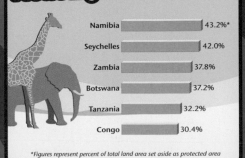

Namibia	43.2%*
Seychelles	42.0%
Zambia	37.8%
Botswana	37.2%
Tanzania	32.2%
Congo	30.4%

Figures represent percent of total land area set aside as protected area

The Great Sphinx at Giza in Egypt

AFRICA

PHYSICAL

LAND AREA
11,608,000 sq mi
(30,065,000 sq km)

HIGHEST POINT
Kilimanjaro,
Tanzania
19,340 ft (5,895 m)

LOWEST POINT
Lake Assal, Djibouti
-509 ft (-155 m)

LONGEST RIVER
Nile
4,400 mi (7,081 km)

LARGEST LAKE
Victoria
26,800 sq mi
(69,500 sq km)

POLITICAL

POPULATION
1,171,356,000

LARGEST COUNTRY
Algeria
919,595 sq mi
(2,381,741 sq km)

LARGEST METROPOLITAN AREA
Cairo, Egypt
Pop. 18,772,000

MOST DENSELY POPULATED COUNTRY
Mauritius 1,603 people
per sq mi (619 per sq km)

ASIA

EUROPE

Atlantic Ocean

Mediterranean Sea

Red Sea

Nile River

Africa–Asia boundary

TROPIC OF CANCER

Azores (Portugal)

Madeira Islands (Portugal)

Canary Islands (Spain)

Strait of Gibraltar

CABO VERDE

Dakar
Banjul
GAMBIA
SENEGAL
Nouakchott
MAURITANIA
Western Sahara (Morocco)

Rabat
Casablanca
MOROCCO
Marrakech
Fez

Oran
Algiers
Constantine

ALGERIA

Tunis
TUNISIA
Tripoli
Benghazi

LIBYA

MALI
Tombouctou (Timbuktu)
BURKINA FASO
Niamey
NIGER

CHAD

EGYPT
Alexandria
Cairo
Port Said
Suez

SUDAN
Omdurman
Khartoum
DARFUR

ERITREA
Asmara

266

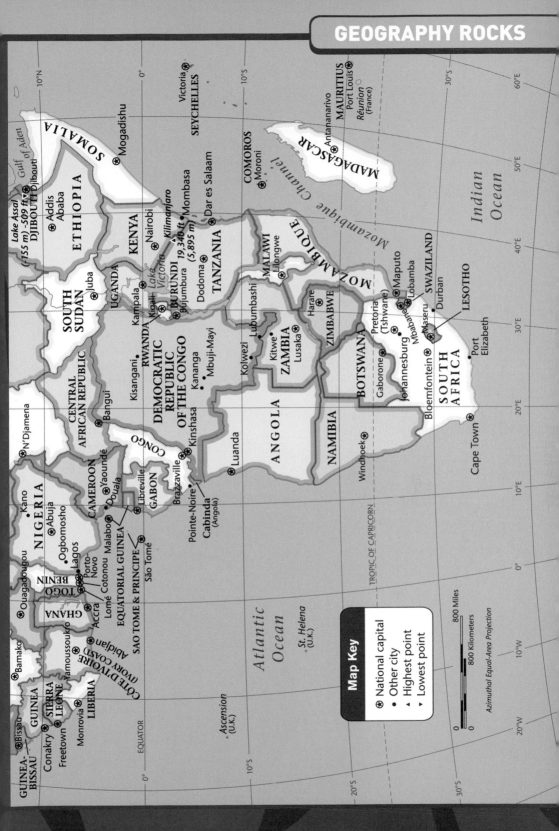

Map Key

⊛ National capital
• Other city
▲ Highest point
▼ Lowest point

Azimuthal Equal-Area Projection

800 Miles
800 Kilometers

SOMALIA
Mogadishu
Gulf of Aden
Lake Assal (-155 m) -509 ft ▼
DJIBOUTI Djibouti
ETHIOPIA
Addis Ababa
Juba
SOUTH SUDAN
UGANDA
Kampala
Nairobi
KENYA
Kilimanjaro 19,340 ft (5,895 m) ▲
Mombasa
Dar es Salaam
TANZANIA
Dodoma
Lake Victoria
RWANDA Kigali
BURUNDI Bujumbura
DEMOCRATIC REPUBLIC OF THE CONGO
Kisangani
Mbuji-Mayi
Kananga
Kinshasa
Lubumbashi
MALAWI Lilongwe
Harare
ZIMBABWE
Kolwezi
Kitwe
ZAMBIA Lusaka
MOZAMBIQUE
Mozambique Channel
COMOROS Moroni
SEYCHELLES Victoria
MADAGASCAR
Antananarivo
MAURITIUS Port Louis
Réunion (France)
Indian Ocean
Maputo
SWAZILAND Lobamba
Mbabane
LESOTHO Maseru
Durban
Pretoria (Tshwane)
Johannesburg
BOTSWANA Gaborone
Bloemfontein
SOUTH AFRICA
Port Elizabeth
NAMIBIA Windhoek
Cape Town
ANGOLA
Luanda
CONGO Brazzaville
Pointe-Noire
Cabinda (Angola)
GABON Libreville
CAMEROON Yaoundé
Douala
EQUATORIAL GUINEA Malabo
SAO TOME & PRINCIPE São Tomé
CENTRAL AFRICAN REPUBLIC Bangui
N'Djamena
NIGERIA Abuja Kano
Ogbomosho
Lagos
Porto-Novo
BENIN Cotonou
TOGO Lomé
GHANA Accra
Ouagadougou
Yamoussoukro
CÔTE D'IVOIRE (IVORY COAST)
Abidjan
LIBERIA Monrovia
SIERRA LEONE Freetown
GUINEA Conakry
GUINEA-BISSAU Bissau
Bamako
St. Helena (U.K.)
Ascension (U.K.)
Atlantic Ocean
TROPIC OF CAPRICORN
EQUATOR

267

SPOTLIGHT ON
ANTARCTICA

**Emperor penguin
with chick**

> Apart from humans, emperor penguins are the only warm-blooded animal to stay on Antarctica for the winter.

> Millions of years ago, forests grew on Antarctica.

This frozen continent may be a cool place to visit, but unless you're a penguin, you probably wouldn't want to hang out in Antarctica for long. The fact that it's the coldest, windiest, and driest continent helps explain why humans never colonized this ice-covered land surrounding the South Pole.

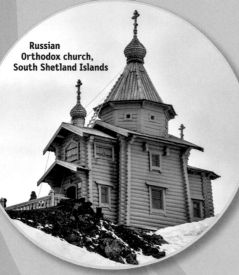

Russian Orthodox church, South Shetland Islands

Slippery Landing

Flying into Antarctica is tricky, as many airport runways are made of blue ice. These runways need to be specially prepared to keep the planes from skidding.

Supersize Seals

Southern elephant seals spend most of their time in the frigid Antarctic waters. Adult males can grow to be 20 feet (6 m) long and weigh as much as a hippo.

Going the Distance

Each year, a few hundred runners from around the world compete in the Antarctica Marathon and Half-Marathon, a hilly and twisty race along the continent's icy peninsula.

Not All Ice

The Antarctic Peninsula is called the "Banana Belt" since it has a milder climate and gets just 14 to 20 inches (35 to 50 cm) of annual precipitation, about the same as Denver, Colorado, U.S.A.

Earth's Largest Deserts

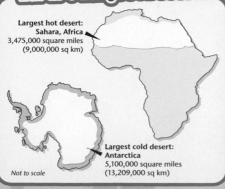

Largest hot desert:
Sahara, Africa
3,475,000 square miles
(9,000,000 sq km)

Largest cold desert:
Antarctica
5,100,000 square miles
(13,209,000 sq km)

Not to scale

Weddell seal

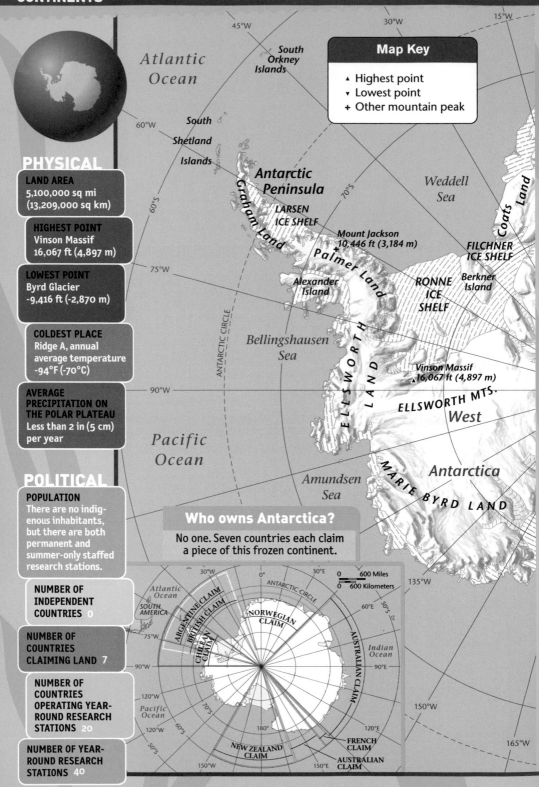

Atlantic
Ocean

South
Orkney
Islands

Map Key
▲ Highest point
▼ Lowest point
+ Other mountain peak

45°W   30°W   15°W

South
Shetland
Islands

60°W

South

**Antarctic
Peninsula**

Graham Land

LARSEN
ICE SHELF

Mount Jackson
10,446 ft (3,184 m)

Weddell
Sea

Coats Land

FILCHNER
ICE SHELF

PHYSICAL

LAND AREA
5,100,000 sq mi
(13,209,000 sq km)

HIGHEST POINT
Vinson Massif
16,067 ft (4,897 m)

LOWEST POINT
Byrd Glacier
-9,416 ft (-2,870 m)

COLDEST PLACE
Ridge A, annual
average temperature
-94°F (-70°C)

**AVERAGE
PRECIPITATION ON
THE POLAR PLATEAU**
Less than 2 in (5 cm)
per year

Palmer Land

Alexander
Island

RONNE
ICE
SHELF

Berkner
Island

75°W

ANTARCTIC CIRCLE

Bellingshausen
Sea

E L L S W O R T H   L A N D

90°W

Vinson Massif
▲16,067 ft (4,897 m)

ELLSWORTH MTS.

West

Pacific
Ocean

Amundsen
Sea

M A R I E   B Y R D   L A N D

Antarctica

POLITICAL

POPULATION
There are no indig-
enous inhabitants,
but there are both
permanent and
summer-only staffed
research stations.

**NUMBER OF
INDEPENDENT
COUNTRIES** 0

**NUMBER OF
COUNTRIES
CLAIMING LAND** 7

**NUMBER OF
COUNTRIES
OPERATING YEAR-
ROUND RESEARCH
STATIONS** 20

**NUMBER OF YEAR-
ROUND RESEARCH
STATIONS** 40

Who owns Antarctica?

No one. Seven countries each claim
a piece of this frozen continent.

30°W   0°   30°E   0 ___ 600 Miles
Atlantic   ANTARCTIC CIRCLE   0 ___ 600 Kilometers
Ocean
SOUTH   NORWEGIAN   60°E   135°W
AMERICA   CLAIM

ARGENTINE CLAIM
BRITISH CLAIM
CHILEAN CLAIM

75°W   AUSTRALIAN CLAIM   Indian
Ocean

90°W   90°E

120°W   150°E

Pacific
Ocean   120°E   150°W

FRENCH
CLAIM

NEW ZEALAND   AUSTRALIAN
CLAIM   CLAIM

180°   150°E   165°W

ANTARCTICA

FIMBUL
ICE SHELF

RIISER-LARSEN
ICE SHELF

QUEEN MAUD LAND

ENDERBY
LAND

Indian
Ocean

0°

15°E

30°E

45°E

60°E

Valkyrie
Dome

MacKenzie Bay   75°E

Lambert
Glacier

AMERY ICE SHELF

AMERICAN

HIGHLAND

WEST
ICE SHELF

Ridge A +

East

POLAR PLATEAU

South Pole

Antarctica

90°E

SHACKLETON
ICE SHELF

T
R
A
N
S
A
N
T
A
R
C
T
I
C

M
O
U
N
T
A
I
N
S

80°S

105°E

ROSS
ICE
SHELF

Byrd Glacier
-9,416 ft (-2,870 m)

Roosevelt
Island

Taylor
Glacier

Ross Island

Mount Erebus
12,448 ft
(3,794 m)

W
I
L
K
E
S

L
A
N
D

70°S

120°E

Ross
Sea

V
I
C
T
O
R
I
A

L
A
N
D

Talos
Dome

180°

• South
Magnetic
Pole (2015)

60°S

Indian
Ocean

0   600 Miles

0   600 Kilometers

Azimuthal Equidistant Projection

150°E

135°E

271

SPOTLIGHT ON
ASIA

Red panda

The Chinese name for red panda is *hun-ho*, which means "fire fox."

Mountains cover 75 percent of Kyrgyzstan.

Made up of 46 countries, Asia is the world's largest continent. Just how big is it? From western Turkey to the eastern tip of Russia, Asia spans nearly half the globe! Home to four billion citizens—that's three out of five people on the planet—Asia's population is bigger than that of all the other continents combined.

Safdarjung's Tomb, Delhi, India

Bear It

The dog-size sun bear is native to the dense forests of Southeast Asia. Its short fur keeps it cool in the tropical heat. Contrary to their name, they are mostly active at night.

Stellar Schools

A recent study shows that Asian schools are the top of the class in math and science. Singapore schools rank the highest in the world, followed by Hong Kong, South Korea, and Japan.

Young Mountains

Stretching across South Asia, the Himalaya include Mount Everest, the world's tallest peak. Formed about 50 million years ago, it's one of the youngest mountain ranges on Earth.

Flower Power

Thailand is one of the world's top orchid exporters. You can find more than 1,000 species of the flower growing wild in Thai forests.

World's Tallest Buildings

Asia is home to four of the five tallest buildings in the world.

Burj Khalifa	Shanghai Tower	Makkah Clock Royal Tower	One World Trade Center	CTF Finance Center
Dubai, U.A.E.	Shanghai, China	Mecca, Saudi Arabia	New York, U.S.A.	Guangzhou, China
2,717 feet (828 m)	2,073 feet (632 m)	1,972 feet (601 m)	1,776 feet (541 m)	1,739 feet (530 m)

Kuala Lumpur, Malaysia

ASIA

PHYSICAL

LAND AREA
17,208,000 sq mi
(44,570,000 sq km)

HIGHEST POINT
Mount Everest,
China–Nepal
29,035 ft (8,850 m)

LOWEST POINT
Dead Sea,
Israel–Jordan
-1,388 ft (-423 m)

LONGEST RIVER
Yangtze, China
3,880 mi (6,244 km)

**LARGEST LAKE
ENTIRELY IN ASIA**
Lake Baikal, Russia
12,200 sq mi
(31,500 sq km)

POLITICAL

POPULATION
4,396,678,000

**LARGEST
METROPOLITAN AREA**
Tokyo, Japan
Pop. 38,001,000

**LARGEST COUNTRY
ENTIRELY IN ASIA**
China
3,705,405 sq mi
(9,596,960 sq km)

**MOST DENSELY
POPULATED COUNTRY**
Singapore
21,729 people
per sq mi
(8,395 per sq km)

EUROPE

PERU

Nizhniy Tagil
Yekaterinburg
Tyumen'
Magnitogorsk
Chelyabinsk
Omsk

Europe
Asia

Mediterranean Sea

Dardanelles
Bosporus
Izmir
TURKEY
ARMENIA
GEORGIA
Ankara
Tbilisi
TURKMENISTAN
Astana

LEBANON
Yerevan
Baku
Qaraghandy
KAZAKHSTAN

Beirut
SYRIA
Damascus
UZBEKISTAN
Bishkek
Jerusalem
Amman
AZERBAIJAN
Ashgabat
Tashkent
Almaty
ISRAEL
Dead Sea
-1,388 ft
(-423 m)
Baghdad
Tehran
Samarqand
Dushanbe
KYRGYZSTAN
JORDAN
IRAQ
Mashhad
TAJIKISTAN

Medina
Basra
IRAN
AFGHANISTAN
Hotan
KUWAIT
Kuwait
City
Kabul
Islamabad
Rawalpindi
Jeddah
SAUDI ARABIA
Manama
Faisalabad
Lahore
Mecca
Riyadh
Doha
Dubai
Delhi
BAHRAIN
Abu Dhabi
PAKISTAN
New Delhi
NEPAL
QATAR
Jaipur
Kanpur

Sanaa
Muscat
Karachi
Indore
Bhopal
YEMEN
OMAN
Surat
Aden
UNITED ARAB
EMIRATES
Mumbai
(Bombay)
INDIA
Pune

AFRICA
Arabian
Sea
Hyderabad
Bengaluru
(Bangalore)

EQUATOR
Chennai
(Madras)
SRI
LANKA
Colombo
Sri Jayewardenepura Kotte
Male
MALDIVES

Indian Ocean

0   800 Miles
0   800 Kilometers
Two-point Equidistant Projection

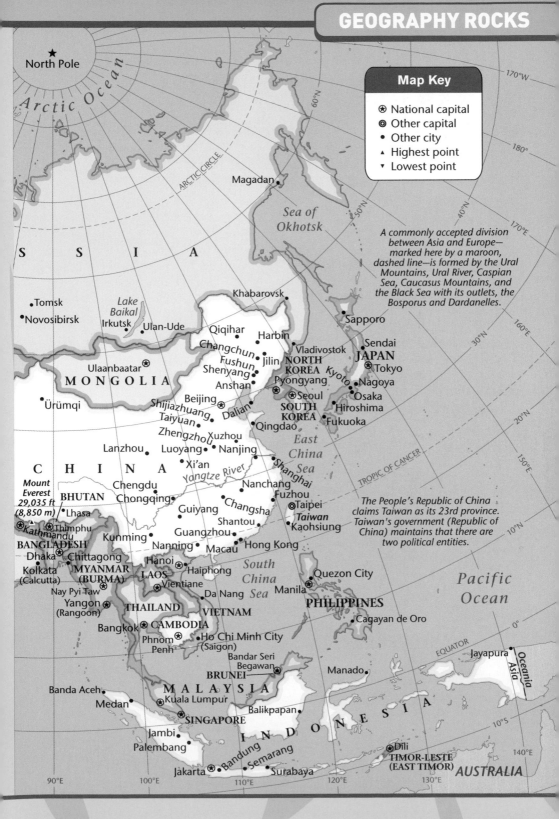

★ North Pole

Arctic Ocean

Map Key

⊗ National capital
◎ Other capital
• Other city
▲ Highest point
▼ Lowest point

R U S S I A

Magadan

Sea of Okhotsk

A commonly accepted division between Asia and Europe—marked here by a maroon, dashed line—is formed by the Ural Mountains, Ural River, Caspian Sea, Caucasus Mountains, and the Black Sea with its outlets, the Bosporus and Dardanelles.

•Tomsk
•Novosibirsk

Lake Baikal
Irkutsk •Ulan-Ude

Khabarovsk

Sapporo

Qiqihar
Changchun
Fushun
Shenyang
Anshan
Jilin
Vladivostok

NORTH KOREA
Pyongyang

Sendai
JAPAN
Tokyo
Kyoto
Nagoya
Osaka
Hiroshima
Fukuoka

Ulaanbaatar ⊗

M O N G O L I A

•Ürümqi

Beijing
Shijiazhuang
Taiyuan
Dalian
Qingdao

Seoul ⊗
SOUTH KOREA

Lanzhou
Zhengzhou
Luoyang
Xuzhou
Nanjing

East China Sea

C H I N A
Xi'an
Yangtze River
Shanghai

Chengdu
Chongqing
Nanchang
Changsha
Fuzhou
◎Taipei
Taiwan

Mount Everest 29,035 ft (8,850 m) ▲

BHUTAN
•Lhasa
Thimphu

Guiyang
Shantou
Kaohsiung

The People's Republic of China claims Taiwan as its 23rd province. Taiwan's government (Republic of China) maintains that there are two political entities.

⊗Kathmandu
BANGLADESH
Dhaka⊗ •Chittagong
Kolkata (Calcutta)

Kunming
Guangzhou
Nanning
Macau
Hong Kong

Hanoi
Haiphong
LAOS
Vientiane

South China Sea

Quezon City

Manila

MYANMAR (BURMA)
Nay Pyi Taw⊗
Yangon⊗ (Rangoon)

THAILAND
Bangkok⊗
CAMBODIA
Phnom Penh⊗

Da Nang
VIETNAM
Ho Chi Minh City (Saigon)

PHILIPPINES
•Cagayan de Oro

Pacific Ocean

Banda Aceh•

Bandar Seri Begawan

BRUNEI
M A L A Y S I A
Kuala Lumpur⊗
Balikpapan

Manado

Jayapura
Oceania
Asia

Medan•

SINGAPORE⊗

I N D O N E S I A

Jambi•
Palembang•
Bandung
Semarang
Jakarta⊗
Surabaya

•Dili
TIMOR-LESTE (EAST TIMOR)

AUSTRALIA

EQUATOR

TROPIC OF CANCER

ARCTIC CIRCLE

170°W
180°
170°E
160°E
150°E
140°E
130°E
120°E
110°E
100°E
90°E

60°N
50°N
40°N
30°N
20°N
10°N
0°
10°S

SPOTLIGHT ON
AUSTRALIA,
NEW ZEALAND, AND OCEANIA

In Australia, "Bluey" is a nickname for redheads.

The Twelve Apostles limestone rock stacks were once called the Sow and Piglets.

Twelve Apostles rock stacks, Victoria, Australia

G'day, mate! This vast region, covering almost 3.3 million square miles (8.5 million sq km), includes Australia—the world's smallest and flattest continent—and New Zealand, as well as a fleet of mostly tiny islands scattered across the Pacific Ocean. Also known as "down under," all of the countries in this region are in the Southern Hemisphere, and below the Equator.

Maori children of New Zealand in ceremonial costume

Snowy Spot

It does snow down under! From June through September, the Australian Alps, stretching through New South Wales and into Victoria, gets about 6.5 feet (2 m) of snow.

Horse Country

Mobs of wild horses, known as brumbies, roam throughout Australia. It's believed they escaped into the bush when European settlers arrived in the country 150 years ago.

Plenty of Wool

With more sheep than people, Australia and New Zealand are among the world's top producers of wool. Sheep shearing and wool handling competitions are held in both countries.

Protected Waters

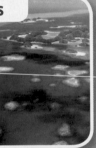

The South Pacific island nation of Palau is making big waves as the future home of what may be the world's largest marine sanctuary. Plans include a block on fishing and drilling.

Australia
Sizing Up the Great Barrier Reef

Just how big is the Great Barrier Reef Marine Park? It's approximately as large as:

Great Barrier Reef Marine Park

Germany

Vietnam

Australia

or the Republic of Congo

*Based on an area of 133,000 square miles (344,400 sq km)

Sydney Harbour Bridge in Sydney, Australia

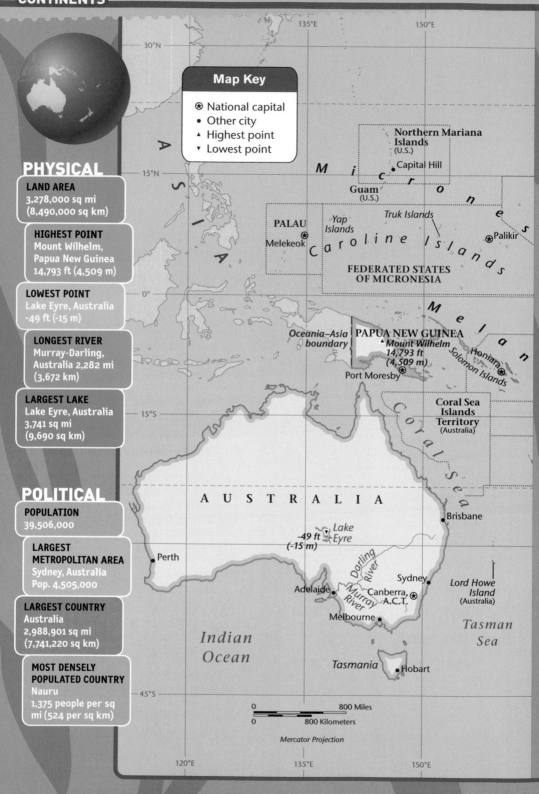

Map Key

- ⊛ National capital
- • Other city
- ▲ Highest point
- ▼ Lowest point

PHYSICAL

LAND AREA
3,278,000 sq mi
(8,490,000 sq km)

HIGHEST POINT
Mount Wilhelm,
Papua New Guinea
14,793 ft (4,509 m)

LOWEST POINT
Lake Eyre, Australia
-49 ft (-15 m)

LONGEST RIVER
Murray-Darling,
Australia 2,282 mi
(3,672 km)

LARGEST LAKE
Lake Eyre, Australia
3,741 sq mi
(9,690 sq km)

POLITICAL

POPULATION
39,506,000

**LARGEST
METROPOLITAN AREA**
Sydney, Australia
Pop. 4,505,000

LARGEST COUNTRY
Australia
2,988,901 sq mi
(7,741,220 sq km)

**MOST DENSELY
POPULATED COUNTRY**
Nauru
1,375 people per sq
mi (524 per sq km)

Northern Mariana
Islands
(U.S.)
•Capital Hill

Guam
(U.S.)

PALAU
Melekeok ⊛

Yap
Islands

Truk Islands

⊛ Palikir

Caroline Islands

FEDERATED STATES
OF MICRONESIA

Melan

Oceania–Asia
boundary

PAPUA NEW GUINEA
▲ Mount Wilhelm
14,793 ft
(4,509 m)

Port Moresby

Honiara•
Solomon Islands ⊛

Coral Sea
Islands
Territory
(Australia)

Coral Sea

AUSTRALIA

Brisbane•

-49 ft
(-15 m)
▼ Lake
Eyre

Perth•

Darling
River

Sydney•
Lord Howe
Island
(Australia)

Adelaide•

Murray
River

Canberra,
A.C.T. ⊛

Melbourne•

Indian
Ocean

Tasman
Sea

Tasmania

Hobart•

| 0 | 800 Miles |
| 0 | 800 Kilometers |

Mercator Projection

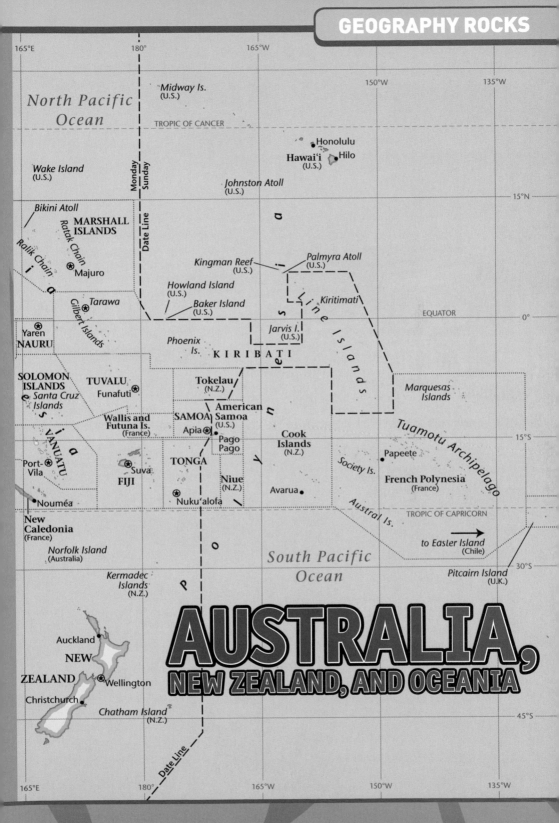

North Pacific Ocean

Midway Is. (U.S.)

TROPIC OF CANCER

Wake Island (U.S.)

Honolulu
Hawai'i
(U.S.)
Hilo

Johnston Atoll (U.S.)

Monday Sunday

Date Line

Bikini Atoll

MARSHALL ISLANDS

Ralik Chain
Ratak Chain

Majuro

Kingman Reef (U.S.)
Palmyra Atoll (U.S.)

Howland Island (U.S.)

Kiritimati

Baker Island (U.S.)

EQUATOR

Tarawa

Gilbert Islands

Jarvis I. (U.S.)

15°N

Yaren
NAURU

Phoenix Is.

KIRIBATI

Line Islands

SOLOMON ISLANDS

TUVALU

Tokelau (N.Z.)

Marquesas Islands

Santa Cruz Islands

Funafuti

American Samoa (U.S.)

Wallis and Futuna Is. (France)

SAMOA
Apia

VANUATU

Pago Pago

Cook Islands (N.Z.)

Tuamotu Archipelago

Port-Vila

Suva

TONGA

Papeete

Society Is.

15°S

FIJI

Niue (N.Z.)

French Polynesia (France)

Nouméa

Nuku'alofa

Avarua

Austral Is.

TROPIC OF CAPRICORN

New Caledonia (France)

Norfolk Island (Australia)

to Easter Island (Chile)

South Pacific Ocean

Pitcairn Island (U.K.)

30°S

Kermadec Islands (N.Z.)

AUSTRALIA,
NEW ZEALAND, AND OCEANIA

Auckland

NEW

ZEALAND
Wellington

Christchurch

Chatham Island (N.Z.)

Date Line

45°S

165°E   180°   165°W   150°W   135°W

SPOTLIGHT ON
EUROPE

Amsterdam, Netherlands, is home to 165 canals.

The first circus was held in Rome, Italy.

Amsterdam, Netherlands

A cluster of islands and peninsulas jutting west from Asia, Europe is bordered by the Atlantic and Arctic Oceans and more than a dozen seas. Here you'll find a variety of scenery, from mountains to countryside to coastlines. Europe is also known for its rich culture and fascinating history, which make it one of the most visited continents on Earth.

Hedgehog

Blue Bloods

There are 12 surviving monarchies in western Europe. Denmark's royal family takes the crown for Europe's longest-running monarchy, having lasted more than 1,000 years.

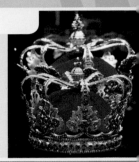

Fiery Mountain

Italy's Mount Etna, one of the most active volcanoes on Earth, erupts almost every year. Towering 10,900 feet (3,322 m) above Sicily, it can be seen from much of the island.

Magic Kingdom

Disney World's famous Cinderella castle was modeled after the Neuschwanstein Castle, a 19th-century fortress built for King Ludwig II in southwest Bavaria in Germany.

Just Visiting

More than 580 million people visit Europe each year, making it the most popular continent to travel to. The top destinations within Europe? France, Spain, and Italy.

Europe's 6 Most-Visited Cities*

1. **London, England**
   18.82 million visitors

2. **Paris, France**
   16.06 million visitors

3. **Istanbul, Turkey**
   12.56 million visitors

4. **Barcelona, Spain**
   7.63 million visitors

5. **Amsterdam, Netherlands**
   7.44 million visitors

6. **Rome, Italy**
   7.41 million visitors

*International visitors in 2015

Traditional dance performed in Greece

PHYSICAL

LAND AREA
3,841,000 sq mi
(9,947,000 sq km)

HIGHEST POINT
El'brus, Russia
18,510 ft (5,642 m)

LOWEST POINT
Caspian Sea
-92 ft (-28 m)

LONGEST RIVER
Volga, Russia
2,290 mi
(3,685 km)

**LARGEST LAKE
ENTIRELY IN EUROPE**
Ladoga, Russia
6,900 sq mi
(17,872 sq km)

POLITICAL

POPULATION
741,652,000

**LARGEST
METROPOLITAN AREA**
Moscow, Russia
Pop. 12,166,000

**LARGEST COUNTRY
ENTIRELY IN EUROPE**
Ukraine
233,030 sq mi
(603,550 sq km)

**MOST DENSELY
POPULATED COUNTRY**
Monaco
47,500 people per sq
mi (19,000 per sq km)

Map Key

- ✪ National capital
- • Other city
- ▫ Small country
- ▲ Highest point
- ▾ Lowest point

30°W   20°W   10°W   0°

Jan Mayen
(Norway)

Reykjavík
ICELAND

ARCTIC CIRCLE

60°N

*Norwegian
Sea*

Faroe Islands
(Denmark)

PRIME MERIDIAN

N O R

Shetland
Islands

Orkney Islands

Oslo

SCOTLAND

Göteborg

Glasgow
N. IRELAND
Belfast Edinburgh

*North
Sea*

DENMARK
Copenhagen ✪

**IRELAND
(ÉIRE)**
Dublin ✪

UNITED KINGDOM

Kiel

Liverpool •Manchester
WALES   Birmingham
Cardiff •ENGLAND
London ✪

Hamburg
NETH. Berlin ✪
The
Hague• Amsterdam

50°N

*Atlantic
Ocean*

Brussels ✪
BELGIUM

GERMANY

Frankfurt
LUX. Prague ✪

✪ Paris

Nantes

Munich
LIECH.

F R A N C E Zürich
Bern
SWITZ.

AUSTRIA
Ljubljana
SLOV.

Bay of
Biscay

Bordeaux Lyon

Milan
Turin Venice
Genoa

Oporto

40°N

PORTUGAL

Bilbao
Valladolid

Toulouse

MONACO
Nice
Marseille

**SAN
MARINO**

ITALY

ANDORRA
Madrid ✪ •Zaragoza

Lisbon

S P A I N
Valencia•

Barcelona

Corsica
(France)

**VATICAN
CITY** ▫
Rome ✪

10°W

Seville• Murcia•
Málaga•

Balearic Is.
(Spain)

Sardinia
(Italy)

Naples•

•Gibraltar (U.K.)

M e d i t e r r a

Palermo•

Messina

Catania
n e a n Sicily

0   400 Miles
0   400 Kilometers

Azimuthal Equidistant Projection

A F R I C A

Valletta•
MALTA

0°   10°E

EUROPE

A commonly accepted division between Asia and Europe—marked here by a maroon, dashed line—is formed by the Ural Mountains, Ural River, Caspian Sea, Caucasus Mountains, and the Black Sea with its outlets, the Bosporus and Dardanelles.

Barents Sea

ASIA

RUSSIA

NORWAY

SWEDEN

FINLAND

Murmansk

Archangel

Lake Ladoga

Helsinki

Stockholm

Tallinn

St. Petersburg

ESTONIA

Baltic Sea

Riga

LATVIA

Kaliningrad (Russia)

LITHUANIA

Vitsyebsk

Kaunas

Vilnius

Minsk

Gdańsk

BELARUS

POLAND

Warsaw

Homyel'

Bydgoszcz

Łódź

Wrocław

Kraków

CZECH REP. (CZECHIA)

L'viv

UKRAINE

Kiev

Vinnytsya

Poltava

Donets'k

Vienna

SLOVAKIA

Bratislava

Budapest

HUNGARY

MOLDOVA

Chişinău

Zagreb

CROATIA

ROMANIA

Odesa

Simferopol'

BOSNIA & HERZEGOVINA

Belgrade

Bucharest

Sevastopol'

Sarajevo

SERBIA

MONTENEGRO

KOSOVO

Prishtina

BULGARIA

Varna

Podgorica

Skopje

Sofia

Tirana

MACED.

ALBANIA

Thessaloniki

Istanbul

Bosporus

Dardanelles

GREECE

TURKEY

Athens

Sea

Crete

NORTHERN CYPRUS

Nicosia

CYPRUS

Tver'

Yaroslavl'

Volga River

Kazan'

Ufa

Moscow

Nizhniy Novgorod

Samara

Orenburg

Ryazan'

Penza

Smolensk

Saratov

Bryansk

Kursk

KAZAKHSTAN

Kharkiv

Volgograd

Astrakhan'

Rostov

Dnipropetrovs'k

-92 ft (-28 m)

Caspian Sea

El'brus (5,642 m) 18,510 ft

Groznyy

Sochi

GEORGIA

Baku

AZERBAIJAN

Black Sea

10°E 20°E 30°E 40°E 50°E 60°E 70°E

20°E 30°E 40°E

60°N

50°N

40°N

SPOTLIGHT ON
NORTH AMERICA

Chichén Itzá, a Maya temple on Mexico's Yucatan Peninsula, has 365 steps —one for each day of the calendar year.

Honduras is the only Central American country that doesn't have a volcano.

Castillo Kukulkan Temple of Chichén Itzá, Mexico

From the Great Plains of the United States and Canada to the rain forests of Panama, North America stretches 5,500 miles (8,850 km) from north to south. The third largest continent, North America can be divided into five regions: the mountainous west (including parts of Mexico and Central America's western coast), the Great Plains, the Canadian Shield, the varied eastern region (including Central America's lowlands and coastal plains), and the Caribbean.

Rodeo cowboy

Taking Flight

Millions of monarchs migrate up to 3,000 miles (4,828 km) to Mexico every year from the United States and Canada. They're the only butterflies to make such a massive journey.

Back to Its Roots

Same mountain, new official name: Formerly called Mount McKinley, Denali now officially goes by the Native Alaskan name it was given thousands of years ago.

Early Life

The 20,000-year-old stone tools and animal bones discovered in the Bluefish caves in Yukon Territory, Canada, may be the continent's first evidence of human activity.

Horse jawbone

Tale of the Shrew

Found throughout most of Canada and the U.S., the northern short-tailed shrew is North America's only native venomous mammal. The mouse-size animal uses its venom to paralyze prey.

North America's 5 Most Visited National Parks*

1. Great Smoky Mountains, U.S.A. 10.1 million
2. Grand Canyon, U.S.A. 4.8 million
3. Yosemite, U.S.A. 3.9 million
4. Banff, Canada 3.6 million**
5. Yellowstone, U.S.A. 3.5 million

*2014 (National Park Service); **2014-2015 Parks Canada

Snowy owl

PHYSICAL

LAND AREA
9,449,000 sq mi
(24,474,000 sq km)

HIGHEST POINT
Denali, Alaska
20,320 ft (6,194 m)

LOWEST POINT
Death Valley, California
-282 ft (-86 m)

LONGEST RIVER
Mississippi–Missouri,
United States
3,780 mi (6,083 km)

LARGEST LAKE
Lake Superior,
U.S.–Canada
31,700 sq mi
(82,100 sq km)

POLITICAL

POPULATION
573,373,000

LARGEST COUNTRY
Canada
3,855,103 sq mi
(9,984,670 sq km)

LARGEST METROPOLITAN AREA
Mexico City, Mexico
Pop. 20,999,000

MOST DENSELY POPULATED COUNTRY
Barbados /1,675 people
per sq mi (647 per sq km)

Map Key
⊛ National capital
• Other city
▲ Highest point
▸ Lowest point

EUROPE

ASIA

Arctic Ocean

North Pole

ARCTIC CIRCLE

Greenland
(Denmark)

C A N A D A

Alaska
(U.S.)
(Mount McKinley) Denali
(6,190 m) 20,310 ft ▲
Anchorage

Edmonton
Calgary
Winnipeg
Seattle
Vancouver
Victoria
Thunder Bay
Montreal

20°W
40°W
40°W
40°N
60°N
60°N
80°N
160°W
180°
40°N

0 800 Miles
0 800 Kilometers
Azimuthal Equidistant Projection

286

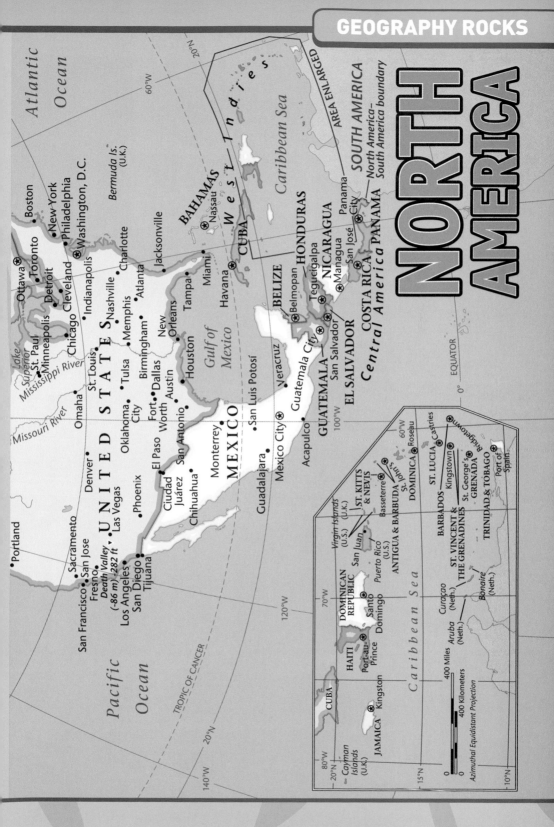

NORTH AMERICA

Atlantic Ocean

Pacific Ocean

Gulf of Mexico

Caribbean Sea

West Indies

UNITED STATES

MEXICO

BAHAMAS

CUBA

BELIZE

GUATEMALA

HONDURAS

EL SALVADOR

NICARAGUA

COSTA RICA

PANAMA

SOUTH AMERICA

AREA ENLARGED

North America–
South America boundary

Central America

EQUATOR

TROPIC OF CANCER

Lake Superior

Mississippi River

Missouri River

Portland
San Francisco
Sacramento
San Jose
Fresno
Las Vegas
Los Angeles
San Diego
Tijuana
Death Valley -282 ft
(-86 m)
Denver
Phoenix
El Paso
Ciudad Juárez
Chihuahua
Omaha
Oklahoma City
Tulsa
Fort Worth
Dallas
Austin
San Antonio
St. Louis
Memphis
Birmingham
New Orleans
Houston
Monterrey
Guadalajara
Mexico City
Acapulco
San Luis Potosí
Veracruz
Guatemala City
San Salvador
Tegucigalpa
Belmopan
Managua
San José
Panama City
St. Paul
Minneapolis
Chicago
Indianapolis
Nashville
Atlanta
Charlotte
Jacksonville
Tampa
Miami
Havana
Nassau
Detroit
Cleveland
Toronto
Ottawa
Boston
New York
Philadelphia
Washington, D.C.

Bermuda Is. (U.K.)

Caribbean Sea

CUBA
Kingston
JAMAICA
Cayman Islands (U.K.)

HAITI
Port-au-Prince
DOMINICAN REPUBLIC
Santo Domingo

Puerto Rico (U.S.)
San Juan
Virgin Islands (U.S.) (U.K.)

ST. KITTS & NEVIS
Basseterre
St. John's
ANTIGUA & BARBUDA

DOMINICA
Roseau

ST. LUCIA
Castries

BARBADOS
Bridgetown

ST. VINCENT & THE GRENADINES
Kingstown
St. George's
GRENADA

TRINIDAD & TOBAGO
Port of Spain

Curaçao (Neth.)
Aruba (Neth.)
Bonaire (Neth.)

400 Miles
400 Kilometers

Azimuthal Equidistant Projection

SPOTLIGHT ON
SOUTH AMERICA

In addition to llamas and alpacas, you might find ocelots, condors, and spectacled bears at Machu Picchu.

More than 700,000 different kinds of insects live in Brazil.

Llamas and alpacas, Machu Picchu, Peru

South America is bordered by three major bodies of water—the Caribbean Sea, Atlantic Ocean, and Pacific Ocean. The world's fourth largest continent extends over a range of climates from tropical in the north to subarctic in the south. South America produces a rich diversity of natural resources, including nuts, fruits, sugar, grains, coffee, and chocolate.

A boy celebrates Carnival in Río de Janeiro, Brazil.

High Sands

Peru's Cerro Blanco is home to the world's highest sand dune. At 3,858 feet (1,176 m), it's more than 1,000 feet (305 m) taller than Dubai's Burj Khalifa—the world's tallest building.

Clean Air

The southern tip of South America has some of the world's freshest air. Ushuaia, Argentina, has no pollutants in the air much of the year. A remote location and frequent rain play a part.

Big Bird

The Andean condor, which lives exclusively in the mountains and valleys of the Andes, is the largest raptor in the world and the largest flying bird in South America.

Living in Isolation

Brazil's Amazon rain forest is home to more isolated tribes than anywhere on the planet. There are thought to be at least 77 groups with little to no contact with the outside world.

World's Deepest Canyon

Peru's Cotahuasi Canyon is more than 11,500 feet (3,500 m) deep!

Almost twice as deep as the Grand Canyon — 6,000 feet (1,111 m) —

Burj Khalifa 2,717 feet (828 m)

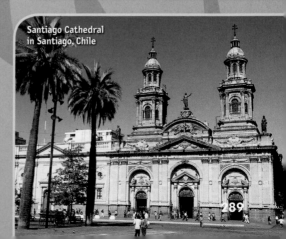

Santiago Cathedral in Santiago, Chile

PHYSICAL

LAND AREA
6,880,000 sq mi
(17,819,000 sq km)

HIGHEST POINT
Cerro Aconcagua,
Argentina
22,831 ft (6,959 m)

LOWEST POINT
Laguna del Carbón,
Argentina
-344 ft (-105 m)

LONGEST RIVER
Amazon
4,150 mi (6,679 km)

LARGEST LAKE
Lake Maracaibo,
Venezuela
5,127 sq mi
(13,280 sq km)

POLITICAL

POPULATION
413,870,000

LARGEST COUNTRY
Brazil
3,287,612 sq mi
(8,514,877 sq km)

LARGEST METROPOLITAN AREA
São Paulo, Brazil
Pop. 21,066,000

**MOST DENSELY POPULATED
COUNTRY**
Ecuador / 149 people per
sq mi (57 per sq km)

Map Key
⊛ National capital
• Other city
▲ Highest point
▼ Lowest point

Central
America

Caribbean
Sea

South America–
North America
boundary

Barranquilla
Maracaibo
Lake
Maracaibo
Medellín
⊛ Bogotá
Cali
COLOMBIA

Caracás
Valencia
Barquisimeto
VENEZUELA

⊛ Quito
ECUADOR

Guayaquil

Trujillo

Lima ⊛

Cusco

P E R U

B O L I V I A

Georgetown
Paramaribo
Cayenne
French Guiana
(France)
GUYANA
SURINAME

Manaus

Amazon River

B R A Z I L

Belém

Fortaleza
Natal
Recife
Salvador
(Bahia)

⊛ Brasília

EQUATOR

10°N
0°
10°S

80°W
70°W
60°W
50°W
40°W

290

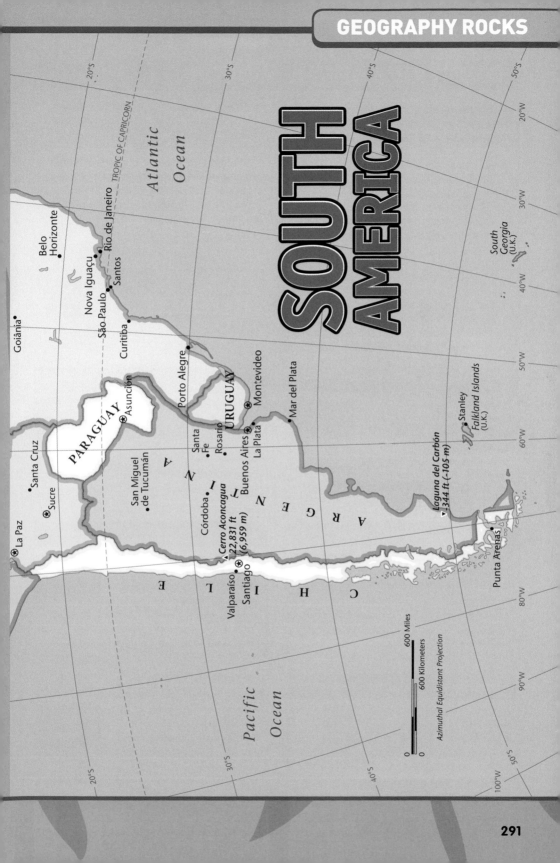

SOUTH AMERICA

Atlantic Ocean

Pacific Ocean

TROPIC OF CAPRICORN

PARAGUAY

URUGUAY

ARGENTINA

CHILE

La Paz

Sucre

Santa Cruz

Goiânia

Belo Horizonte

Nova Iguaçu

Rio de Janeiro

Santos

São Paulo

Curitiba

Porto Alegre

Asunción

San Miguel de Tucumán

Córdoba

Cerro Aconcagua
△ 22,831 ft
(6,959 m)

Valparaíso
Santiago

Santa Fe

Rosario

Buenos Aires

La Plata

Montevideo

Mar del Plata

Laguna del Carbón
▽ 344 ft (-105 m)

Punta Arenas

Stanley
Falkland Islands
(U.K.)

South Georgia
(U.K.)

600 Miles

600 Kilometers

Azimuthal Equidistant Projection

0

0

20°S

30°S

40°S

50°S

20°S

30°S

40°S

20°W

30°W

40°W

50°W

60°W

80°W

90°W

100°W

50°W

291

COUNTRIES OF THE WORLD

The following pages present a general overview of all 195 independent countries recognized by the National Geographic Society, including the newest nation, South Sudan, which gained independence in 2011.

The flags of each independent country symbolize diverse cultures and histories. The statistical data cover highlights of geography and demography and provide a brief overview of each country. They present general characteristics and are not intended to be comprehensive. For example, not every language spoken in a specific country can be listed. Thus, languages shown are the most representative of that area. This is also true of the religions mentioned.

A country is defined as a political body with its own independent government, geographical space, and, in most cases, laws, military, and taxes.

Disputed areas such as Northern Cyprus and Taiwan, and dependencies of independent nations, such as Bermuda and Puerto Rico, are not included in this listing.

Note the color key at the bottom of the pages and the locator map below, which assign a color to each country based on the continent on which it is located. All information is accurate as of press time.

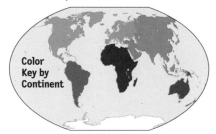

Color Key by Continent

Afghanistan

Area: 251,773 sq mi (652,090 sq km)
Population: 32,247,000
Capital: Kabul, pop. 4,436,000
Currency: afghani
Religions: Sunni Muslim, Shiite Muslim
Languages: Afghan Persian (Dari), Pashto, Turkic languages (primarily Uzbek and Turkmen), Baluchi, 30 minor languages (including Pashai)

Albania

Area: 11,100 sq mi (28,748 sq km)
Population: 2,892,000
Capital: Tirana, pop. 445,000
Currency: lek
Religions: Muslim, Albanian Orthodox, Roman Catholic
Languages: Albanian, Greek, Vlach, Romani, Slavic dialects

Algeria

Area: 919,595 sq mi (2,381,741 sq km)
Population: 39,948,000
Capital: Algiers, pop. 2,559,000
Currency: Algerian dinar
Religion: Sunni Muslim
Languages: Arabic, French, Berber dialects

Andorra

Area: 181 sq mi (469 sq km)
Population: 78,000
Capital: Andorra la Vella, pop. 23,000
Currency: euro
Religion: Roman Catholic
Languages: Catalan, French, Castilian, Portuguese

Angola

Area: 481,354 sq mi (1,246,700 sq km)
Population: 25,000,000
Capital: Luanda, pop. 5,288,000
Currency: kwanza
Religions: indigenous beliefs, Roman Catholic, Protestant
Languages: Portuguese, Bantu, and other African languages

Antigua and Barbuda

Area: 171 sq mi (442 sq km)
Population: 90,000
Capital: St. John's, pop. 22,000
Currency: East Caribbean dollar
Religions: Anglican, Seventh-day Adventist, Pentecostal, Moravian, Roman Catholic, Methodist, Baptist, Church of God, other Christian
Languages: English, local dialects

Argentina

Area: 1,073,518 sq mi (2,780,400 sq km)
Population: 42,426,000
Capital: Buenos Aires, pop. 15,024,000
Currency: Argentine peso
Religion: Roman Catholic
Languages: Spanish, English, Italian, German, French

Armenia

Area: 11,484 sq mi (29,743 sq km)
Population: 3,017,000
Capital: Yerevan, pop. 1,049,000
Currency: dram
Religions: Armenian Apostolic, other Christian
Language: Armenian

Australia

Area: 2,988,901 sq mi (7,741,220 sq km)
Population: 23,888,000
Capital: Canberra, A.C.T., pop. 415,000
Currency: Australian dollar
Religions: Roman Catholic, Anglican
Language: English

Austria

Area: 32,378 sq mi (83,858 sq km)
Population: 8,616,000
Capital: Vienna, pop. 1,743,000
Currency: euro
Religions: Roman Catholic, Protestant, Muslim
Language: German

Azerbaijan

Area: 33,436 sq mi (86,600 sq km)
Population: 9,651,000
Capital: Baku, pop. 2,317,000
Currency: Azerbaijani manat
Religion: Muslim
Language: Azerbaijani (Azeri)

Bahamas

Area: 5,382 sq mi (13,939 sq km)
Population: 377,000
Capital: Nassau, pop. 267,000
Currency: Bahamian dollar
Religions: Baptist, Anglican, Roman Catholic, Pentecostal, Church of God
Languages: English, Creole

Bahrain

Area: 277 sq mi (717 sq km)
Population: 1,412,000
Capital: Manama, pop. 398,000
Currency: Bahraini dinar
Religions: Shiite Muslim, Sunni Muslim, Christian
Languages: Arabic, English, Farsi, Urdu

Bangladesh

Area: 55,598 sq mi (143,998 sq km)
Population: 160,411,000
Capital: Dhaka, pop. 16,982,000
Currency: taka
Religions: Muslim, Hindu
Languages: Bangla (Bengali), English

5 cool things about AUSTRALIA

1. Australia's outback is home to the world's largest population of wild camels.

2. The dangerous bulldog ant—whose bite can be fatal to humans—is found exclusively in Australia.

3. Kangaroos as tall as a professional basketball player once roamed around Australia.

4. You can ride a single train from one coast of Australia to another—a total of 2,704 miles (4,352 km).

5. The term "selfie" is said to have originated in Australia.

Barbados

Area: 166 sq mi (430 sq km)
Population: 278,000
Capital: Bridgetown, pop. 90,000
Currency: Barbadian dollar
Religions: Anglican, Pentecostal, Methodist, other Protestant, Roman Catholic
Language: English

Belarus

Area: 80,153 sq mi (207,595 sq km)
Population: 9,524,000
Capital: Minsk, pop. 1,905,000
Currency: Belarusian ruble
Religions: Eastern Orthodox, other (includes Roman Catholic, Protestant, Jewish, Muslim)
Languages: Belarusian, Russian

Belgium

Area: 11,787 sq mi (30,528 sq km)
Population: 11,211,000
Capital: Brussels, pop. 2,029,000
Currency: euro
Religions: Roman Catholic, other (includes Protestant)
Languages: Dutch, French

Belize

Area: 8,867 sq mi (22,965 sq km)
Population: 368,000
Capital: Belmopan, pop. 17,000
Currency: Belizean dollar
Religions: Roman Catholic, Protestant (includes Pentecostal, Seventh-day Adventist, Mennonite, Methodist)
Languages: Spanish, Creole, Mayan dialects, English, Garifuna (Carib), German

Benin

Area: 43,484 sq mi (112,622 sq km)
Population: 10,583,000
Capitals: Porto-Novo, pop. 268,000; Cotonou, pop. 680,000
Currency: Communauté Financière Africaine franc
Religions: Christian, Muslim, Vodoun
Languages: French, Fon, Yoruba, tribal languages

Bhutan

Area: 17,954 sq mi (46,500 sq km)
Population: 757,000
Capital: Thimphu, pop. 152,000
Currencies: ngultrum; Indian rupee
Religions: Lamaistic Buddhist, Indian- and Nepalese-influenced Hindu
Languages: Dzongkha, Tibetan dialects, Nepalese dialects

Bolivia

Area: 424,164 sq mi (1,098,581 sq km)
Population: 10,476,000
Capitals: La Paz, pop. 1,800,000; Sucre, pop. 358,000
Currency: boliviano
Religions: Roman Catholic, Protestant (includes Evangelical Methodist)
Languages: Spanish, Quechua, Aymara

There are **NO MOTOR VEHICLES** on Bolivia's Isla del Sol—**VISITORS MUST HIKE OR TRAVEL BY BOAT.**

Bosnia and Herzegovina

Area: 19,741 sq mi (51,129 sq km)
Population: 3,650,000
Capital: Sarajevo, pop. 322,000
Currency: konvertibilna marka (convertible mark)
Religions: Muslim, Orthodox, Roman Catholic
Languages: Bosnian, Croatian, Serbian

Botswana

Area: 224,607 sq mi (581,730 sq km)
Population: 2,140,000
Capital: Gaborone, pop. 247,000
Currency: pula
Religions: Christian, Badimo
Languages: Setswana, Kalanga

Brazil

Area: 3,287,612 sq mi
(8,514,877 sq km)
Population: 204,519,000
Capital: Brasília, pop. 4,074,000
Currency: real
Religions: Roman Catholic, Protestant
Language: Portuguese

Bulgaria

Area: 42,855 sq mi
(110,994 sq km)
Population: 7,181,000
Capital: Sofia, pop. 1,222,000
Currency: lev
Religions: Bulgarian Orthodox, Muslim
Languages: Bulgarian, Turkish, Roma

Brunei

Area: 2,226 sq mi (5,765 sq km)
Population: 413,000
Capital: Bandar Seri Begawan,
pop. 14,000
Currency: Bruneian dollar
Religions: Muslim, Buddhist, Christian, other
(includes indigenous beliefs)
Languages: Malay, English, Chinese

Burkina Faso

Area: 105,869 sq mi
(274,200 sq km)
Population: 18,450,000
Capital: Ouagadougou,
pop. 2,565,000
Currency: Communauté Financière Africaine franc
Religions: Muslim, indigenous beliefs, Christian
Languages: French, native African languages

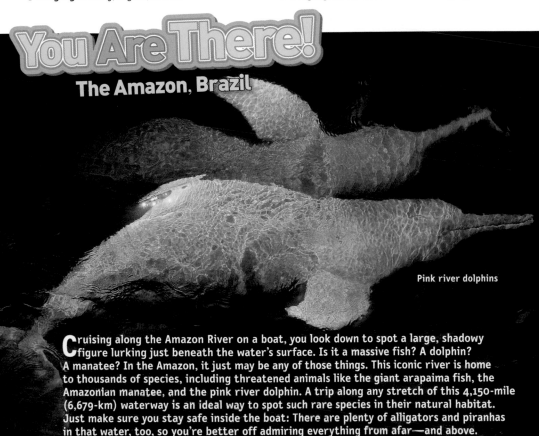

You Are There!
The Amazon, Brazil

Pink river dolphins

Cruising along the Amazon River on a boat, you look down to spot a large, shadowy figure lurking just beneath the water's surface. Is it a massive fish? A dolphin? A manatee? In the Amazon, it just may be any of those things. This iconic river is home to thousands of species, including threatened animals like the giant arapaima fish, the Amazonian manatee, and the pink river dolphin. A trip along any stretch of this 4,150-mile (6,679-km) waterway is an ideal way to spot such rare species in their natural habitat. Just make sure you stay safe inside the boat: There are plenty of alligators and piranhas in that water, too, so you're better off admiring everything from afar—and above.

● Asia ● Europe ● North America ● South America

Burundi

Area: 10,747 sq mi (27,834 sq km)
Population: 10,742,000
Capital: Bujumbura, pop. 707,000
Currency: Burundi franc
Religions: Roman Catholic, indigenous beliefs, Muslim, Protestant
Languages: Kirundi, French, Swahili

Cabo Verde

Area: 1,558 sq mi (4,036 sq km)
Population: 514,000
Capital: Praia, pop. 145,000
Currency: Cape Verdean escudo
Religions: Roman Catholic (infused with indigenous beliefs), Protestant (mostly Church of the Nazarene)
Languages: Portuguese, Crioulo

Cambodia

Area: 69,898 sq mi (181,035 sq km)
Population: 15,417,000
Capital: Phnom Penh, pop. 1,684,000
Currency: riel
Religion: Theravada Buddhist
Language: Khmer

Cameroon

Area: 183,569 sq mi (475,442 sq km)
Population: 23,739,000
Capital: Yaoundé, pop. 2,930,000
Currency: Communauté Financière Africaine franc
Religions: indigenous beliefs, Christian, Muslim
Languages: 24 major African language groups, English, French

You Are There!

Vancouver Island, British Columbia, Canada

Picture this: You're cruising along around Vancouver Island on a ferry boat when you head out to the deck just in time to see a giant, shiny, black and white object go flying in the air before plunging back into the water with a huge splash. An orca! Hundreds of these massive mammals—plus other whales including humpbacks, greys and minkes—can be found in the waters surrounding Vancouver Island. So it's no wonder this place is one of the world's top whale-watching spots. But there's more than just whales to see as you wonder around Vancouver Island: Sea lions swim alongside octopuses, and you may spot a bald eagle soaring up above or a grizzly bear snagging salmon along the shores. So keep your eyes peeled—and be sure to bring your binoculars!

COLOR KEY ● Africa ● Australia, New Zealand, and Oceania

Canada

Area: 3,855,101 sq mi
(9,984,670 sq km)
Population: 35,833,000
Capital: Ottawa, pop. 1,306,000
Currency: Canadian dollar
Religions: Roman Catholic, Protestant (includes United Church, Anglican), other Christian
Languages: English, French

Central African Republic

Area: 240,535 sq mi
(622,984 sq km)
Population: 5,552,000
Capital: Bangui, pop. 781,000
Currency: Communauté Financière Africaine franc
Religions: indigenous beliefs, Protestant, Roman Catholic, Muslim
Languages: French, Sangho, tribal languages

Chad

Area: 495,755 sq mi
(1,284,000 sq km)
Population: 13,707,000
Capital: N'Djamena, pop. 1,212,000
Currency: Communauté Financière Africaine franc
Religions: Muslim, Catholic, Protestant, animist
Languages: French, Arabic, Sara, more than 120 languages and dialects

Chile

Area: 291,930 sq mi
(756,096 sq km)
Population: 18,025,000
Capital: Santiago, pop. 6,472,000
Currency: Chilean peso
Religions: Roman Catholic, Evangelical
Language: Spanish

China

Area: 3,705,406 sq mi
(9,596,961 sq km)
Population: 1,371,920,000
Capital: Beijing, pop. 19,520,000
Currency: renminbi (yuan)
Religions: Taoist, Buddhist, Christian
Languages: Standard Chinese or Mandarin, Yue, Wu, Minbei, Minnan, Xiang, Gan, Hakka dialects

Colombia

Area: 440,831 sq mi
(1,141,748 sq km)
Population: 48,218,000
Capital: Bogotá, pop. 9,558,000
Currency: Colombian peso
Religion: Roman Catholic
Language: Spanish

Comoros

Area: 863 sq mi (2,235 sq km)
Population: 764,000
Capital: Moroni, pop. 56,000
Currency: Comoran franc
Religion: Sunni Muslim
Languages: Arabic, French, Shikomoro

Congo

Area: 132,047 sq mi (342,000 sq km)
Population: 4,755,000
Capital: Brazzaville, pop. 1,827,000
Currency: Communauté Financière Africaine franc
Religions: Christian, animist
Languages: French, Lingala, Monokutuba, local languages

Costa Rica

Area: 19,730 sq mi
(51,100 sq km)
Population: 4,832,000
Capital: San José, pop. 1,160,000
Currency: Costa Rican colón
Religions: Roman Catholic, Evangelical
Languages: Spanish, English

Côte d'Ivoire (Ivory Coast)

Area: 124,503 sq mi
(322,462 sq km)
Population: 23,281,000
Capitals: Abidjan, pop. 4,708,000; Yamoussoukro, pop. 259,000
Currency: Communauté Financière Africaine franc
Religions: Muslim, indigenous beliefs, Christian
Languages: French, Dioula, other native dialects

Croatia

Area: 21,831 sq mi
(56,542 sq km)
Population: 4,215,000
Capital: Zagreb, pop. 687,000
Currency: kuna
Religions: Roman Catholic, Orthodox
Language: Croatian

NECKTIES ORIGINATED IN CROATIA.

Cuba

Area: 42,803 sq mi
(110,860 sq km)
Population: 11,139,000
Capital: Havana, pop. 2,146,000
Currency: Cuban peso
Religions: Roman Catholic, Protestant, Jehovah's Witnesses, Jewish, Santería
Language: Spanish

Cyprus

Area: 3,572 sq mi (9,251 sq km)
Population: 1,153,000
Capital: Nicosia, pop. 251,000
Currencies: euro; new Turkish lira in Northern Cyprus
Religions: Greek Orthodox, Muslim, Maronite, Armenian Apostolic
Languages: Greek, Turkish, English

Czech Republic (Czechia)

Area: 30,450 sq mi (78,866 sq km)
Population: 10,551,000
Capital: Prague, pop. 1,303,000
Currency: koruny
Religion: Roman Catholic
Language: Czech

Democratic Republic of the Congo

Area: 905,365 sq mi
(2,344,885 sq km)
Population: 73,340,000
Capital: Kinshasa, pop. 11,116,000
Currency: Congolese franc
Religions: Roman Catholic, Protestant, Kimbanguist, Muslim, syncretic sects, indigenous beliefs
Languages: French, Lingala, Kingwana, Kikongo, Tshiluba

Denmark

Area: 16,640 sq mi (43,098 sq km)
Population: 5,676,000
Capital: Copenhagen, pop. 1,255,000
Currency: Danish krone
Religions: Evangelical Lutheran, other Protestant, Roman Catholic
Languages: Danish, Faroese, Greenlandic, German, English as second language

Djibouti

Area: 8,958 sq mi
(23,200 sq km)
Population: 900,000
Capital: Djibouti, pop. 522,000
Currency: Djiboutian franc
Religions: Muslim, Christian
Languages: French, Arabic, Somali, Afar

Dominica

Area: 290 sq mi (751 sq km)
Population: 68,000
Capital: Roseau, pop. 15,000
Currency: East Caribbean dollar
Religions: Roman Catholic, Seventh-day Adventist, Pentecostal, Baptist, Methodist, other Christian
Languages: English, French patois

Dominican Republic

Area: 18,704 sq mi
(48,442 sq km)
Population: 10,508,000
Capital: Santo Domingo, pop. 2,873,000
Currency: Dominican peso
Religion: Roman Catholic
Language: Spanish

COLOR KEY ● Africa ● Australia, New Zealand, and Oceania

Ecuador

Area: 109,483 sq mi
(283,560 sq km)
Population: 16,279,000
Capital: Quito, pop. 1,699,000
Currency: U.S. dollar
Religion: Roman Catholic
Languages: Spanish, Quechua, other
Amerindian languages

Egypt

Area: 386,874 sq mi
(1,002,000 sq km)
Population: 89,074,000
Capital: Cairo, pop. 18,419,000
Currency: Egyptian pound
Religions: Muslim (mostly Sunni), Coptic Christian
Languages: Arabic, English, French

El Salvador

Area: 8,124 sq mi
(21,041 sq km)
Population: 6,366,000
Capital: San Salvador,
pop. 1,097,000
Currency: U.S. dollar
Religions: Roman Catholic, Protestant
Languages: Spanish, Nahua

5 cool things about EL SALVADOR

1. El Salvador is the smallest country in Central America; at its longest, it is only 88 miles (142 km) long.

2. Known as the Land of Volcanoes, there are over 20 active volcanoes in El Salvador.

3. Green toucans can be found in the cloud forest on Monte Cristo Mountain.

4. In 2005, 13,380 people gathered to brush their teeth together at a world record-setting event in San Salvador.

5. El Salvador's coastlines are popular spots for surfers from around the world.

Equatorial Guinea

Area: 10,831 sq mi (28,051 sq km)
Population: 805,000
Capital: Malabo, pop. 145,000
Currency: Communauté
Financière Africaine franc
Religions: Christian (predominantly Roman Catholic),
pagan practices
Languages: Spanish, French, Fang, Bubi

Equatorial Guinea is a nesting site FOR ENDANGERED SEA TURTLES.

Eritrea

Area: 45,406 sq mi
(117,600 sq km)
Population: 5,200,000
Capital: Asmara, pop. 775,000
Currency: nakfa
Religions: Muslim, Coptic Christian, Roman Catholic
Languages: Afar, Arabic, Tigre, Kunama, Tigrinya, other
Cushitic languages

Estonia

Area: 17,462 sq mi (45,227 sq km)
Population: 1,311,000
Capital: Tallinn, pop. 392,000
Currency: euro
Religions: Evangelical Lutheran, Orthodox
Languages: Estonian, Russian

Ethiopia

Area: 426,373 sq mi
(1,104,300 sq km)
Population: 98,148,000
Capital: Addis Ababa,
pop. 3,168,000
Currency: birr
Religions: Christian, Muslim, traditional
Languages: Amharic, Oromigna, Tigrinya, Guaragigna

Fiji

Area: 7,095 sq mi
(18,376 sq km)
Population: 867,000
Capital: Suva, pop. 176,000
Currency: Fijian dollar
Religions: Christian (Methodist, Roman Catholic, Assembly of God), Hindu (Sanatan), Muslim (Sunni)
Languages: English, Fijian, Hindustani

France

Area: 210,026 sq mi
(543,965 sq km)
Population: 64,347,000
Capital: Paris, pop. 10,764,000
Currency: euro
Religions: Roman Catholic, Muslim
Language: French

Finland

Area: 130,558 sq mi
(338,145 sq km)
Population: 5,476,000
Capital: Helsinki, pop. 1,170,000
Currency: euro
Religion: Lutheran Church of Finland
Languages: Finnish, Swedish

Gabon

Area: 103,347 sq mi (267,667 sq km)
Population: 1,751,000
Capital: Libreville, pop. 695,000
Currency: Communauté Financière Africaine franc
Religions: Christian, animist
Languages: French, Fang, Myene, Nzebi, Bapounou/Eschira, Bandjabi

You Are There!

Fiji Barrier Reef

After slipping on some fins and a snorkel mask, you plunge into the turquoise Pacific Ocean. The water is so clear, you can see straight to the bottom as the sunlight filters down in glittering rays around you. This is what it's like to snorkel in Fiji: a network of some 320 islands all surrounded by about 4,000 square miles (10,360 sq km) of coral reef. Hundreds of species, like turtles, seabirds, and fish, call the "Soft Coral Capital of the World" home. A dip into the waters will welcome you with breathtaking sights, like schools of tropical fish in a rainbow of colors and giant clams that grow as long as a baseball bat. It's like swimming in your very own aquarium!

COLOR KEY ● Africa ● Australia, New Zealand, and Oceania

Gambia

Area: 4,361 sq mi (11,295 sq km)
Population: 2,022,000
Capital: Banjul, pop. 489,000
Currency: dalasi
Religions: Muslim, Christian
Languages: English, Mandinka, Wolof, Fula, other indigenous vernaculars

Georgia

Area: 26,911 sq mi (69,700 sq km)
Population: 3,804,000
Capital: Tbilisi, pop. 1,150,000
Currency: lari
Religions: Orthodox Christian, Muslim, Armenian-Gregorian
Languages: Georgian, Russian, Armenian, Azeri, Abkhaz

Germany

Area: 137,847 sq mi (357,022 sq km)
Population: 81,132,000
Capital: Berlin, pop. 3,547,000
Currency: euro
Religions: Protestant, Roman Catholic, Muslim
Language: German

Ghana

Area: 92,100 sq mi (238,537 sq km)
Population: 27,673,000
Capital: Accra, pop. 2,242,000
Currency: Ghana cedi
Religions: Christian (Pentecostal/Charismatic, Protestant, Roman Catholic, other), Muslim, traditional beliefs
Languages: Asante, Ewe, Fante, Boron (Brong), Dagomba, Dangme, Dagarte (Dagaba), Akyem, Ga, English

Greece

Area: 50,949 sq mi (131,957 sq km)
Population: 11,521,000
Capital: Athens, pop. 3,060,000
Currency: euro
Religion: Greek Orthodox
Languages: Greek, English, French

Grenada

Area: 133 sq mi (344 sq km)
Population: 111,000
Capital: St. George's, pop. 38,000
Currency: East Caribbean dollar
Religions: Roman Catholic, Anglican, other Protestant
Languages: English, French patois

Guatemala

Area: 42,042 sq mi (108,889 sq km)
Population: 16,184,000
Capital: Guatemala City, pop. 2,874,000
Currency: quetzal
Religions: Roman Catholic, Protestant, indigenous Maya beliefs
Languages: Spanish, 23 official Amerindian languages

Guinea

Area: 94,926 sq mi (245,857 sq km)
Population: 10,986,000
Capital: Conakry, pop. 1,886,000
Currency: Guinean franc
Religions: Muslim, Christian, indigenous beliefs
Languages: French, ethnic languages

Guinea-Bissau

Area: 13,948 sq mi (36,125 sq km)
Population: 1,788,000
Capital: Bissau, pop. 473,000
Currency: Communauté Financière Africaine franc
Religions: indigenous beliefs, Muslim, Christian
Languages: Portuguese, Crioulo, African languages

Guyana

Area: 83,000 sq mi (214,969 sq km)
Population: 743,000
Capital: Georgetown, pop. 124,000
Currency: Guyanese dollar
Religions: Christian, Hindu, Muslim
Languages: English, Amerindian dialects, Creole, Hindustani, Urdu

Haiti

Area: 10,714 sq mi (27,750 sq km)
Population: 10,924,000
Capital: Port-au-Prince, pop. 2,376,000
Currency: gourde
Religions: Roman Catholic, Protestant (Baptist, Pentecostal, other)
Languages: French, Creole

Honduras

Area: 43,433 sq mi (112,492 sq km)
Population: 8,340,000
Capital: Tegucigalpa, pop. 1,101,000
Currency: lempira
Religions: Roman Catholic, Protestant
Languages: Spanish, Amerindian dialects

Hungary

Area: 35,919 sq mi (93,030 sq km)
Population: 9,835,000
Capital: Budapest, pop. 1,717,000
Currency: forint
Religions: Roman Catholic, Calvinist, Lutheran
Language: Hungarian

Iceland

Area: 39,769 sq mi (103,000 sq km)
Population: 331,000
Capital: Reykjavík, pop. 184,000
Currency: Icelandic krona
Religion: Lutheran Church of Iceland
Languages: Icelandic, English, Nordic languages, German

India

Area: 1,269,221 sq mi (3,287,270 sq km)
Population: 1,314,098,000
Capital: New Delhi, pop. 24,953,000 (part of Delhi metropolitan area)
Currency: Indian rupee
Religions: Hindu, Muslim
Languages: Hindi, 21 other official languages, Hindustani (popular Hindi/Urdu variant in the north)

Indonesia

Area: 742,308 sq mi (1,922,570 sq km)
Population: 255,742,000
Capital: Jakarta, pop. 10,176,000
Currency: Indonesian rupiah
Religions: Muslim, Protestant, Roman Catholic
Languages: Bahasa Indonesia (modified form of Malay), English, Dutch, Javanese, local dialects

Iran

Area: 636,296 sq mi (1,648,000 sq km)
Population: 78,483,000
Capital: Tehran, pop. 8,353,000
Currency: Iranian rial
Religions: Shiite Muslim, Sunni Muslim
Languages: Persian, Turkic, Kurdish, Luri, Baluchi, Arabic

Iraq

Area: 168,754 sq mi (437,072 sq km)
Population: 37,056,000
Capital: Baghdad, pop. 6,483,000
Currency: Iraqi dinar
Religions: Shiite Muslim, Sunni Muslim
Languages: Arabic, Kurdish, Assyrian, Armenian

Ireland (Éire)

Area: 27,133 sq mi (70,273 sq km)
Population: 4,630,000
Capital: Dublin, pop. 1,155,000
Currency: euro
Religions: Roman Catholic, Church of Ireland
Languages: Irish (Gaelic), English

Israel

Area: 8,550 sq mi (22,145 sq km)
Population: 8,375,000
Capital: Jerusalem, pop. 829,000
Currency: new Israeli sheqel
Religions: Jewish, Muslim
Languages: Hebrew, Arabic, English

COLOR KEY ● Africa ● Australia, New Zealand, and Oceania

Italy

Area: 116,345 sq mi
(301,333 sq km)
Population: 62,467,000
Capital: Rome, pop. 3,697,000
Currency: euro
Religions: Roman Catholic, Protestant, Jewish, Muslim
Languages: Italian, German, French, Slovene

Japan

Area: 145,902 sq mi (377,887 sq km)
Population: 126,867,000
Capital: Tokyo, pop. 37,833,000
Currency: yen
Religions: Shinto, Buddhist
Language: Japanese

Jamaica

Area: 4,244 sq mi
(10,991 sq km)
Population: 2,727,000
Capital: Kingston, pop. 587,000
Currency: Jamaican dollar
Religions: Protestant (Church of God, Seventh-day Adventist, Pentecostal, Baptist, Anglican, other)
Languages: English, English patois

Jordan

Area: 34,495 sq mi
(89,342 sq km)
Population: 8,118,000
Capital: Amman, pop. 1,148,000
Currency: Jordanian dinar
Religions: Sunni Muslim, Christian
Languages: Arabic, English

You Are There!
Tanjung Puting, Indonesia

There are only two places on the planet where you can spot a wild orangutan—the islands of Borneo and Sumatra. To get a glance of these big orange apes in person, head to Indonesia's Tanjung Puting National Park on the island of Borneo. Here, you can travel with a tour group deep within the forest to ogle orangutans. Tour guides dole out bananas and vitamin-rich milk to lure the animals as visitors stand at a safe distance to watch the apes in action. Don't forget to bring your camera: Orangutans—which share much of the same genetic code as humans—just may strike some funny poses as you snap away!

● Asia ● Europe ● North America ● South America

Kazakhstan

Area: 1,049,155 sq mi
(2,717,300 sq km)
Population: 17,544,000
Capital: Astana, pop. 741,000
Currency: tenge
Religions: Muslim, Russian Orthodox
Languages: Kazakh (Qazaq), Russian

Kiribati

Area: 313 sq mi (811 sq km)
Population: 113,000
Capital: Tarawa, pop. 46,000
Currency: Australian
dollar
Religions: Roman Catholic, Protestant
(Congregational)
Languages: I-Kiribati, English

Kenya

Area: 224,081 sq mi (580,367 sq km)
Population: 44,306,000
Capital: Nairobi, pop. 3,768,000
Currency: Kenyan shilling
Religions: Protestant, Roman Catholic, Muslim,
indigenous beliefs
Languages: English, Kiswahili, many indigenous
languages

Kosovo

Area: 4,203 sq mi (10,887 sq km)
Population: 1,802,000
Capital: Prishtina, pop. 207,500
Currency: euro
Religions: Muslim, Serbian Orthodox, Roman Catholic
Languages: Albanian, Serbian, Bosnian,
Turkish, Roma

You Are There!
Bokeo Nature Reserve, Laos

Up for an adventure? Head to the Bokeo Nature Reserve, a lush rain forest in northern Laos. There, you can take a three-day tour exploring the depths of this wilderness while looking out for some of the area's most coveted wildlife, including tigers, black bears, clouded leopards, and black-crested gibbons. Shoot down a series of zip lines cutting through the rain forest's canopy, then cool off in a swimming hole found at the base of a rushing waterfall. And when you need a place to rest your head? Spend the night in a tree house nestled 130 feet (40 m) aboveground. No need to set an alarm clock: The gibbons' screeching call will wake you right up.

Kuwait

Area: 6,880 sq mi (17,818 sq km)
Population: 3,838,000
Capital: Kuwait City, pop. 2,680,000
Currency: Kuwaiti dinar
Religions: Sunni Muslim, Shiite Muslim
Languages: Arabic, English

Kyrgyzstan

Area: 77,182 sq mi (199,900 sq km)
Population: 5,951,000
Capital: Bishkek, pop. 858,000
Currency: som
Religions: Muslim, Russian Orthodox
Languages: Kyrgyz, Uzbek, Russian

Laos

Area: 91,429 sq mi (236,800 sq km)
Population: 6,903,000
Capital: Vientiane, pop. 946,000
Currency: kip
Religions: Buddhist, animist
Languages: Lao, French, English, various ethnic languages

Latvia

Area: 24,938 sq mi (64,589 sq km)
Population: 1,978,000
Capital: Riga, pop. 629,000
Currency: Latvian lat
Religions: Lutheran, Roman Catholic, Russian Orthodox
Languages: Latvian, Russian, Lithuanian

Lebanon

Area: 4,036 sq mi (10,452 sq km)
Population: 6,185,000
Capital: Beirut, pop. 2,179,000
Currency: Lebanese pound
Religions: Muslim, Christian
Languages: Arabic, French, English, Armenian

Lesotho

Area: 11,720 sq mi (30,355 sq km)
Population: 1,924,000
Capital: Maseru, pop. 267,000
Currencies: loti; South African rand
Religions: Christian, indigenous beliefs
Languages: Sesotho, English, Zulu, Xhosa

Liberia

Area: 43,000 sq mi (111,370 sq km)
Population: 4,503,000
Capital: Monrovia, pop. 1,224,000
Currency: Liberian dollar
Religions: Christian, indigenous beliefs, Muslim
Languages: English, some 20 ethnic languages

Libya

Area: 679,362 sq mi (1,759,540 sq km)
Population: 6,317,000
Capital: Tripoli, pop. 1,126,000
Currency: Libyan dinar
Religion: Sunni Muslim
Languages: Arabic, Italian, English

Liechtenstein

Area: 62 sq mi (160 sq km)
Population: 38,000
Capital: Vaduz, pop. 5,000
Currency: Swiss franc
Religions: Roman Catholic, Protestant
Languages: German, Alemannic dialect

Lithuania

Area: 25,212 sq mi (65,300 sq km)
Population: 2,911,000
Capital: Vilnius, pop. 519,000
Currency: litas
Religions: Roman Catholic, Russian Orthodox
Languages: Lithuanian, Russian, Polish

Luxembourg

Area: 998 sq mi (2,586 sq km)
Population: 569,000
Capital: Luxembourg, pop. 107,000
Currency: euro
Religions: Roman Catholic, Protestant, Jewish, Muslim
Languages: Luxembourgish, German, French

Maldives

Area: 115 sq mi (298 sq km)
Population: 347,000
Capital: Male, pop. 156,000
Currency: rufiyaa
Religion: Sunni Muslim
Languages: Maldivian Dhivehi, English

Macedonia

Area: 9,928 sq mi (25,713 sq km)
Population: 2,070,000
Capital: Skopje, pop. 501,000
Currency: Macedonian denar
Religions: Macedonian Orthodox, Muslim
Languages: Macedonian, Albanian, Turkish

Of the 1,190 islands that make up the Maldives, **SOME 1,000 ARE UNINHABITED.**

Madagascar

Area: 226,658 sq mi (587,041 sq km)
Population: 23,047,000
Capital: Antananarivo, pop. 2,487,000
Currency: Madagascar ariary
Religions: indigenous beliefs, Christian, Muslim
Languages: English, French, Malagasy

Mali

Area: 478,841 sq mi (1,240,192 sq km)
Population: 16,749,000
Capital: Bamako, pop. 2,386,000
Currency: Communauté Financière Africaine franc
Religions: Muslim, indigenous beliefs
Languages: Bambara, French, numerous African languages

Malawi

Area: 45,747 sq mi (118,484 sq km)
Population: 17,174,000
Capital: Lilongwe, pop. 867,000
Currency: Malawian kwacha
Religions: Christian, Muslim
Languages: Chichewa, Chinyanja, Chiyao, Chitumbuka

Malta

Area: 122 sq mi (316 sq km)
Population: 431,000
Capital: Valletta, pop. 197,000
Currency: euro
Religion: Roman Catholic
Languages: Maltese, English

Malaysia

Area: 127,355 sq mi (329,847 sq km)
Population: 30,789,000
Capital: Kuala Lumpur, pop. 6,629,000
Currency: ringgit
Religions: Muslim, Buddhist, Christian, Hindu
Languages: Bahasa Malaysia, English, Chinese, Tamil, Telugu, Malayalam, Panjabi, Thai, indigenous languages

Marshall Islands

Area: 70 sq mi (181 sq km)
Population: 55,000
Capital: Majuro, pop. 31,000
Currency: U.S. dollar
Religions: Protestant, Assembly of God, Roman Catholic
Language: Marshallese

Mauritania

Area: 397,955 sq mi (1,030,700 sq km)
Population: 3,641,000
Capital: Nouakchott, pop. 945,000
Currency: ouguiya
Religion: Muslim
Languages: Arabic, Pulaar, Soninke, French, Hassaniya, Wolof

Mauritius

Area: 788 sq mi (2,040 sq km)
Population: 1,263,000
Capital: Port Louis, pop. 135,000
Currency: Mauritian rupee
Religions: Hindu, Roman Catholic, Muslim, other Christian
Languages: Creole, Bhojpuri, French

Mexico

Area: 758,449 sq mi (1,964,375 sq km)
Population: 127,017,000
Capital: Mexico City, pop. 20,843,000
Currency: Mexican peso
Religions: Roman Catholic, Protestant
Languages: Spanish, Mayan, other indigenous languages

5 cool things about MEXICO

1. Tabasco sauce and Chihuahua dogs share their names with two states in Mexico.

2. A Mexican flag larger than an Olympic swimming pool is the biggest flag flown from a flagpole—so far.

3. Built on a bed of a dried-out lake, Mexico City has sunk 26 feet (8 m) in the last 100 years.

4. The volcano rabbit is found only on the slopes of volcanoes in central Mexico.

5. Founded in 1551, Universidad Nacional Autónoma de México (UNAM) is North America's oldest university.

Micronesia

Area: 271 sq mi (702 sq km)
Population: 103,000
Capital: Palikir, pop. 7,000
Currency: U.S. dollar
Religions: Roman Catholic, Protestant
Languages: English, Trukese, Pohnpeian, Yapese, other indigenous languages

Moldova

Area: 13,050 sq mi (33,800 sq km)
Population: 4,109,000
Capital: Chisinau, pop. 721,000
Currency: Moldovan leu
Religion: Eastern Orthodox
Languages: Moldovan, Russian, Gagauz

Monaco

Area: 0.8 sq mi (2.0 sq km)
Population: 38,000
Capital: Monaco, pop. 38,000
Currency: euro
Religion: Roman Catholic
Languages: French, English, Italian, Monegasque

Mongolia

Area: 603,909 sq mi (1,564,116 sq km)
Population: 3,029,000
Capital: Ulaanbaatar, pop. 1,334,000
Currency: togrog/tugrik
Religions: Buddhist Lamaist, Shamanist, Christian
Languages: Khalkha Mongol, Turkic, Russian

Montenegro

Area: 5,333 sq mi (13,812 sq km)
Population: 622,000
Capital: Podgorica, pop. 165,000
Currency: euro
Religions: Orthodox, Muslim, Roman Catholic
Languages: Serbian (Ijekavian dialect), Bosnian, Albanian, Croatian

Morocco

Area: 172,414 sq mi
(446,550 sq km)
Population: 34,121,000
Capital: Rabat, pop. 1,932,000
Currency: Moroccan dirham
Religion: Muslim
Languages: Arabic, Berber dialects, French

Myanmar (Burma)

Area: 261,218 sq mi
(676,552 sq km)
Population: 52,147,000
Capitals: Nay Pyi Taw, pop.
1,016,000; Yangon (Rangoon), pop. 4,802,000
Currency: kyat
Religions: Buddhist, Christian, Muslim
Languages: Burmese, minority ethnic languages

Mozambique

Area: 308,642 sq mi
(799,380 sq km)
Population: 25,736,000
Capital: Maputo, pop. 1,174,000
Currency: metical
Religions: Roman Catholic, Muslim, Zionist Christian
Languages: Emakhuwa, Xichangana, Portuguese,
Elomwe, Cisena, Echuwabo, other local languages

Namibia

Area: 318,261 sq mi
(824,292 sq km)
Population: 2,482,000
Capital: Windhoek, pop. 356,000
Currencies: Namibian dollar;
South African rand
Religions: Lutheran, other Christian, indigenous beliefs
Languages: Afrikaans, German, English

You Are There!

Namib-Naukluft National Park, Namibia

Sand dunes as tall as a skyscraper? Only in this national park, where high winds form these star-shaped dunes in the Sossusvlei area. Here they rise from the ground like reddish orange mountains. One of the world's largest national parks, Namib-Naukluft covers an area about the size of Costa Rica and is home to an array of animals such as Hartmann's mountain zebras, leopards, and flamingos. The park's main attraction, of course, is its amazing dunes.

Nauru

Area: 8 sq mi (21 sq km)
Population: 11,000
Capital: Yaren, pop. 10,000
Currency: Australian dollar
Religions: Protestant, Roman Catholic
Languages: Nauruan, English

Nepal

Area: 56,827 sq mi (147,181 sq km)
Population: 28,039,000
Capital: Kathmandu, pop. 1,142,000
Currency: Nepalese rupee
Religions: Hindu, Buddhist, Muslim, Kirant
Languages: Nepali, Maithali, Bhojpuri, Tharu, Tamang, Newar, Magar

Netherlands

Area: 16,034 sq mi (41,528 sq km)
Population: 16,942,000
Capital: Amsterdam, pop. 1,084,000
Currency: euro
Religions: Roman Catholic, Dutch Reformed, Calvinist, Muslim
Languages: Dutch, Frisian

New Zealand

Area: 104,454 sq mi (270,534 sq km)
Population: 4,598,000
Capital: Wellington, pop. 380,000
Currency: New Zealand dollar
Religions: Anglican, Roman Catholic, Presbyterian, other Christian
Languages: English, Maori

Nicaragua

Area: 50,193 sq mi (130,000 sq km)
Population: 6,262,000
Capital: Managua, pop. 951,000
Currency: gold cordoba
Religions: Roman Catholic, Evangelical
Language: Spanish

Niger

Area: 489,191 sq mi (1,267,000 sq km)
Population: 18,884,000
Capital: Niamey, pop. 1,058,000
Currency: Communauté Financière Africaine franc
Religions: Muslim, other (includes indigenous beliefs and Christian)
Languages: French, Hausa, Djerma

Nigeria

Area: 356,669 sq mi (923,768 sq km)
Population: 181,839,000
Capital: Abuja, pop. 2,301,000
Currency: naira
Religions: Muslim, Christian, indigenous beliefs
Languages: English, Hausa, Yoruba, Igbo (Ibo), Fulani

North Korea

Area: 46,540 sq mi (120,538 sq km)
Population: 24,983,000
Capital: Pyongyang, pop. 2,856,000
Currency: North Korean won
Religions: Buddhist, Confucianist, some Christian and syncretic Chondogyo
Language: Korean

Norway

Area: 125,004 sq mi (323,758 sq km)
Population: 5,194,000
Capital: Oslo, pop. 970,000
Currency: Norwegian krone
Religion: Church of Norway (Lutheran)
Languages: Bokmal Norwegian, Nynorsk Norwegian, Sami

Oman

Area: 119,500 sq mi (309,500 sq km)
Population: 4,201,000
Capital: Muscat, pop. 812,000
Currency: Omani rial
Religions: Ibadhi Muslim, Sunni Muslim, Shiite Muslim, Hindu
Languages: Arabic, English, Baluchi, Urdu, Indian dialects

Pakistan

Area: 307,374 sq mi
(796,095 sq km)
Population: 199,047,000
Capital: Islamabad, pop. 1,297,000
Currency: Pakistani rupee
Religions: Sunni Muslim, Shiite Muslim
Languages: Punjabi, Sindhi, Siraiki, Pashto, Urdu, Baluchi, Hindko, English

Palau

Area: 189 sq mi (489 sq km)
Population: 18,000
Capital: Melekeok, pop. 1,000
Currency: U.S. dollar
Religions: Roman Catholic, Protestant, Modekngei, Seventh-day Adventist
Languages: Palauan, Filipino, English, Chinese

Panama

Area: 29,157 sq mi (75,517 sq km)
Population: 3,980,000
Capital: Panama City, pop. 1,638,000
Currencies: balboa; U.S. dollar
Religions: Roman Catholic, Protestant
Languages: Spanish, English

Papua New Guinea

Area: 178,703 sq mi (462,840 sq km)
Population: 7,745,000
Capital: Port Moresby, pop. 338,000
Currency: kina
Religions: indigenous beliefs, Roman Catholic, Lutheran, other Protestant
Languages: Melanesian Pidgin, 820 indigenous languages

Paraguay

Area: 157,048 sq mi
(406,752 sq km)
Population: 7,020,000
Capital: Asunción, pop. 2,307,000
Currency: guarani
Religions: Roman Catholic, Protestant
Languages: Spanish, Guarani

Peru

Area: 496,224 sq mi
(1,285,216 sq km)
Population: 31,152,000
Capital: Lima, pop. 9,722,000
Currency: nuevo sol
Religion: Roman Catholic
Languages: Spanish, Quechua, Aymara, minor Amazonian languages

Philippines

Area: 115,831 sq mi
(300,000 sq km)
Population: 102,965,000
Capital: Manila, pop. 12,764,000
Currency: Philippine peso
Religions: Roman Catholic, Muslim, other Christian
Languages: Filipino (based on Tagalog), English

Poland

Area: 120,728 sq mi
(312,685 sq km)
Population: 38,478,000
Capital: Warsaw, pop. 1,718,000
Currency: zloty
Religion: Roman Catholic
Language: Polish

Portugal

Area: 35,655 sq mi
(92,345 sq km)
Population: 10,349,000
Capital: Lisbon, pop. 2,869,000
Currency: euro
Religion: Roman Catholic
Languages: Portuguese, Mirandese

Qatar

Area: 4,448 sq mi
(11,521 sq km)
Population: 2,395,000
Capital: Doha, pop. 699,000
Currency: Qatari rial
Religions: Muslim, Christian
Languages: Arabic; English commonly a second language

Romania

Area: 92,043 sq mi
(238,391 sq km)
Population: 19,839,000
Capital: Bucharest, pop. 1,872,000
Currency: new leu
Religions: Eastern Orthodox, Protestant,
Roman Catholic
Languages: Romanian, Hungarian

Russia

Area: 6,592,850 sq mi
(17,075,400 sq km)
Population: 144,302,000
Capital: Moscow, pop. 12,063,000
Currency: ruble
Religions: Russian Orthodox, Muslim
Languages: Russian, many minority languages

*Note: Russia is in both Europe and Asia, but its capital is in Europe,
so it is classified here as a European country.*

Rwanda

Area: 10,169 sq mi
(26,338 sq km)
Population: 11,331,000
Capital: Kigali, pop. 1,223,000
Currency: Rwandan franc
Religions: Roman Catholic, Protestant,
Adventist, Muslim
Languages: Kinyarwanda, French, English, Kiswahili

Samoa

Area: 1,093 sq mi (2,831 sq km)
Population: 194,000
Capital: Apia, pop. 37,000
Currency: tala
Religions: Congregationalist, Roman Catholic,
Methodist, Church of Jesus Christ of Latter-day
Saints, Assembly of God, Seventh-day Adventist
Languages: Samoan (Polynesian), English

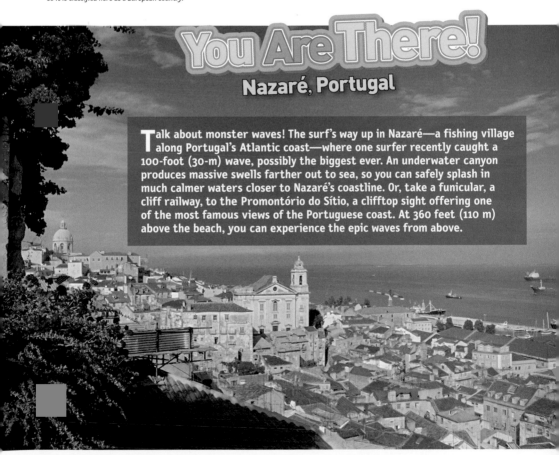

You Are There!
Nazaré, Portugal

Talk about monster waves! The surf's way up in Nazaré—a fishing village along Portugal's Atlantic coast—where one surfer recently caught a 100-foot (30-m) wave, possibly the biggest ever. An underwater canyon produces massive swells farther out to sea, so you can safely splash in much calmer waters closer to Nazaré's coastline. Or, take a funicular, a cliff railway, to the Promontório do Sítio, a clifftop sight offering one of the most famous views of the Portuguese coast. At 360 feet (110 m) above the beach, you can experience the epic waves from above.

● Asia ● Europe ● North America ● South America

San Marino

Area: 24 sq mi (61 sq km)
Population: 33,000
Capital: San Marino, pop. 4,000
Currency: euro
Religion: Roman Catholic
Language: Italian

Sao Tome and Principe

Area: 386 sq mi (1,001 sq km)
Population: 196,000
Capital: São Tomé, pop. 71,000
Currency: dobra
Religions: Roman Catholic, Evangelical
Language: Portuguese

Saudi Arabia

Area: 756,985 sq mi (1,960,582 sq km)
Population: 31,565,000
Capital: Riyadh, pop. 6,195,000
Currency: Saudi riyal
Religion: Muslim
Language: Arabic

Senegal

Area: 75,955 sq mi (196,722 sq km)
Population: 14,690,000
Capital: Dakar, pop. 3,393,000
Currency: Communauté Financière Africaine franc
Religions: Muslim, Christian (mostly Roman Catholic)
Languages: French, Wolof, Pulaar, Jola, Mandinka

Serbia

Area: 29,913 sq mi (77,474 sq km)
Population: 7,097,000
Capital: Belgrade, pop. 1,181,000
Currency: Serbian dinar
Religions: Serbian Orthodox, Roman Catholic, Muslim
Languages: Serbian, Hungarian

Seychelles

Area: 176 sq mi (455 sq km)
Population: 93,000
Capital: Victoria, pop. 26,000
Currency: Seychelles rupee
Religions: Roman Catholic, Anglican, other Christian
Languages: Creole, English

Sierra Leone

Area: 27,699 sq mi (71,740 sq km)
Population: 6,503,000
Capital: Freetown, pop. 986,000
Currency: leone
Religions: Muslim, indigenous beliefs, Christian
Languages: English, Mende, Temne, Krio

Singapore

Area: 255 sq mi (660 sq km)
Population: 5,541,000
Capital: Singapore, pop. 5,500,000
Currency: Singapore dollar
Religions: Buddhist, Muslim, Taoist, Roman Catholic, Hindu, other Christian
Languages: Mandarin, English, Malay, Hokkien, Cantonese, Teochew, Tamil

Slovakia

Area: 18,932 sq mi (49,035 sq km)
Population: 5,424,000
Capital: Bratislava, pop. 403,000
Currency: euro
Religions: Roman Catholic, Protestant, Greek Catholic
Languages: Slovak, Hungarian

Slovenia

Area: 7,827 sq mi (20,273 sq km)
Population: 2,064,000
Capital: Ljubljana, pop. 279,000
Currency: euro
Religions: Roman Catholic, Muslim, Orthodox
Languages: Slovene, Croatian, Serbian

COLOR KEY ● Africa ● Australia, New Zealand, and Oceania

Solomon Islands

Area: 10,954 sq mi (28,370 sq km)
Population: 642,000
Capital: Honiara, pop. 73,000
Currency: Solomon Islands dollar
Religions: Church of Melanesia, Roman Catholic, South Seas Evangelical, other Christian
Languages: Melanesian pidgin, 120 indigenous languages

Somalia

Area: 246,201 sq mi (637,657 sq km)
Population: 11,123,000
Capital: Mogadishu, pop. 2,014,000
Currency: Somali shilling
Religion: Sunni Muslim
Languages: Somali, Arabic, Italian, English

South Africa

Area: 470,693 sq mi (1,219,090 sq km)
Population: 55,041,000
Capitals: Pretoria (Tshwane), pop. 1,991,000; Bloemfontein, pop. 496,000; Cape Town, pop. 3,624,000
Currency: rand
Religions: Zion Christian, Pentecostal, Catholic, Methodist, Dutch Reformed, Anglican, other Christian
Languages: IsiZulu, IsiXhosa, Afrikaans, Sepedi, English

5 cool things about SOUTH AFRICA

1. There are over six million trees in the city of Johannesburg, placing it among the world's largest man-made urban forests.

2. South Africa's Namaqua National Park is home to the speckled padloper, believed to be the world's smallest tortoise.

3. June, July, and August are a great time to hit the slopes at a ski resort in South Africa's Drakensberg mountains.

4. You can ride a cable car over 3,500 feet (1,070 m) in five minutes to the top of Cape Town's Table Mountain.

5. South Africa has 11 official languages.

South Korea

Area: 38,321 sq mi (99,250 sq km)
Population: 50,714,000
Capital: Seoul, pop. 9,775,000
Currency: South Korean won
Religions: Christian, Buddhist
Languages: Korean, English

South Sudan

Area: 248,777 sq mi (644,329 sq km)
Population: 12,152,000
Capital: Juba, pop. 307,000
Currency: South Sudan pound
Religions: animist, Christian
Languages: English, Arabic, regional languages (Dinke, Nuer, Bari, Zande, Shilluk)

Spain

Area: 195,363 sq mi (505,988 sq km)
Population: 46,368,000
Capital: Madrid, pop. 6,133,000
Currency: euro
Religion: Roman Catholic
Languages: Castilian Spanish, Catalan, Galician, Basque

Sri Lanka

Area: 25,299 sq mi (65,525 sq km)
Population: 20,869,000
Capitals: Colombo, pop. 704,000; Sri Jayewardenepura Kotte, pop. 128,000
Currency: Sri Lankan rupee
Religions: Buddhist, Muslim, Hindu, Christian
Languages: Sinhala, Tamil

St. Kitts and Nevis

Area: 104 sq mi (269 sq km)
Population: 46,000
Capital: Basseterre, pop. 14,000
Currency: East Caribbean dollar
Religions: Anglican, other Protestant, Roman Catholic
Language: English

St. Lucia

Area: 238 sq mi (616 sq km)
Population: 175,000
Capital: Castries, pop. 22,000
Currency: East Caribbean dollar
Religions: Roman Catholic, Seventh-day Adventist, Pentecostal
Languages: English, French patois

Sweden

Area: 173,732 sq mi (449,964 sq km)
Population: 9,805,000
Capital: Stockholm, pop. 1,464,000
Currency: Swedish krona
Religion: Lutheran
Languages: Swedish, Sami, Finnish

St. Vincent and the Grenadines

Area: 150 sq mi (389 sq km)
Population: 110,000
Capital: Kingstown, pop. 27,000
Currency: East Caribbean dollar
Religions: Anglican, Methodist, Roman Catholic
Languages: English, French patois

Switzerland

Area: 15,940 sq mi (41,284 sq km)
Population: 8,293,000
Capital: Bern, pop. 358,000
Currency: Swiss franc
Religions: Roman Catholic, Protestant, Muslim
Languages: German, French, Italian, Romansh

Sudan

Area: 718,722 sq mi (1,861,484 sq km)
Population: 40,884,000
Capital: Khartoum, pop. 5,000,000
Currency: Sudanese pound
Religions: Sunni Muslim, indigenous beliefs, Christian
Languages: Arabic, Nubian, Ta Bedawie, many diverse dialects of Nilotic, Nilo-Hamitic, Sudanic languages

Syria

Area: 71,498 sq mi (185,180 sq km)
Population: 17,065,000
Capital: Damascus, pop. 2,574,000
Currency: Syrian pound
Religions: Sunni, other Muslim (includes Alawite, Druze), Christian
Languages: Arabic, Kurdish, Armenian, Aramaic, Circassian

Suriname

Area: 63,037 sq mi (163,265 sq km)
Population: 576,000
Capital: Paramaribo, pop. 234,000
Currency: Suriname dollar
Religions: Hindu, Protestant (predominantly Moravian), Roman Catholic, Muslim, indigenous beliefs
Languages: Dutch, English, Sranang Tongo, Hindustani, Javanese

Tajikistan

Area: 55,251 sq mi (143,100 sq km)
Population: 8,452,000
Capital: Dushanbe, pop. 801,000
Currency: somoni
Religions: Sunni Muslim, Shiite Muslim
Languages: Tajik, Russian

Swaziland

Area: 6,704 sq mi (17,363 sq km)
Population: 1,286,000
Capitals: Mbabane, pop. 66,000; Lobamba, pop. 4,600
Currency: lilangeni
Religions: Zionist, Roman Catholic, Muslim
Languages: English, siSwati

Tanzania

Area: 364,900 sq mi (945,087 sq km)
Population: 52,291,000
Capitals: Dar es Salaam, pop. 5,116,000; Dodoma, pop. 228,000
Currency: Tanzanian shilling
Religions: Muslim, indigenous beliefs, Christian
Languages: Kiswahili, Kiunguja, English, Arabic, local languages

Thailand

Area: 198,115 sq mi
(513,115 sq km)
Population: 65,121,000
Capital: Bangkok, pop. 9,098,000
Currency: baht
Religions: Buddhist, Muslim
Languages: Thai, English, ethnic dialects

GIANT STINGRAYS that grow to be THE SIZE OF CARS live in Thailand's Mae Klong River.

Timor-Leste (East Timor)

Area: 5,640 sq mi
(14,609 sq km)
Population: 1,245,000
Capital: Dili, pop. 228,000
Currency: U.S. dollar
Religion: Roman Catholic
Languages: Tetum, Portuguese, Indonesian, English, indigenous languages

Togo

Area: 21,925 sq mi (56,785 sq km)
Population: 7,231,000
Capital: Lomé, pop. 930,000
Currency: Communauté Financière Africaine franc
Religions: indigenous beliefs, Christian, Muslim
Languages: French, Ewe, Mina, Kabye, Dagomb

Tonga

Area: 289 sq mi (748 sq km)
Population: 103,000
Capital: Nuku'alofa, pop. 25,000
Currency: pa'anga
Religion: Christian
Languages: Tongan, English

Trinidad and Tobago

Area: 1,980 sq mi (5,128 sq km)
Population: 1,351,000
Capital: Port of Spain, pop. 34,000
Currency: Trinidad and Tobago dollar
Religions: Roman Catholic, Hindu, Anglican, Baptist
Languages: English, Caribbean Hindustani, French, Spanish, Chinese

Tunisia

Area: 63,170 sq mi
(163,610 sq km)
Population: 11,026,000
Capital: Tunis, pop. 1,978,000
Currency: Tunisian dinar
Religion: Muslim
Languages: Arabic, French

Turkey

Area: 300,948 sq mi
(779,452 sq km)
Population: 78,215,000
Capital: Ankara, pop. 4,644,000
Currency: new Turkish lira
Religion: Muslim (mostly Sunni)
Languages: Turkish, Kurdish, Dimli (Zaza), Azeri, Kabardian, Gagauz

Turkmenistan

Area: 188,456 sq mi
(488,100 sq km)
Population: 5,373,000
Capital: Ashgabat, pop. 735,000
Currency: Turkmen manat
Religions: Muslim, Eastern Orthodox
Languages: Turkmen, Russian, Uzbek

Tuvalu

Area: 10 sq mi (26 sq km)
Population: 12,000
Capital: Funafuti, pop. 6,000
Currencies: Australian dollar; Tuvaluan dollar
Religion: Church of Tuvalu (Congregationalist)
Languages: Tuvaluan, English, Samoan, Kiribati

Uganda

Area: 93,104 sq mi
(241,139 sq km)
Population: 40,141,000
Capital: Kampala, pop. 1,863,000
Currency: Ugandan shilling
Religions: Protestant, Roman Catholic, Muslim
Languages: English, Ganda, other local languages, Kiswahili, Arabic

United Arab Emirates

Area: 30,000 sq mi
(77,700 sq km)
Population: 9,577,000
Capital: Abu Dhabi,
pop. 1,114,000
Currency: Emirati dirham
Religion: Muslim
Languages: Arabic, Persian, English, Hindi, Urdu

Ukraine

Area: 233,090 sq mi
(603,700 sq km)
Population: 42,828,000
Capital: Kiev, pop. 2,917,000
Currency: hryvnia
Religions: Ukrainian Orthodox, Orthodox, Ukrainian Greek Catholic
Languages: Ukrainian, Russian

United Kingdom

Area: 93,788 sq mi
(242,910 sq km)
Population: 65,092,000
Capital: London, pop. 10,189,000
Currency: British pound
Religions: Anglican, Roman Catholic, Presbyterian, Methodist
Languages: English, Welsh, Scottish form of Gaelic

You Are There!
Dubai, United Arab Emirates

Can you say dream destination? There's tons to do in Dubai, a city sitting on the coast of the Persian Gulf in the United Arab Emirates. Need a quick itinerary? First, take a lightning-quick elevator ride up to the top of Burj Khalifa, the tallest building in the world. From 148 stories up, watch the cars and people, as tiny as ants, mill below you. Once you're back on the ground, head on over to Ski Dubai, the Middle East's first indoor ski resort. No matter the weather, you can schuss down the slopes on man-made snow at this giant arena, complete with a black diamond run and a chairlift. While you're there, check out the resident king and gentoo penguins—you can even feed and hug one if you'd like. End your day with a fountain and light show on Burj Khalifa Lake in downtown Dubai. With the spray synched up to music and lights, it's literally a can't-miss sight: The water sprays as high as a 50-story building, making it the world's largest dancing fountain.

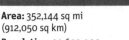
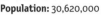

United States

Area: 3,794,083 sq mi
(9,826,630 sq km)
Population: 321,234,000
Capital: Washington, D.C.,
pop. 646,449
Currency: U.S. dollar
Religions: Protestant, Roman Catholic
Languages: English, Spanish

Uruguay

Area: 68,037 sq mi
(176,215 sq km)
Population: 3,562,000
Capital: Montevideo, pop. 1,698,000
Currency: Uruguayan peso
Religion: Roman Catholic
Language: Spanish

Uzbekistan

Area: 172,742 sq mi
(447,400 sq km)
Population: 31,291,000
Capital: Tashkent,
pop. 2,241,000
Currency: Uzbekistani sum
Religions: Muslim (mostly Sunni), Eastern Orthodox
Languages: Uzbek, Russian, Tajik

Vanuatu

Area: 4,707 sq mi (12,190 sq km)
Population: 278,000
Capital: Port Vila, pop. 53,000
Currency: vatu
Religions: Presbyterian, Anglican, Roman Catholic,
other Christian, indigenous beliefs
Languages: more than 100 local languages, pidgin
(known as Bislama or Bichelama)

Vatican City

Area: 0.2 sq mi (0.4 sq km)
Population: 1,000
Capital: Vatican City, pop. 1,000
Currency: euro
Religion: Roman Catholic
Languages: Italian, Latin, French

Venezuela

Area: 352,144 sq mi
(912,050 sq km)
Population: 30,620,000
Capital: Caracas, pop. 2,912,000
Currency: bolivar
Religion: Roman Catholic
Languages: Spanish, numerous indigenous dialects

Vietnam

Area: 127,844 sq mi
(331,114 sq km)
Population: 91,714,000
Capital: Hanoi, pop. 3,470,000
Currency: dong
Religions: Buddhist, Roman Catholic
Languages: Vietnamese, English, French, Chinese, Khmer

Yemen

Area: 207,286 sq mi
(536,869 sq km)
Population: 26,737,000
Capital: Sanaa, pop. 2,833,000
Currency: Yemeni rial
Religions: Muslim, including Shaf'i (Sunni)
and Zaydi (Shiite)
Language: Arabic

Zambia

Area: 290,586 sq mi
(752,614 sq km)
Population: 15,474,000
Capital: Lusaka, pop. 2,078,000
Currency: Zambian kwacha
Religions: Christian, Muslim, Hindu
Languages: English, Bemba, Kaonda, Lozi, Lunda, Luvale,
Nyanja, Tonga, about 70 other indigenous languages

Zimbabwe

Area: 150,872 sq mi
(390,757 sq km)
Population: 17,354,000
Capital: Harare, pop. 1,495,000
Currency: Zimbabwean dollar
Religions: Syncretic (part Christian, part indigenous
beliefs), Christian, indigenous beliefs
Languages: English, Shona, Sindebele, tribal dialects

THE POLITICAL UNITED STATES

9:00 AM PACIFIC TIME

10:00 AM MOUNTAIN TIME

Cape Flattery

Seattle
Olympia Tacoma
Spokane
WASHINGTON
Yakima
Portland
Columbia
Salem
Eugene
OREGON
Medford
Klamath Falls
Eureka
Redding

Great Falls
Missouri
Butte Helena
MONTANA
Billings
Cody
Yellowstone L.
Boise
Idaho Falls
Snake
Pocatello
WYOMING
Casper
N. Platte
Cheyenne
Laramie
Fort Collins
S. Platte
Boulder
Denver
COLORADO
Colorado Springs
Pueblo

Minot
NORTH DAKOTA
Bismarck
Aberdeen
SOUTH DAKOTA
Pierre
Rapid City
Missouri
NEBRASKA
Grand Island
Platte

Sacramento
Reno
Carson City
Lake Tahoe
Great Basin
NEVADA
Sierra Nevada
San Francisco
Oakland
San Jose
Salinas
Fresno
Mojave
Bakersfield
Point Conception
Los Angeles
Long Beach
Riverside
San Diego

Great Salt Lake
Ogden
Salt Lake City
Provo
UTAH
Lake Powell
St. George
Colorado
Grand Junction

Las Vegas
Lake Mead
Desert
Grand Canyon
Salton Sea
Phoenix Mesa
Yuma
ARIZONA
Flagstaff
Tucson

KANSAS
Dodge City
Arkansas
Wichita

Santa Fe
Albuquerque
Amarillo
NEW MEXICO
Roswell
Las Cruces
El Paso
Rio Grande

OKLAH
Oklahoma City
Lawton
Wichita Falls
Red
Lubbock
Fort Worth
Midland
Abilene
Odessa
Waco
TEXAS

7:00 AM
HAWAI'I-
ALEUTIAN
TIME

North Slope
Brooks Range
Yukon
Alaska Range
Juneau
Anchorage
ALASKA
Alaska Peninsula
ALEUTIAN ISLANDS

0   400 miles
0   400 kilometers

Kaua'i
Ni'ihau
O'ahu
Moloka'i
Honolulu
Lana'i   Maui
Kaho'olawe
Hilo   Hawai'i
HAWAI'I

0   150 mi
0   150 km

7:00 AM
HAWAI'I-
ALEUTIAN
TIME

8:00 AM
ALASKA TIME

Austin
San Antonio
Corpus Christi
Laredo
Rio Grande
Brownsville

The United States is made up of 50 states joined like a giant quilt. Each is unique, but together they make a national fabric held together by a constitution and a federal government. State boundaries, outlined in dotted lines on the map, set apart internal political units within the country. The national capital—Washington, D.C.—is marked by a star in a double circle. The capital of each state is marked by a star in a single circle.

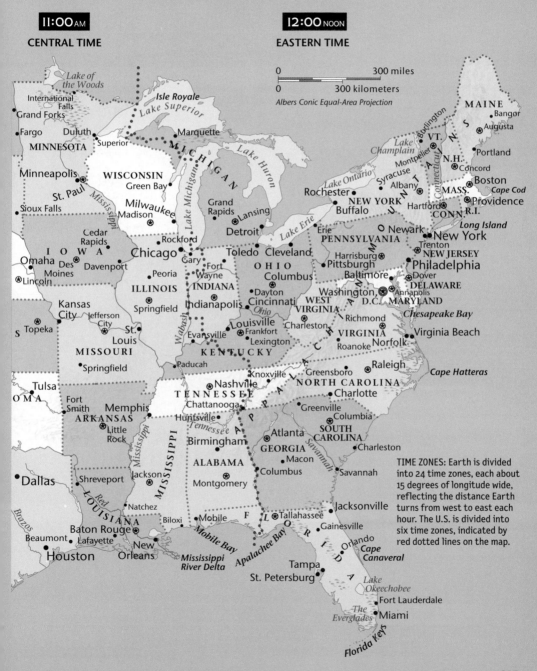

11:00 AM
CENTRAL TIME

12:00 NOON
EASTERN TIME

0 — 300 miles
0 — 300 kilometers
Albers Conic Equal-Area Projection

TIME ZONES: Earth is divided into 24 time zones, each about 15 degrees of longitude wide, reflecting the distance Earth turns from west to east each hour. The U.S. is divided into six time zones, indicated by red dotted lines on the map.

319

THE PHYSICAL UNITED STATES

CASCADE RANGE

Mt. St. Helens
8,366 ft, 2,550 m

Mt. Rainier
14,411 ft
4,392 m

Snake

Columbia

Mt. Hood
11,239 ft
3,425 m

Blue Mountains

Great Sandy Desert

Columbia Plateau

Snake River Plain

Snake

Flathead Lake

Bitterroot Range

Salmon River Mountains

Yellowstone Lake

Grand Teton
13,770 ft
4,197 m

Absaroka Range

ROCKY

Milk

Fort Peck Lake

Missouri

Yellowstone

Bighorn Mts.

Laramie Mts.

Little Missouri

GREAT

Lake Sakakawea

Heart

White Butte
3,506 ft
1,069 m

Lake Oahe

Missouri

Geographical Center of the 50 United States

White

James

Black Hills

Harney Peak
7,242 ft
2,207 m

Niobrara

N. Platte

Sand Hills

PLAINS

Sierra Nevada

Sacramento Valley

San Joaquin Valley

San Joaquin

Lake Tahoe

Great Salt Lake

Wasatch Range

Uinta Mts.

Great Divide Basin

Front Range

MOUNTAINS

Great Basin

Mt. Whitney
14,494 ft
4,418 m

Death Valley

Lowest Point in North America
-282 ft, -86 m

Mojave Desert

Lake Mead

Grand Canyon

Lake Powell

Colorado

San Juan Mts.

Mt. Elbert
14,433 ft
4,399 m

Pikes Peak
14,110 ft
4,301 m

S. Platte

Geographical Center of the 48 Contiguous United States.

Smoky Hills

Arkansas

Red Hills

Black Mesa
4,973 ft
1,516 m

Platte

Canadian

Colorado Plateau

Painted Desert

Colorado

Humphreys Peak
12,637 ft
3,852 m

Salt

Sangre de Cristo Mts.

Rio Grande

Cimarron

Llano Estacado

Channel Islands

Salton Sea

Imperial Valley

Gila

Sonoran Desert

Sacramento Mts.

Guadalupe Peak
8,749 ft
2,667 m

Pecos

Brazos

Colorado

Edwards Plateau

0   400 miles
0   400 kilometers

North Slope

Brooks Range

Yukon

(Mt. McKinley) Denali
6,190 m; 20,310 ft

Highest Point in North America

Alaska Range

Alexander Archipelago

Aleutian Islands

Alaska Peninsula

Rio Grande

Kaua'i

Ni'ihau

O'ahu

Moloka'i

Lana'i   Maui

Kaho'olawe

Hawai'i

Mauna Kea
13,679 ft
4,169 m

0   150 miles
0   150 kilometers

ALASKA AND HAWAII:
In addition to the states
located on the main landmass,
the U.S. has two states—Alaska
and Hawaii—that are not directly
connected to the other 48 states.
If Alaska and Hawaii were shown in
their correct relative sizes and locations,
the map would not fit on these pages.

Stretching from the Atlantic Ocean in the east to the Pacific Ocean in the west, the United States is the third largest country (by area) in the world. Its physical diversity ranges from mountains to fertile plains and dry deserts. Shading on the map indicates changes in elevation, while colors show different vegetation patterns.

0 — 400 miles

0 — 400 kilometers

Albers Conic Equal-Area Projection

NATURAL VEGETATION

- NEEDLELEAF FOREST
- BROADLEAF FOREST
- MIXED FOREST
- GRASSLAND
- TROPICAL VEGETATION
- DESERT
- TUNDRA

THE STATES

From sea to shining sea, the United States of America is a nation of diversity. In the 241 years since its creation, the nation has grown to become home to a wide range of peoples, industries, and cultures. The following pages present a general overview of all 50 states in the U.S.

The country is generally divided into five large regions: the Northeast, the Southeast, the Midwest, the Southwest, and the West. Though loosely defined, these zones tend to share important similarities, including climate, history, and geography. The color key below provides a guide to which states are in each region.

Flags of each state and highlights of demography and industry are also included. These details offer a brief overview of each state.

In addition, each state's official flower and bird are identified.

Color Key by Region

Alabama

Area: 52,419 sq mi (135,765 sq km)
Population: 4,849,377
Capital: Montgomery, pop. 200,481
Largest city: Birmingham, pop. 212,247
Industry: Retail and wholesale trade, services, government, finance, insurance, real estate, transportation, construction, communication
State flower/bird: Camellia/northern flicker

Alaska

Area: 663,267 sq mi (1,717,862 sq km)
Population: 736,732
Capital: Juneau, pop. 32,406
Largest city: Anchorage, pop. 301,010
Industry: Petroleum products, government, services, trade
State flower/bird: Forget-me-not/willow ptarmigan

Arizona

Area: 113,998 sq mi (295,256 sq km)
Population: 6,731,484
Capital: Phoenix, pop. 1,537,058
Largest city: Phoenix, pop. 1,537,058
Industry: Real estate, manufactured goods, retail, state and local government, transportation and public utilities, wholesale trade, health services
State flower/bird: Saguaro/cactus wren

Arkansas

Area: 53,179 sq mi (137,732 sq km)
Population: 2,966,369
Capital: Little Rock, pop. 197,706
Largest city: Little Rock, pop. 197,706
Industry: Services, food processing, paper products, transportation, metal products, machinery, electronics
State flower/bird: Apple blossom/mockingbird

California

Area: 163,696 sq mi (423,972 sq km)
Population: 38,802,500
Capital: Sacramento, pop. 485,199
Largest city: Los Angeles, pop. 3,928,864
Industry: Electronic components and equipment, computers and computer software, tourism, food processing, entertainment, clothing
State flower/bird: Golden poppy/California quail

Colorado

Area: 104,094 sq mi (269,602 sq km)
Population: 5,355,866
Capital: Denver, pop. 663,862
Largest city: Denver, pop. 663,862
Industry: Real estate, government, durable goods, communications, health and other services, nondurable goods, transportation
State flower/bird: Columbine/lark bunting

The lyrics to "America the Beautiful" WERE INSPIRED BY THE VIEW ATOP Colorado's Pikes Peak.

COLOR KEY ● Northeast ● Southeast

Connecticut

Area: 5,543 sq mi (14,357 sq km)
Population: 3,596,677
Capital: Hartford, pop. 124,705
Largest city: Bridgeport, pop. 147,612
Industry: Transportation equipment, metal products, machinery, electrical equipment, printing and publishing, scientific instruments, insurance
State flower/bird: Mountain laurel/robin

Delaware

Area: 2,489 sq mi (6,447 sq km)
Population: 935,614
Capital: Dover, pop. 37,355
Largest city: Wilmington, pop. 71,817
Industry: Food processing, chemicals, rubber and plastic products, scientific instruments, printing and publishing, financial services
State flower/bird: Peach blossom/blue hen chicken

Florida

Area: 65,755 sq mi (170,304 sq km)
Population: 19,893,297
Capital: Tallahassee, pop. 188,107
Largest city: Jacksonville, pop. 853,382
Industry: Tourism, health services, business services, communications, banking, electronic equipment, insurance
State flower/bird: Orange blossom/mockingbird

Georgia

Area: 59,425 sq mi (153,910 sq km)
Population: 10,097,343
Capital: Atlanta, pop. 456,002
Largest city: Atlanta, pop. 456,002
Industry: Textiles and clothing, transportation equipment, food processing, paper products, chemicals, electrical equipment, tourism
State flower/bird: Cherokee rose/brown thrasher

Hawaii

Area: 10,931 sq mi (28,311 sq km)
Population: 1,419,561
Capital: Honolulu, pop. 350,399
Largest city: Honolulu, pop. 350,399
Industry: Tourism, trade, finance, food processing, petroleum refining, stone, clay, glass products
State flower/bird: Hibiscus/Hawaiian goose (nene)

Idaho

Area: 83,570 sq mi (216,447 sq km)
Population: 1,634,464
Capital: Boise, pop. 216,282
Largest city: Boise, pop. 216,282
Industry: Electronics and computer equipment, tourism, food processing, forest products, mining
State flower/bird: Syringa (Lewis's mock orange)/ mountain bluebird

At 7,900 feet (2,408 m) deep, Idaho's HELLS CANYON is the deepest gorge in the United States.

Illinois

Area: 57,914 sq mi (149,998 sq km)
Population: 12,880,580
Capital: Springfield, pop. 116,809
Largest city: Chicago, pop. 2,722,389
Industry: Industrial machinery, electronic equipment, food processing, chemicals, metals, printing and publishing, rubber and plastics, motor vehicles
State flower/bird: Violet/cardinal

Indiana

Area: 36,418 sq mi (94,322 sq km)
Population: 6,596,855
Capital: Indianapolis, pop. 848,788
Largest city: Indianapolis, pop. 848,788
Industry: Transportation equipment, steel, pharmaceutical and chemical products, machinery, petroleum, coal
State flower/bird: Peony/cardinal

Iowa

Area: 56,272 sq mi (145,743 sq km)
Population: 3,107,126
Capital: Des Moines, pop. 209,220
Largest city: Des Moines, pop. 209,220
Industry: Real estate, health services, industrial machinery, food processing, construction
State flower/bird: Wild rose/American goldfinch

Kansas

Area: 82,277 sq mi (213,097 sq km)
Population: 2,904,021
Capital: Topeka, pop. 127,215
Largest city: Wichita, pop. 388,413
Industry: Aircraft manufacturing, transportation equipment, construction, food processing, printing and publishing, health care
State flower/bird: Sunflower/western meadowlark

DODGE CITY, KANSAS, is one of the windiest cities in the United States.

Kentucky

Area: 40,409 sq mi (104,659 sq km)
Population: 4,413,457
Capital: Frankfort, pop. 27,557
Largest city: Louisville, pop. 612,780
Industry: Manufacturing, services, government, finance, insurance, real estate, retail trade, transportation, wholesale trade, construction, mining
State flower/bird: Goldenrod/cardinal

Louisiana

Area: 51,840 sq mi (134,265 sq km)
Population: 4,649,676
Capital: Baton Rouge, pop. 228,895
Largest city: New Orleans, pop. 384,320
Industry: Chemicals, petroleum products, food processing, health services, tourism, oil and natural gas extraction, paper products
State flower/bird: Magnolia/brown pelican

Maine

Area: 35,385 sq mi (91,646 sq km)
Population: 1,330,089
Capital: Augusta, pop. 18,705
Largest city: Portland, pop. 66,666
Industry: Health services, tourism, forest products, leather products, electrical equipment
State flower/bird: White pine cone and tassel/chickadee

Maryland

Area: 12,407 sq mi (32,133 sq km)
Population: 5,976,407
Capital: Annapolis, pop. 38,856
Largest city: Baltimore, pop. 622,793
Industry: Real estate, federal government, health services, business services, engineering services
State flower/bird: Black-eyed Susan/northern (Baltimore) oriole

Massachusetts

Area: 10,555 sq mi (27,336 sq km)
Population: 6,745,408
Capital: Boston, pop. 655,884
Largest city: Boston, pop. 655,884
Industry: Electrical equipment, machinery, metal products, scientific instruments, printing and publishing, tourism
State flower/bird: Mayflower/chickadee

Michigan

Area: 96,716 sq mi (250,495 sq km)
Population: 9,909,877
Capital: Lansing, pop. 114,620
Largest city: Detroit, pop. 680,250
Industry: Motor vehicles and parts, machinery, metal products, office furniture, tourism, chemicals
State flower/bird: Apple blossom/robin

Minnesota

Area: 86,939 sq mi (225,172 sq km)
Population: 5,457,173
Capital: St. Paul, pop. 297,640
Largest city: Minneapolis, pop. 407,207
Industry: Real estate, banking and insurance, industrial machinery, printing and publishing, food processing, scientific equipment
State flower/bird: Showy lady's slipper/common loon

Mississippi

Area: 48,430 sq mi (125,434 sq km)
Population: 2,994,079
Capital: Jackson, pop. 171,155
Largest city: Jackson, pop. 171,155
Industry: Petroleum products, health services, electronic equipment, transportation, banking, forest products, communications
State flower/bird: Magnolia/mockingbird

Missouri

Area: 69,704 sq mi (180,534 sq km)
Population: 6,063,589
Capital: Jefferson City, pop. 43,132
Largest city: Kansas City, pop. 470,800
Industry: Transportation equipment, food processing, chemicals, electrical equipment, metal products
State flower/bird: Hawthorn/eastern bluebird

Montana

Area: 147,042 sq mi (380,840 sq km)
Population: 1,023,579
Capital: Helena, pop. 29,943
Largest city: Billings, pop. 108,869
Industry: Forest products, food processing, mining, construction, tourism
State flower/bird: Bitterroot/western meadowlark

Nebraska

Area: 77,354 sq mi (200,346 sq km)
Population: 1,881,503
Capital: Lincoln, pop. 272,996
Largest city: Omaha, pop. 446,599
Industry: Food processing, machinery, electrical equipment, printing and publishing
State flower/bird: Goldenrod/western meadowlark

Nevada

Area: 110,561 sq mi (286,352 sq km)
Population: 2,839,099
Capital: Carson City, pop. 54,522
Largest city: Las Vegas, pop. 613,599
Industry: Tourism and gaming, mining, printing and publishing, food processing, electrical equipment
State flower/bird: Sagebrush/mountain bluebird

New Hampshire

Area: 9,350 sq mi (24,216 sq km)
Population: 1,326,813
Capital: Concord, pop. 42,444
Largest city: Manchester, pop. 110,448
Industry: Machinery, electronics, metal products
State flower/bird: Purple lilac/purple finch

New Jersey

Area: 8,721 sq mi (22,588 sq km)
Population: 8,938,175
Capital: Trenton, pop. 84,034
Largest city: Newark, pop. 280,579
Industry: Machinery, electronics, metal products, chemicals
State flower/bird: Violet/American goldfinch

New Mexico

Area: 121,590 sq mi (314,917 sq km)
Population: 2,085,572
Capital: Santa Fe, pop. 70,297
Largest city: Albuquerque, pop. 557,169
Industry: Electronic equipment, state and local government, real estate, business services, federal government, oil and gas extraction, health services
State flower/bird: Yucca/roadrunner

ALBUQUERQUE, NEW MEXICO, is considered the hot air ballooning capital of the world.

New York

Area: 54,556 sq mi (141,300 sq km)
Population: 19,746,227
Capital: Albany, pop. 98,566
Largest city: New York City, pop. 8,491,079
Industry: Printing and publishing, machinery, computer products, finance, tourism
State flower/bird: Rose/eastern bluebird

North Carolina

Area: 53,819 sq mi (139,390 sq km)
Population: 9,943,964
Capital: Raleigh, pop. 439,896
Largest city: Charlotte, pop. 809,958
Industry: Real estate, health services, chemicals, tobacco products, finance, textiles
State flower/bird: Flowering dogwood/cardinal

● Midwest ● Southwest ● West

North Dakota

Area: 70,700 sq mi (183,113 sq km)
Population: 739,482
Capital: Bismarck, pop. 68,896
Largest city: Fargo, pop. 115,863
Industry: Services, government, finance, construction, transportation, oil and gas
State flower/bird: Wild prairie rose/ western meadowlark

Ohio

Area: 44,825 sq mi (116,097 sq km)
Population: 11,594,163
Capital: Columbus, pop. 835,957
Largest city: Columbus, pop. 835,957
Industry: Transportation equipment, metal products, machinery, food processing, electrical equipment
State flower/bird: Scarlet carnation/cardinal

Oklahoma

Area: 69,898 sq mi (181,036 sq km)
Population: 3,878,051
Capital: Oklahoma City, pop. 620,602
Largest city: Oklahoma City, pop. 620,602
Industry: Manufacturing, services, government, finance, insurance, real estate
State flower/bird: Mistletoe/scissor-tailed flycatcher

5 cool things about OKLAHOMA

1. The first shopping cart debuted in 1937 at Humpty Dumpty markets in Oklahoma City.

2. Central Oklahoma has more tornadoes per square mile than anywhere on Earth.

3. Oklahoma is home to over 200 man-made lakes—more than any other state in the country.

4. Bushyhead, Cookietown, and Slapout are all names of places in Oklahoma.

5. There's a totem pole as tall as a nine-story building in Foyil, Oklahoma.

Oregon

Area: 98,381 sq mi (254,806 sq km)
Population: 3,970,239
Capital: Salem, pop. 161,637
Largest city: Portland, pop. 619,360
Industry: Real estate, retail and wholesale trade, electronic equipment, health services, construction, forest products, business services
State flower/bird: Oregon grape/western meadowlark

Pennsylvania

Area: 46,055 sq mi (119,283 sq km)
Population: 12,787,209
Capital: Harrisburg, pop. 49,082
Largest city: Philadelphia, pop. 1,560,297
Industry: Machinery, printing and publishing, forest products, metal products
State flower/bird: Mountain laurel/ruffed grouse

Rhode Island

Area: 1,545 sq mi (4,002 sq km)
Population: 1,055,173
Capital: Providence, pop. 179,154
Largest city: Providence, pop. 179,154
Industry: Health services, business services, silver and jewelry products, metal products
State flower/bird: Violet/Rhode Island red

South Carolina

Area: 32,020 sq mi (82,932 sq km)
Population: 4,832,482
Capital: Columbia, pop. 132,067
Largest city: Columbia, pop. 132,067
Industry: Service industries, tourism, chemicals, textiles, machinery, forest products
State flower/bird: Yellow jessamine/Carolina wren

South Dakota

Area: 77,117 sq mi (199,732 sq km)
Population: 853,175
Capital: Pierre, pop. 14,054
Largest city: Sioux Falls, pop. 168,586
Industry: Finance, services, manufacturing, government, retail trade, transportation and utilities, wholesale trade, construction, mining
State flower/bird: Pasqueflower/ring-necked pheasant

COLOR KEY ● Northeast ● Southeast

Tennessee

Area: 42,143 sq mi (109,151 sq km)
Population: 6,549,352
Capital: Nashville, pop. 644,014
Largest city: Memphis, pop. 656,861
Industry: Service industries, chemicals, transportation equipment, processed foods, machinery
State flower/bird: Iris/mockingbird

MOON PIES were first sold in a Chattanooga, Tennessee, bakery 100 years ago.

Texas

Area: 268,581 sq mi (695,624 sq km)
Population: 26,956,958
Capital: Austin, pop. 912,791
Largest city: Houston, pop. 2,239,558
Industry: Chemicals, machinery, electronics and computers, food products, petroleum and natural gas, transportation equipment
State flower/bird: Bluebonnet/mockingbird

Utah

Area: 84,899 sq mi (219,888 sq km)
Population: 2,942,902
Capital: Salt Lake City, pop. 190,884
Largest city: Salt Lake City, pop. 190,884
Industry: Government, manufacturing, real estate, construction, health services, business services, banking
State flower/bird: Sego lily/California gull

Vermont

Area: 9,614 sq mi (24,901 sq km)
Population: 626,562
Capital: Montpelier, pop. 7,671
Largest city: Burlington, pop. 42,211
Industry: Health services, tourism, finance, real estate, computer components, electrical parts, printing and publishing, machine tools
State flower/bird: Red clover/hermit thrush

Virginia

Area: 42,774 sq mi (110,785 sq km)
Population: 8,326,289
Capital: Richmond, pop. 217,853
Largest city: Virginia Beach, pop. 450,980
Industry: Food processing, communication and electronic equipment, transportation equipment, printing, shipbuilding, textiles
State flower/bird: Flowering dogwood/cardinal

Washington

Area: 71,300 sq mi (184,666 sq km)
Population: 7,061,530
Capital: Olympia, pop. 49,218
Largest city: Seattle, pop. 668,342
Industry: Aerospace, tourism, food processing, forest products, paper products, industrial machinery, printing and publishing, metals, computer software
State flower/bird: Coast rhododendron/Amer. goldfinch

West Virginia

Area: 24,230 sq mi (62,755 sq km)
Population: 1,850,326
Capital: Charleston, pop. 50,404
Largest city: Charleston, pop. 50,404
Industry: Tourism, coal mining, chemicals, metal manufacturing, forest products, stone, clay, oil, glass products
State flower/bird: Rhododendron/cardinal

Wisconsin

Area: 65,498 sq mi (169,639 sq km)
Population: 5,757,564
Capital: Madison, pop. 245,691
Largest city: Milwaukee, pop. 599,642
Industry: Industrial machinery, paper products, food processing, metal products, electronic equipment, transportation
State flower/bird: Wood violet/robin

Wyoming

Area: 97,814 sq mi (253,337 sq km)
Population: 584,153
Capital: Cheyenne, pop. 62,845
Largest city: Cheyenne, pop. 62,845
Industry: Oil and natural gas, mining, generation of electricity, chemicals, tourism
State flower/bird: Indian paintbrush/western meadowlark

● Midwest ● Southwest ● West

THE TERRITORIES

The United States has 14 territories— political divisions that are not states. Three of these are in the Caribbean Sea, and the other eleven are in the Pacific Ocean.

St. John, U.S. Virgin Islands

Convention Center, San Juan, Puerto Rico

Talofofo Falls, Guam

U.S. CARIBBEAN TERRITORIES

Puerto Rico

Area: 3,508 sq mi (9,086 sq km)
Population: 3,548,397
Capital: San Juan, pop. 365,575
Languages: Spanish, English

U.S. Virgin Islands

Area: 149 sq mi (386 sq km)
Population: 104,000
Capital: Charlotte Amalie, pop. 52,000
Languages: English, Spanish or Spanish Creole, French or French Creole

U.S. PACIFIC TERRITORIES

American Samoa

Area: 77 sq mi (199 sq km)
Population: 54,000
Capital: Pago Pago, pop. 48,000
Language: Samoan

Guam

Area: 217 sq mi (561 sq km)
Population: 162,000
Capital: Hagåtña (Agana), pop. 143,000
Languages: English, Chamorro, Philippine languages

Northern Mariana Islands

Area: 184 sq mi (477 sq km)
Population: 52,000
Capital: Saipan, pop. 49,000
Languages: Philippine languages, Chinese, Chamorro, English

Other U.S. Territories

Baker Island, Howland Island, Jarvis Island, Johnston Atoll, Kingman Reef, Midway Islands, Palmyra Atoll, Wake Island, Navassa Island (in the Caribbean)

Figures for capital cities vary widely between sources because of differences in the way the area is defined and other projection methods.

THE U.S. CAPITAL

District of Columbia

Area: 68 sq mi (177 sq km)
Population: 658,893

Abraham Lincoln, who was President during the Civil War and a strong opponent of slavery, is remembered in the Lincoln Memorial, located at the opposite end of the National Mall from the U.S. Capitol Building.

COLOR KEY • Territories • Northeast

DESTINATION GUIDE

San Antonio, Texas

The Alamo

Bats flying out of Bracken Cave

Tower of the Americas

Deep in the heart of Texas you'll find San Antonio, a town that's bursting with both famous historical sights and glitzy modern attractions. Here are just a few of the many things you can do while visiting.

WHAT TO DO:

REMEMBER THE ALAMO: A trip to San Antonio isn't complete without a stop at this landmark—the site where a band of Texans held out for 13 days against Mexican soldiers in 1836 while defending their freedom. Learn more about their story as you walk the grounds of this historical site.

SEARCH FOR SPARKLE: Pan for precious gems at National Bridge Caverns, where you'll find the largest mining sluice in Texas. Then stick around for the evening entertainment: On summer nights, millions of bats spiral out of Bracken Cave on a hunt for insects.

A NEW VIEW: Check out San Antonio from 750 feet (229 m) above by traveling to the top of the Tower of the Americas in downtown San Antonio. Take in the panoramic view, then head to the tower's theater for a 4-D movie ride that'll take you on a high-flying trip across Texas.

WALK THE RIVER: The place to be in San Antonio? The town's jazzy River Walk, packed with restaurants, shops, and other sights. Take a stroll or rent a bike and hit the trails—there are about 15 miles (24 km) of riverfront paths to pedal along.

From 1836 to 1846, Texas was an independent nation called the Republic of Texas.

Streets in San Antonio include Bacon Road, Can't Stop Street, and Buggywhip Drive.

More than 2.5 million people visit the Alamo every year.

The River Walk

Wacky World →

Check out these **bizarre attractions** from around the UNITED KINGDOM.

Move over, Big Ben and Parliament: Next time you're cruising around England, make a pit stop at some truly peculiar places found throughout the country. You'll have plenty to write home about after visiting these weird and wacky attractions!

Dog Collar Museum
Where: Kent, England
Why it's wacky: Check out a collection of more than 100 dog collars from five centuries, ranging from spiky iron ones worn by hunting hounds to 21st-century chic neckwear for pampered pooches.

The Gnome Reserve and Wildflower Garden
Where: near West Putford, England
Why it's wacky: More than 2,000 gnome and pixie figurines—the world's largest collection—are scattered amid four acres (1.6 ha) of countryside. Visitors are encouraged to wear pointy hats (provided at the park's entrance) so they don't scare the gnomes.

Dennis Severs' House

Where: London, England
Why it's wacky: Stroll through this "living museum," and you'll get the sense that its 18th-century occupants are still residing there and just left the room. Wait—was that a whisper coming from the next room? Hello? Is anybody home?

The Crooked House

Where: Himley, England
Why it's wacky: Built in 1765, part of this brick house has shifted due to unstable ground, leaving one end four feet (1.2 m) lower than the other. Now a restaurant, the floors have been leveled for safety, but the house's walls remain off-kilter for an unbalanced look.

Wild Vacation

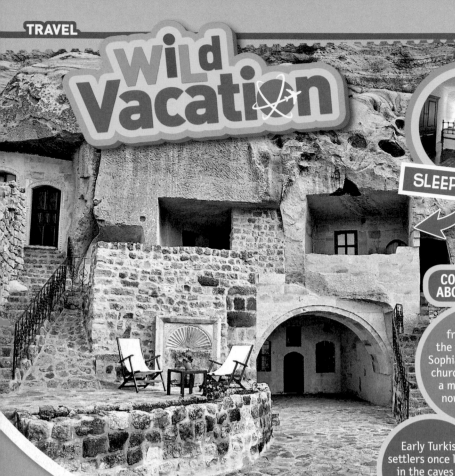

SLEEP HERE!

COOL THINGS ABOUT TURKEY

Dating from A.D. 537, the famous Hagia Sophia was built as a church, turned into a mosque, and is now a museum.

Early Turkish settlers once lived in the caves of the Cappadocia region.

Yogurt was invented in Turkey and is a main ingredient in local food—from soups to desserts.

King Midas may not have really turned all he touched into gold. But he did rule over the kingdom of Phrygia, in what is now Turkey, in the eighth century B.C.

Cave Hotel

YUNAK EVLERI HOTEL

WHERE Cappadocia region, Turkey

WHY IT'S COOL Here's a hotel that really rocks. The Yunak Evleri is built into caves left by volcanic activity ten million years ago. Follow narrow passageways and stone stairs to rooms that are a cool 57°F (14°C). Spend the day hiking rocky terrain, exploring caverns, or hot air ballooning over "fairy chimneys"—tall rock formations that dot the skyline. At night you won't have to worry about being awakened by eruptions since the Cappadocia volcanoes are now dormant. So they're "sleeping," too!

THINGS TO DO IN TURKEY

Ride a camel to tour the bizarre rock formations around Cappadocia.

Take a boat ride up the Bosporus strait to get from Asia to Europe in 15 minutes.

Haggle with shopkeepers in the bustling market of Istanbul's Grand Bazaar.

EXTREME WEIRDNESS

From **AROUND** the **WORLD**

AT EASE, GORILLAS!

GORILLA FOOLS HUMANS

WHAT Ape robot

WHERE Bristol, England

DETAILS Call it *Planet of the Fake Apes.* The Bristol Zoo Gardens' "Wow! Gorillas" exhibit featured an animatronic ape and several five-foot (1.5-m)-tall fiberglass gorilla sculptures. The sculptures were later painted and decorated by local artists. What's next—papier-mâché penguins?

STRAW MAN

WHAT Straw bears

WHERE Heldra, Germany

DETAILS Somebody went overboard with their winter coat. In colder months, some Germans have a tradition of wearing outfits made of straw while attending seasonal festivals. These "straw bears" date back to an old belief that the outfits would scare winter away. All this guy needs is a straw scarf.

MEET STRAW MAN, TIN MAN'S LONG-LOST COUSIN.

BIIIGGG BINOCULARS

WHAT Binocular-shaped entrance

WHERE Venice, California, U.S.A.

DETAILS Did somebody ask for a better view? Sculptors Claes Oldenburg and Coosje van Bruggen designed this 45-foot (14-m)-tall set of binoculars that now serves as an office entrance for Google. So *that's* what they mean by "Internet search."

NOT SURE HOW TO WATCH BIRDS WITH THESE.

1 When building a waterslide, a construction crew follows the manufacturer's directions and puts the slide together piece by piece at the park. It's like assembling a **HUGE TOY RACETRACK!**

2 Riders inside a **CLEAR TUNNEL** pass through **A POOL OF SHARKS** on the Leap of Faith waterslide in the Bahamas.

3 **WATERSLIDES** made out of *STAINLESS STEEL ARE FASTER* than those that are made out of fiberglass.

4 Riders reach speeds of **65 miles an hour (105 kph)** on the Insano waterslide at Beach Park in Fortaleza, Brazil.

17 SPLASHY FACTS ABOUT WATER

5 THERE ARE MORE THAN **1,200 water parks** IN NORTH AMERICA.

6 In 2011, more than two million people visited Typhoon Lagoon in Orlando. That's about the same as the entire population of Slovenia, in eastern Europe.

7 A group raft ride in Wisconsin Dells, U.S.A., plunges riders into a 58-foot (18-m)-long tunnel with fake fog and lightning. **It's like riding into a hurricane.**

8 THE 145,000-SQUARE-FOOT (13,471-SQ-M) WAVE PALACE AT SIAM PARK IN SPAIN'S CANARY ISLANDS USES **185,000 gallons** (700,301 L) of salt water TO CREATE HUGE, OCEANLIKE WAVES FOR SURFERS.

9 New water parks are designed to **CONSERVE WATER.** They generally use less water than people living in a neighborhood of about the same size do.

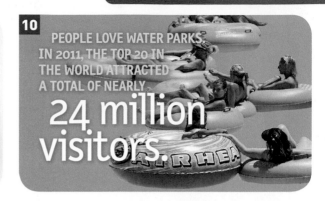

10 PEOPLE LOVE WATER PARKS. IN 2011, THE TOP 20 IN THE WORLD ATTRACTED A TOTAL OF NEARLY **24 million visitors.**

11 TEN OF THE TOP 20 WATER PARKS IN THE WORLD ARE IN ASIA; 6 ARE IN THE UNITED STATES, AND 4 OF THOSE ARE IN FLORIDA.

12 The tight turns of the Constrictor ride at Wet 'N Wild in Phoenix, Arizona, U.S.A., make riders feel like they are traveling inside a giant snake.

13 The mile-(1.6-km)-long Raging River inner tube ride in Texas's Schlitterbahn (German for "slippery road") takes some 45 minutes to complete.

PARKS

14 Yas Waterworld in Abu Dhabi, in the United Arab Emirates, spreads across 37 acres (15 ha). That's more than 330 NBA-size basketball courts!

15 In 24 hours, a man in Erding, Germany, covered 94.5 miles (152 km) riding one waterslide 427 times. That's about the distance between New York City and Philadelphia, U.S.A.!

16 SURFERS TRY TO **GET AIR** ON NINE-FOOT (2.7-M)-HIGH WAVES IN THE WAVE POOL AT SUNWAY LAGOON IN MALAYSIA.

17 Wisconsin Dells calls itself the **"Waterpark Capital of the World."** The town boasts more than 20 indoor and outdoor water parks.

QUIZ WHIZ

Is your geography knowledge off the map? Quiz yourself to find out!
ANSWERS BELOW

1 Where in the world can you find sand dunes as tall as skyscrapers?
a. Namibia
b. Dubai
c. Croatia
d. Antarctica

2 Which species of insect makes an annual migration from Canada and the U.S.A. to Mexico?
a. cricket
b. monarch butterfly
c. rhinoceros beetle
d. banana moth

3 _____ is also known as the "Soft Coral Capital of the World."

4 What are the only ways to get to Bolivia's Isla del Sol?
a. boat or hike
b. rocket ship or UFO
c. car or truck
d. plane or train

5 **True or false?** There are pink lakes in Australia.

Not **STUMPED** yet? Check out the *NATIONAL GEOGRAPHIC KIDS QUIZ WHIZ* collection for more crazy **GEOGRAPHY** questions!

HOMEWORK HELP

Finding Your Way Around

Every map has a story to tell, but first you have to know how to read one. Maps represent information by using a language of symbols. Knowing how to read these symbols provides access to a wide range of information. Look at the scale and compass rose or arrow to understand distance and direction (see box below).

To find out what each symbol on a map means, you must use the key. It's your secret decoder—identifying information by each symbol on the map.

Latitude

Longitude

90°N (North Pole)
75°N
60°N
45°N
30°N
15°N
0° (Equator)
15°S
30°S
45°S

LATITUDE AND LONGITUDE

Latitude and longitude lines (above) help us determine locations on Earth. Every place on Earth has a special address called absolute location. Imaginary lines called lines of latitude run west to east, parallel to the Equator. These lines measure distance in degrees north or south from the Equator (0° latitude) to the North Pole (90°N) or to the South Pole (90°S). One degree of latitude is approximately 70 miles (113 km).

Lines of longitude run north to south, meeting at the Poles. These lines measure distance in degrees east or west from 0° longitude (prime meridian) to 180° longitude. The prime meridian runs through Greenwich, England.

SCALE AND DIRECTION

The scale on a map can be shown as a fraction, as words, or as a line or bar. It relates distance on the map to distance in the real world. Sometimes the scale identifies the type of map projection. Maps may include an arrow or compass rose to indicate north on the map.

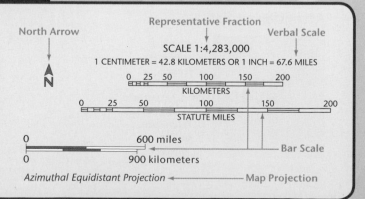

North Arrow

N

Representative Fraction

SCALE 1:4,283,000
1 CENTIMETER = 42.8 KILOMETERS OR 1 INCH = 67.6 MILES

Verbal Scale

0   25   50   100   150   200
KILOMETERS

0   25   50   100   150   200
STATUTE MILES

0   600 miles
0   900 kilometers

Bar Scale

Azimuthal Equidistant Projection ——— Map Projection

GAME ANSWERS

Find the Hidden Animals, page 144

1. **F**, 2. **E**, 3. **D**, 4. **A**, 5. **C**, 6. **B**.

What in the World? page 145

Top row: **island, forest, elephant herd.**
Middle row: **flamingos, camels, coral reef.**
Bottom row: **flower fields, icebergs, hot-air balloon.** Bonus: **You crack me up!**

A-MAZE-ing Mind, page 146

Noun Town, page 148

The 12 compound nouns are: 1. **sleeping bag,** 2. **eggplant,** 3. **catfish,** 4. **bellhop,** 5. **ladybug,** 6. **housework,** 7. **butterfly,** 8. **limelight,** 9. **arrowhead,** 10. **full moon,** 11. **treehouse,** 12. **coffee table.**

Attention on Set, page 149

1. **utensils,** 2. **antennae,** 3. **stencil,** 4. **extension cord,** 5. **tentacle,** 6. **kitten,** 7. **tent,** 8. **Tennessee,** 9. **tennis ball,** 10. **mitten.**

What in the World? page 150

Top row: **corn, tennis ball, sunflowers.**
Middle row: **snake, canary, banana slug.**
Bottom row: **butterfly, honeycomb, lemon.**
Bonus: **Cut it in half.**

Riddle Me This, page 152

1. *sneak*-ers, 2. **zebra,** 3. **tree,** 4. **rain,** 5. **candle,** 6. **footsteps,** 7. **clock,** 8. **goose,** 9. **bottle,** 10. **window.**

Book Boggle, page 155

The eight book titles are:
Treasure Island (1, 11);
Little House on the Prairie (6, 2);
The Lion, the Witch and the Wardrobe (7, 3);
The Lightning Thief (4, 13);
James and the Giant Peach (10, 5);
Diary of a Wimpy Kid (8, 15);
Harry Potter and the Goblet of Fire (14, 9);
and *Green Eggs and Ham* (16, 12).

Dog Daze, page 157

Your World 2017 (8–17)

p. 13 "Kermit's Twin" by Rose Davidson; p. 15 "Camera Ball" by Crispin Boyer; p. 17 "Pet Smuggler Busted!" by Karen De Seve; all other articles in section by Sarah Wassner Flynn

Amazing Animals (18–79)

pp. 20–25 "17 Cutest Animals of 2017" by Sarah Wassner Flynn; pp. 26–27 "Animal Rascals" by Aline Alexander Newman; pp. 28–29 "Sea Otter Shoots Hoops" & "Horse Lives in House" by Kitson Jazynka, "Skateboarding Cat" by Rose Davidson; pp. 30–31 "What Is Taxonomy?" & "Vertebrates"/ "Invertebrates" by Susan K. Donnelly; pp. 32–33 "Mission Animal Rescue: Rhino" by Clare Hodgson Meeker; pp. 34–35 "Wild Hamsters" by Kate Jaimet; pp. 36–37 "Secrets of the Spirit Bear" and "Tough Cats" by Karen De Seve; p. 38 "5 Cool Things About Koalas" by Crispin Boyer; p. 39 "Foxes on Ice" by Karen De Seve; p. 41 "Wolverine!" by Stephanie Warren; pp. 42–43 "Freaky Frogs!" by Ruth A. Musgrave; pp. 44–45 "Goofballs" by Avery Elizabeth Hurt; pp. 46–47 "Big Cats" by Elizabeth Carney; pp. 48–49 "Mission Animal Rescue: Lion" by Scott Elder; p. 50 "Cheetahs: Built for Speed" by Fiona Sunquist; p. 51 "Snow Leopard Secrets" by Karen De Seve; pp. 52–53 "Mission Animal Rescue: Sea Turtle" by Scott Elder; pp. 54–55 "Talking Dolphin" by Ruth A. Musgrave; pp. 56–57 "Parenting, Puffin Style" by Ruth A. Musgrave; pp. 58–59 "Name That Tide Pool Animal" by Nancy Honovich; pp. 60–63 "Awesome Insect Awards" and "Monarchs Hit the Road!" by Sarah Wassner Flynn; p. 64 "What Killed the Dinosaurs?" by Sarah Wassner Flynn; pp. 64–66 "Prehistoric Time Line," "Dino Classification" & "Who Ate What?" by Susan K. Donnelly; pp. 72–73 "How to Speak Cat" by Aline Alexander Newman and Gary Weitzman, D.V.M.; p. 75 "Real Animal Heroes!" by Aline Alexander Newman; pp. 76–77 "Lifestyles of the Rich & Furry" by Patricia J. Murphy

Going Green (80–95)

pp. 82–83 "Saving the Jaguars" by Sarah Wassner Flynn and "Manatee Rescue!" by Scott Elder; pp. 84–87 "17 Cool Things About Going Green," "The Arctic's Disappearing Ice," and "What a Prince!" by Sarah Wassner Flynn; p. 87 "Pollution" by David George Gordon; p. 88 "Food for Thought" by Barton Seaver; pp. 89–90 "Fighting Food Waste" and "6 Tips to Save the Earth" by Sarah Wassner Flynn; pp. 92–93 "Green Extremes" by Sarah Wassner Flynn

Culture Connection (96–121)

pp. 100–101 "*Howl*-oween Pet Party" by Kay Boatner; p. 102 "What's Your Chinese Horoscope?" by Geoff Williams; pp. 104–105 "Archaeologist Fred Hiebert Digs the Past" by Sarah Wassner Flynn; pp. 106–107 "World's Wackiest Houses" by Zachary Petit; pp. 110–111 "Chew on This" by Kay Boatner; pp. 112–113 "Money Around the World!" by Kristin Baird Rattini; pp. 116–117 "Monster Myths" by Kitson Jazynka; pp. 118–119 "World Religions" by Mark Bockenhauer; p. 119 "Technology Meets Tradition" by Sarah Wassner Flynn

Awesome Adventure (122–141)

pp. 124–127 "Dare to Explore" by C.M. Tomlin; pp. 130–131 "Rhian Waller: Keeping Your Cool!" by Margaret Gurevich; pp. 132–133 "Cave of Secrets" by Scott Elder; p. 135 "Frozen in Time" by Sarah Wassner Flynn; p. 136 "Meerkat Close Encounter" by Kitson Jazynka; p. 137 "How to Survive a Killer Bee Attack!" & "How to Survive a Bee Sting!" by Rachel Buchholz; pp. 138–139 "Getting the Shot" by April Capochino Myers

Fun and Games (142–161)

p. 154 "Funny Fill-In" by Jennifer MacKinnon; p. 159 "Funny Fill-In" by Becky Baines

Super Science (162–197)

pp. 166 "Cool Inventions" by Crispin Boyer; p. 167 "Accidents Happen" by Renee Skelton; p. 169 "The Three Domains of Life" by Susan K. Donnelly; pp. 170–171 "You and Your Cells" & "You Have a Lot of Nerve!" by Christina Wilsdon, Patricia Daniels, and Jen Agresta; p. 172 "Your Amazing Brain" by Douglas E. Richards; p. 173 "Check Your Memory" by Jennifer Swanson; p. 174 "Your Amazing Ears" by Sarah Wassner Flynn; pp. 176–177 "That's Gross!" by Crispin Boyer; pp. 178–179 "Big Bang" by David A. Aguilar; p. 178 "Powerful Particle" by Sarah Wassner Flynn; p. 182 "By the Numbers: Solar System" by Julie Beer and Michelle Harris; p. 183 "Dwarf Planets" by Sarah Wassner Flynn; p. 184 "Destination Space: Alien Sea" by Stephanie Warren Drimmer; pp. 186–187 "Constellations" by Sarah Wassner Flynn; p. 189 "Rock Stars" by Steve Tomecek; pp. 190–191 "Name That Rock" by Nancy Honovich; pp. 192–193 "Volcano!" by Renee Skelton; pp. 194–195 "Hot Spot" by Scott Elder

Wonders of Nature (198–221)

pp. 200–201 "17 Freaky Facts About Weather" by Thomas M. Kostigen; p. 202 "Weather and Climate" by Mark Bockenhauer; p. 204 "Types of Clouds" by Kathy Furgang; p. 205 "Make a Barometer" by Nancy Honovich; pp. 206–207 "Typhoon!" & "Earthquake" & "Blizzard!" by Sarah Wassner Flynn; pp. 208–209 "What Is a Tornado?" by Kathy Furgang; p. 210 "How Does Your Garden Grow?" by Susan K. Donnelly; pp. 212–213 "Carnivorous Plants" by Sarah Wassner Flynn; pp. 214–215 "Biomes" by Susan K. Donnelly; pp. 218–219 "Pristine Seas" by Sarah Wassner Flynn

History Happens (222–253)

pp. 224–225 "Jungle of Secrets" by John Micklos, Jr.; pp. 226–227 "Knight Life" by Crispin Boyer; pp. 228–229 "Must-See Sights" by Sarah Wassner Flynn; p. 232 "Mystery of the Stone Giants" by Sean McCollum; p. 233 "Mystery of Atlantis" by John Micklos, Jr.; p. 234 "Treasure!" by Jamie Kiffel-Alech; p. 235 "The Secrets of Stonehenge" by Kristin Baird Rattini; pp. 236–237 "War!" by Susan K. Donnelly and Sarah Wassner Flynn; p. 237 "Cracking the Code" by Sarah Wassner Flynn; pp. 238–239 "The Constitution & the Bill of Rights" & "Branches of Government" by Susan K. Donnelly; p. 240 "The Indian Experience" by Martha B. Sharma; pp. 246–247 "Cool Things About Air Force One" by Scott Elder; pp. 248–249 "Civil Rights" & "Stone of Hope" by Susan K. Donnelly and Sarah Wassner Flynn; pp. 250–251 "8 Daring Women in U.S. History!" by Sarah Wassner Flynn

Geography Rocks (254–337)

pp. 256–262 by Mark Bockenhauer; pp. 264–291 by Sarah Wassner Flynn, Mark Bockenhauer, and Susan K. Donnelly; pp. 292–316 "You Are There!" by Sarah Wassner Flynn; pp. 329–331 "Destination Guide: San Antonio, Texas" and "Wacky World" by Sarah Wassner Flynn; p. 332 "Wild Vacation" by C.M. Tomlin; p. 333 "Extreme Weirdness From Around the World" by Kay Boatner

All "Homework Help" by Vicki Ariyasu

ABBREVIATIONS:

CO: Corbis
GI: Getty Images
IS: iStockphoto
MP: Minden Pictures
NGC: National Geographic Creative
NGS: National Geographic Stock
NPL: Nature Picture Library
SS: Shutterstock
WHHA: White House Historical Association

All Maps

By National Geographic Society unless otherwise noted

All Illustrations & Charts

By Stuart Armstrong unless otherwise noted

Front Cover/Spine

(koala), Suzi Eszterhas/MP; (Big Ben), Sean Gallagher/NGC; (chameleon), Life On White/Photodisc/GI; (rock climber), Christopher Kimmel/Flickr RF/GI; (penguin), Tui De Roy/MP; Spine: (Easter Island statues), Volanthevist/Moment Open/GI; (Big Ben), Sean Gallagher/NGC; (chameleon), Life On White/Photodisc/GI

Back Cover

(Taylor Swift peanut art), Steve Casino; (Earth), Alex Staroseltsev/SS; (chameleon), Thomas Marent/MP; (Easter Island statues), Volanthevist/Moment Open/GI; (lemurs), Pete Oxford/MP; (mountain boarder), Klubovy/E+/GI; (diver and shark), frantisekhojdysz/SS; (hat), Steve Collender/SS

Inside Front Cover

(T-Rex), Jim Zuckerman/CO; (giraffe), Roy Toft/NGC; (polar bear cub), Eric Isselee/SS

Front Matter (2–7)

2-3, Suzi Eszterhas/MP; 5 (UP RT), SS; 5 (LO), Nattapol Sritongcom/SS; 5 (UP LE), ESA; 5 (CTR), Thorsten Milse/Robert Harding World Imagery; 6 (UP), Bruno Morandi/Robert Harding World Imagery; 6 (UP CTR), Menno Boermans/Robert Harding World Imagery; 6 (LO CTR), Paul & Paveena Mckenzie/GI; 6 (LO), RAKITA/SIPA/Newscom; 7 (UP), Frans Lanting/Robert Harding World Imagery; 7 (CTR), Danita Delimont/GI; 7 (LO), Angelo Cavalli/Robert Harding World Imagery

Your World 2016 (8–17)

8-9, ESA; 9 (CTR RT), Steve Collender/SS; 10 (UP LE), GI Inc./NGC; 10 (UP RT), Katherine Feng/MP/NGC; 10 (LO LE), AFP/GI; 11 (UP), Gene Blevins/ZUMA Press/CO; 11 (LO LE), Jurgen Otto; 11 (LO RT), Jurgen Otto; 12 (UP), NASA; 12 (UP CTR), NASA; 12 (LO CTR), NASA; 12 (LO), LOLIWARE Biodegr(edible)s; 13 (UP LE), Mark Thiessen/NGC; 13 (UP RT), Courtesy NG Studios/NGC; 13 (CTR), Stefan Fichtel/NGC; 13 (LO LE), Vera Anderson/WireImage/GI; 13 (LO RT), Brian Kubicki/Costa Rican Amphibian Research Center; 14 (UP), Manabu Ogasawara/GI; 14 (CTR LE), © 20th Century-Fox Film Corporation, TM & Copyright/Courtesy Everett Collection; 14 (CTR RT), © Buena Vista Pictures/Courtesy Everett Collection; 14 (LO), © Universal Pictures/Courtesy Everett Collection; 15 (UP), Panono; 15 (UP CTR), Panono; 15 (LO CTR), AC Manley/SS; 15, Courtesy Kelly Sweet, National Geographic staff; 16 (leaf), jannoon028/SS; 16 (U.S. seal), Joseph Sohm/SS; 16 (tiger), Anan Kaewkhammul/SS; 16 (puppet), Opop0/SS; 16 (bird), NH/SS; 16 (Star Wars), © Copyright Twentieth Century-Fox Film Corporation. All rights reserved/Courtesy Everett Collection; 16 (books), blackred/GI; 16 (yoga), Glenkar/SS; 16 (pumpkins), topseller/SS; 17 (UP LE), omphoto/SS; 17 (UP RT), Steve Casino; 17 (CTR RT), Steve Casino; 17 (CTR LE), Steve Casino; 17 (LO), Tom Nick Cocotos

Amazing Animals (18–79)

18-19, Thorsten Milse/Robert Harding World Imagery; 20 (UP), Fuse/GI; 20 (LO), iculizard/IS; 21 (UP), Alex Mustard/NPL; 21 (LO LE), Dave Watts/NPL; 21 (LO RT), Molly Prottas; 22 (UP LE), Sebastian Kennerknecht/MP; 22 (UP RT), Shanna Love/Ballarat Wildlife Park; 22 (LO), Willie Davis/SS; 23 (UP), ARCO/NPL; 23 (LO LE), Christophe Lehenaff/Alamy; 23 (LO RT), Pete Oxford/NPL/MP; 24 (UP LE), CO/SuperStock; 24 (UP RT), Masatsugu Ohashi/Rex USA; 24 (LO LE), Robert Harding World Imagery/Alamy; 24 (LO RT), Suzi Eszterhas/MP; 25 (UP), W8 Media/Splash News/CO; 25 (LO), Shedd Aquarium/Brenna Hernandez; 26 (LE), Denise Kappa/SS; 26 (CTR), Courtesy Mavis Knight; 26 (LO), Loisik/Dreamstime; 26 (Dentures), botazsolti/SS; 27 (LO LE), Charlie Summers/NPL; 27 (LO), Barry Mansell/NPL; 27 (UP), Erik Lam/SS; 27 (UP LE), Courtesy Dr. Gary Sloniker; 27 (UP CTR), Uatp1/Dreamstime; 28 (UP), Oregon Zoo/photo by Michael Durham; 28 (LO), Oregon Zoo/photo by Michael Durham; 29, Carsten Rehder/AFP/GI; 29 (LO), CB2/ZOB/Newscom; 30 (LE CTR), Eric Isselee/SS; 30 (LO RT), Joel Sartore/NGC; 30 (UP), Mint Images Limited/Alamy; 31 (UP LE), FloridaStock/SS; 31 (LO RT), Karen Massier/IS.com; 31 (UP RT), cbpix/SS; 31 (LE CTR), mashe/SS; 31 (LO), Eric Isselee/SS; 32 (LE), Beverly Joubert/NGC; 32 (RT), Beverly Joubert/NGC; 33, Beverly Joubert/NGC; 34-35, Eric Baccega/NPL; 34 (LO), Eric Baccega/NPL; 35 (UP LE), Eric Baccega/NPL; 35 (UP CTR), Eric Baccega/NPL; 35 (UP), Eric Baccega/NPL; 36 (UP LE), Mark Carwardine/ARDEA; 36 (UP RT), Steven J. Kazlowski/Alamy; 36 (LO LE), Steven J. Kazlowski/Alamy; 37 (UP), Arco Images GmbH/Alamy; 37 (LO), Lisa & Mike Husar/Team Husar; 38 (UP), Jouan & Rius/naturepl.com; 38 (LO), Hotshotsworldwide/Dreamstime.com; 39 (UP), Yva Momatiuk & John Eastcott/MP; 39 (LO), Michio Hoshino/MP; 39 (CTR), Steve Kazloski/NPL; 40, Jean Paul Ferrero/Ardea; 41 (Background), Sergey Gorshkov/MP; 41 (LO), Daniel J. Cox/Oxford Scientific/GI; 41 (RT), A. & J. Visage/Peter Arnold/GI; 42 (UP), Stephen Dalton/naturepl.com; 42 (LO RT), Andrew Murray/naturepl.com; 42 (LO LE), Pete Oxford/naturepl.com; 43 (UP RT), Stephen Dalton/naturepl.com; 43 (UP CTR LE), Thomas Marent/MP; 44 (UP), Heidi & Hans-Juergen Koch/MP; 44 (LO), M. Watson/Ardea; 45 (UP LE), Bianca Lavies/NGC; 45, Mark Payne-Gill/NPL; 45 (LO LE), Bianca Lavies/NGC; 45 (CTR RT), Claus Meyer/MP; 45 (LO RT), Jason Tharp; 45, Mark Payne-Gill/NPL; 45, Mark Payne-Gill/NPL; 46, Staffan Widstrand/naturepl .com; 47 (UP LE), worldswildlifewonders/SS; 47 (UP CTR LE), Kesu/SS; 47 (UP CTR RT), WitR/SS; 47 (UP RT), Eric Isselee/SS; 47 (LE CTR), DLILLC/CO; 47 (RT CTR), Eric Isselee/SS; 47 (LO LE), Eric Isselee/SS; 47 (LO RT), Eric Isselee/SS; 48 (LE CTR), BFF; 48 (LO RT), BFF; 49, Pete Oxford/MP; 50 (UP), Andy Rouse/NHPA/Photoshot; 50 (CTR), Stephen Belcher/MP; 50 (LO LE), Martin Harvey/Photolibrary/GI; 50 (LO RT), Suzi Eszterhas/MP; 51 (UP), Steve Winter/National Geographic Stock; 51 (CTR), Purple Pilchards/Alamy; 51 (LO), NHPA/SuperStock; 52-53, Brian J. Skerry/NGC; 52 (LO), NEAQ Rescue; 53 (UP RT), Terry Dickson/Florida Times-Union; 53 (LO LE), Connie Merigo; 54 (UP), Augusto Leandro Stanzani/ARDEA; 54 (LO), Image Source/Alamy; 54 (CTR), Augusto Leandro Stanzani/ARDEA; 54 (LO RT), Jekyll Island Authority; 55 (UP RT), Arco Images GmbH/Alamy; 55 (LO LE), Eco/UIG/GI; 56 (UP RT), Stefan Huwiler/imagebroker/CO; 56 (CTR), Frans Lanting/CO; 56 (LO), ÊJames Urbach/SuperStock; 57 (LE), age fotostock/SuperStock; 57 (UP RT), Alex Mustard/2020VISION/NPL; 57 (CTR RT), Chris Gomersall/NPL; 57 (LO RT), Jouan & Rius/NPL; 58-59, apsimo1/IS; 59 (UP CTR), Brendan Hunter/IS; 59 (UP RT), Nancy Nehring/IS; 59 (LO LE), Lee Rogers/IS; 59 (LO RT), AtWaG/IS; 59 (UP CTR), Lars Johansson/IS; 60 (UP LE), Stephen Dalton/MP; 60 (UP RT), Nature Production/NPL; 60 (LO), Elio Della Ferrera/MP; 61 (UP LE), Heidi & Hans-Juergen Koch/MP; 61 (LO LE), Studio Times Ltd/MP; 61 (UP RT), Mitsuhiko Imamori/MP; 61 (LO RT), Bruce Davidson/MP; 62 (UP back), Ingo Arndt/NPL; 62 (LO), IS.com/GomezDavid; 63 (LE), Stephen Dalton/NPL; 63 (UP RT), IS.com/Ron Brancato; 63 (CTR RT), IS.com/Sarah Bossert; 63 (LO), Noradoa/SS; 64 (UP), Chris Butler/Science Photo Library/Photo Researchers, Inc.; 64 (CTR), Publiphoto/Photo Researchers, Inc.; 64 (LO), Pixeldust Studios/National GeographicStock.com; 65 (B), Laurie O'Keefe/Photo Researchers, Inc.; 65 (C), Chris Butler/Photo Researchers, Inc.; 65 (D), Publiphoto/Photo Researchers, Inc.; 65 (A), Publiphoto/Photo Researchers, Inc.; 65 (E), image Courtesy Project Exploration; 66 (UP), Paul B. Moore/SS; 66 (LO), Andrea Meyer/SS; 67 (UP LE), Gabriel Lio; 67 (UP RT), Courtesy Royal Tyrrell Museum of Canada; 67 (LO LE), Lida Xing; 67 (LO RT), Dinostar Co. Ltd.; 68 (UP RT), Franco Tempesta; 68-69 (ALL), Franco Tempesta; 70 (UP LE), Marcio Jose Bastos Silva/SS; 70 (UP RT), ShaneKato/IS; 70 (CTR LE), imv/IS; 70 (LO LE), Eric Isselee/IS; 70 (LO RT), John Cancalosi/Alamy; 70 (CTR RT), Eric Isselee/IS; 71 (LO LE), Peter Mukherjee/IS; 71 (UP CTR), Hornbil Images/Alamy; 71 (UP RT), Oli Scarff/GI; 71 (UP LE), Michael Murphy/National Parks and Wildlife Service; 71 (CTR LE), Eduard Kyslynskyy/SS; 71 (CTR RT), Philip Scalia/Alamy; 71 (LO RT), Vudhikrai/SS; 72 (UP), Damien Richard/SS; 72 (LO), kurhan/SS; 73 (LO LE), Igor Shpilenok/NPL; 73 (UP), SJ Allen/SS; 73 (LO), Hulya Ozkok/GI; 74 (UP LE), SJ Allen/SS; 74 (UP RT), Wegner/ARCO/NPL; 74 (LO), PM Images/GI; 75 (UP), Courtesy Carly Riley; 75 (CTR), Courtesy Patricia Peter; 75 (LO), Courtesy James Jett; 76 (RT), Meredith Parmelee/Stone/GI; 76 (LE), Yoshitsugu Kimura/Fifi & Romeo; 77 (UP), Courtesy La Petite Maison; 77 (CTR LE), Britt Erlanson/The Image Bank/GI; 77 (CTR), James Kegley; 77 (CTR RT), James Kegley; 77 (LO LE), Augustus Butera/Taxi/GI; 77 (LO RT), Courtesy Three Dog Bakery LLC; 78 (UP), Alex Mustard/NPL; 78 (CTR), Jean Paul Ferrero/ARDEA; 78 (LO), Hotshotsworldwide/Dreamstime.com; 79 (UP RT), CampCrazy Photography/SS

Going Green (80–95)

80-81, Nattapol Sritongcom/SS; 82 (UP), Steve Winter/NGC; 82 (LO), SA Team/MP; 83 (LO), James R. D. Scott/GI; 83 (UP), Courtesy FWC/Activities were conducted under the

USFWS permit number MA770191; 84 (UP LE), Sathit Plengchawee/Dreamstime.com; 84 (UP RT), Helenbr/Dreams-time; 84 (UP CTR), Johnfoto/Dreamstime; 84 (LO CTR), Raylight3/Dreamstime; 84 (LO LE), Image Source/GI; 84 (LO CTR), Francesco Alessi/Dreamstime; 84 (LO RT), Natthawut Punyosaeng/Dreamstime; 85 (UP LE), AP Photo/Pablo Martinez Monsivais; 85 (UP RT), Hauke Dressler/GI; 85 (UP CTR LE), Anton Starikov/Dreamstime; 85 (UP CTR RT), Eleni Seitanidou/Dreamstime; 85 (LO CTR LE), Feng Yu/Dreamstime; 85 (LO CTR RT), Burachet/Dreamstime; 85 (LO LE), flashgun/iStock Images; 85 (LO RT), Skutvik/Dreamstime; 86 (Background), Mujka Design Inc./IS.com; 87 (CTR), Giorgio Cosulich/GI; 87 (LO), Featureflash/SS; 88 (Back), Brian J. Skerry/NGC; 88 (INSET), CuboImages/Alamy; 89 (LO RT), Adrian Brooks/IMAGEWISE; 90 (LO), Jono Halling; 91 (Back), Walter Zerla/GI; 91 (UP LE), Jiang Hongyan/SS; 91 (UP RT), lucielang/IS; 91 (UP CTR LE), PeJo29/IS; 91 (UP CTR), Imagesbybarbara/IS; 91 (UP CTR RT), toddtaulman/IS; 91 (LO CTR RT), nilsz/IS; 91 (LO CTR LE), talevr/IS; 91 (LO LE), PhotosbyAbby/IS; 91 (LO RT), kedsanee/IS; 92 (UP), Art by Zac Freeman; 92 (LO), Courtesy KWS Infra; 93 (LO), WENN/Newscom; 93 (UP LE), Courtesy Nice Architects; 93 (UP RT), Courtesy Nice Architects; 94 (UP LE), nilsz/IS; 94 (UP RT), SA Team/MP; 94 (LO), Giorgio Cosulich/GI; 95, Alboo03/SS

Culture (96–121)

96-97, Bruno Morandi/Robert Harding World Imagery; 98 (4), Tubol Evgeniya/SS; 98 (1), fotohunter/SS; 98 (7), pattarastock/SS; 98 (10), Shamil Zhumatov/Reuters/CO; 98 (9), Supachita Ae/SS; 98 (6), Maarten Wouters/GI; 99 (11), Dinodia/age fotostock; 99 (14), Zee/Alamy; 99 (15), wacpan/SS; 100-101, James Yamasaki; 100-101 (Back), Lilkar/dreamstime; 100-101 (LO), Lilkar/dreamstime; 100 (UP LE), Heidi Dubourgh Pedersen/GI; 100 (LO RT), Romeo Ranoco/CO; 100 (LO RT), Winnie Au/GI; 101 (UP LE), Philip Carr Photography/Photographers Direct; 101 (UP RT), Maro Hagopian/CO; 103 (RT), Mark Thiessen, NGS; 103 (LE), Mark Thiessen, NGS; 104 (UP), Courtesy Dr. Fred Hiebert; 104 (CTR), Rebecca Hale/NGC; 104 (LO), Courtesy Dr. Fred Hiebert; 105 (UP), Courtesy Dr. Fred Hiebert; 105 (CTR LE), Courtesy Dr. Fred Hiebert; 105 (UP RT), Andre Jenny/Alamy; 105 (LO A), Art Directors & TRIP/Alamy; 105 (LO B), Lenscap/Alamy; 105 (LO C), ArtBabii/Alamy; 105 (LO D), Michael Burrell/Alamy; 105 (LO E), Martin Wierink/Alamy; 105 (LO F), razorpix/Alamy; 106, REX USA/Jaime Jacott; 107 (CTR), Reuters/Danish Siddiqui; 107 (LO), Eduardo Longo; 107 (UP), Simon Dale/ZUMAPRESS/Newscom; 108 (UP RT), Africa Studio/SS; 108 (CTR LE), panda3800/SS; 108 (UP LE), Presselect/Alamy; 108 (LO LE), aa3/SS; 108 (CTR RT), SeanPavonePhoto/SS; 108 (LO RT), Jim1123/IS; 108 (UP RT), Mclein/SS; 109 (UP RT), Charlie Neuman/San Diego Union-Tribune/ZUMA Press/Alamy; 109 (LO CTR), Sethislav/IS; 109 (LO CTR LE), Oliver Arlow/Splash News/CO; 109 (UP CTR RT), bonchan/IS; 109 (LO CTR RT), tenback/IS; 109 (UP CTR LE), holbox/SS; 109 (LO LE), Mikael Andersson/Nordic Photos/GI; 109 (LO RT), Floortje/IS; 109 (UP RT), Catherine Lane/IS; 110 (CTR), Mark Theissen/NGS Staff; 110 (Back), Ver Lyr/SS, 111, Rebecca Hale/NGS Staff; 112 (CTR RT), Zoonar GmbH/Alamy; 112 (LO RT), Ninette Maumus/Alamy; 112 (UP RT), bullet74/

SS; 112 (UP LE), Ivan Vdovin/Alamy; 112 (CTR LE), Fritz Goro/The LIFE Picture Collection/GI; 112 (CTR), PhotoStock-Israel/Alamy; 112 (LO LE), Courtesy The Banknote Book; 113 (LO CTR), D. Hurst/Alamy; 113 (LO LE), Nataliya Evmenenko/dreamstime; 113 (UP RT), Comstock/GI; 113 (UP LE), Ivan Vdovin/Alamy; 113, incamerastock/Alamy; 113, Splash News/NewsCom; 113 (LO RT), Kelley Miller/NGS Staff; 114, Sergey Novikov/SS; 115 (CTR), Gonzalo Ordo–ez; 116 (UP), Dean Macadam; 116 (LO), Dean Macadam; 117 (UP RT), Dean Macadam; 117 (LO RT), Dean Macadam; 117 (LO LE), Dean Macadam; 118 (UP), Randy Olson; 118 (LO LE), Martin Gray/NationalGeographicStock.com; 118 (LO RT), Sam Panthaky/AFP/GI; 119 (LO LE), Reza/NationalGeographicStock.com; 119 (LO RT), Richard Nowitz/NationalGeographicStock.com; 119 (UP), Filippo Monteforte/GI; 120 (UP), Mclein/SS; 120 (CTR), Nataliya Evmenenko/Dreamstime; 120 (LO), Gonzalo Ordo–ez; 121 (UP LE), catwalker/SS; 121 (UP RT), dimitris_k/SS; 121 (UP CTR), oconnell/SS; 121 (LO), Steve Allen/SS

Awesome Adventure (122–141)

122-123, Menno Boermans/Robert Harding World Imagery; 124 (UP RT), John Catto/Alpenglow Pictures; 124 (CTR), Carsten Peter/National Geographic Stock; 124 (CTR LE), Carsten Peter/National Geographic Stock; 125 (UP RT), Charles Trout; 125 (LE), African People & Wildlife Fund; 125 (LO RT), Mitsuaki Iwago/MP; 126 (UP RT), Cory Richards/NGC; 126 (LE), Cory Richards/NGC; 126 (CTR LE), Cory Richards/NGC; 126 (CTR RT), Cory Richards/NGC; 127 (UP RT), Kenneth Garrett/NGS; 127 (LO RT), Robert Campbell; 127 (LOCTR), AP Photo/Kenneth Garrett; 127 (CTR), Scott Bjelland; 128 (7), Charles Brutlag/IS; 128 (UP LE), Sora Devore/NGC; 128 (1), Chokniti Khongchum/SS; 128 (2), Courtesy Jessica Cramp; 128 (3), Snyfer/Dreamstime.com; 128 (4), Sean Macdiarmid/Dreamstime.com; 128 (5), National Geographic Society Cartography Department; 128 (6), Juan Moyano/Dreamstime.com; 128 (8), poomsak suwannasilp/SS; 129 (9), Stuwdamdorp/Alamy; 129 (11), sagir/SS; 129 (12), Helen Sessions/Alamy; 129 (13), Igorp1976/Dreamstime.com; 129 (14), Fixzma/Dreamstime.com; 129 (15), Bloomberg/GI; 129 (16), Kguzel/Dreamstime.com; 129 (17), Image Courtesy Bananagrams; 130-131 (UP), Marco Grob/NGC; 130 (LO), CENGAGE/NGC; 130 (LO CTR), Rhian Waller/NGC; 131 (LO RT), Rhian Waller/NGC; 131 (LO LE), Rhian Waller/National Geographic; 132, Carsten Peter/NGC; 133 (RT), Carsten Peter/NGC; 133 (LE), Carsten Peter/NGC; 134 (CTR), Tyler Stableford/Aurora Photos; 135 (UP), Alasdair Turner/Aurora Photos/CO; 135 (LO LE), Popperfoto/GI; 135 (LO RT), Ashley Cooper pics/Alamy; 136 (UP LE), Will Burrard-Lucas; 136 (UP RT), Will Burrard-Lucas; 136 (CTR), Will Burrard-Lucas; 136 (LO), Will Burrard-Lucas; 137 (UP), Tony Campbell/SS; 137 (CTR RT), PMACD|PHOTOGRAPHY/SS; 138 (CTR), Mattias Klum/NGC; 139 (UP), Brian J. Skerry/NGC; 139 (LO), Michael Nichols/NGC; 140 (UP), Ashley Cooper pics/Alamy; 140 (CTR), Carsten Peter/NGC; 140 (LO), CENGAGE/NGC; 141 (UP RT), Grady Reese/IS.com

Fun and Games (142–161)

142-143, Paul & Paveena Mckenzie/GI; 144 (A), Visuals Unlimited/CO; 144 (B), Donald M. Jones/MP; 144 (C), W. Perry Conway/CO; 144 (D), DLILLC/CO; 144 (E), Thomas Rabeil/NPL; 144 (F), Fred Bavendam/MP; 145 (UP LE), Ira Block/

NGC; 145 (UP CTR), Ekaterina Pokrovsky/Dreamstime.com; 145 (UP RT), imageBROKER/Alamy; 145 (CTR LE), Richard du Toit Photography; 145 (CTR), Firefly Productions/CO; 145 (CTR RT), Eddie Gerald/Alamy; 145 (LO LE), Frans Lemmens/GI; 145 (LO CTR), Fred Hirschmann/Science Faction/GI; 145 (LO RT), Philip Wallick/CO; 146, C-TON; 147 (Background), Dr. Morley Read/SS; 148, Joren Cull; 149, James Yamasaki; 150 (UP LE), RBP Trust/GI; 150 (UP CTR), Stockbyte/GI; 150 (UP RT), Ed Collacott/GI; 150 (CTR LE), George Grall/NGC; 150 (CTR), ARCO/NPL; 150 (CTR RT), Ed Reschke/GI; 150 (LO LE), Charles Smith/CO; 150 (LO CTR), Brian Hagiwara/GI; 150 (LO RT), Francesco Ruggeri/GI; 151 (LO LE), Tom Grill/CO; 151 (UP), Eric Isselee/SS; 151 (LO RT), James Laurie/SS; 151, Tom Grill/CO; 151 (LO CTR), mlorenz/SS; 152, CTON; 153 (UP LE), Chris Ware; 153 (UP RT), Jean Galvao; 153 (CTR RT), Gary Fields; 153 (LO LE), Chris Ware; 154, Art by Jim Paillot; 155, James Yamasaki; 156 (UP), Johan Swanepoel/SS; 156 (CTR LE), s_oleg/SS; 156 (LO LE), Eric Isselee/SS; 156 (CTR RT), Hannamariah/SS; 156 (LO LE), Nick Biemans/SS; 156 (LO RT), Alex Kalmbach/SS; 157, CTON; 158 (CTR LE), Kalmatsuy/SS; 158 (LO), fivespots/SS; 158 (CTR RT), Kris Wiktor/SS; 158 (CTR RT), Chiyacat/SS; 158 (UP), Audrey Snider-Bell/SS; 158 (LO), fivespots/SS; 159, Art by Jason Tharp; 160-161, Strika Entertainment

Super Science (162–197)

162-163, RAKITA/SIPA/Newscom; 164 (4), Neil Fraser/Alamy; 164 (5), Bloomberg/GI; 164 (8), Chris Farina/CO; 164 (1), Everett Collection, Inc.; 164 (6), Rex Features/Rex USA; 165 (10), Joe Raedle/GI; 165 (13), Steve Marcus/Reuters/CO; 165 (17), Matthew Putney/Waterloo Courier/AP Photo; 165 (15), Lightspring/SS; 165 (9), Julie Jacobson/AP Photo; 165 (14), Julie Jacobson/AP Photo; 166 (UP), Georges Gobet/AFP/GI; 166 (UP CTR RT), Carlos Fernández Isoird; 166 (LO LE), 3Doodler; 166 (LO CTR RT), 3Doodler; 166 (LO RT), 3Doodler; 167 (UP), Art By Joe Rocco; 167 (LO), Art By Joe Rocco; 168 (LO), David Aguilar; 169 (E), Marie C. Fields/SS; 169 (D), Fedor A. Sidorov/SS; 169 (F), sgame/SS; 169 (A), Sebastian Kaulitzki/SS; 169 (B), Steve Gschmeissner/Photo Researchers, Inc.; 169 (C), Volker Steger/Christian Bardele/Photo Researchers, Inc.; 169 (G), Benjamin Jessop/IS.com; 170 (UP), Brand X/GI; 170 (LO), SSPL/Science Museum/GI; 171 (LO), martan/SS; 171 (UP), Mike Agliolo/Science Source; 172, Cynthia Turner; 173 (UP), Dreamstime; 174 (UP), Cynthia Turner; 174 (LO), Jason Lugo/GI; 174, Cynthia Turner; 175, JasonDoiy/IS; 176 (1), Science Photo Library/Alamy; 176-177 (UP), Irochka/Dreamstime; 177 (3), Sebastian Kaulitzki/SS; 177 (4), Photo Researchers/GI; 177 (RT CTR), Liubov Grigoryeva/Dreamstime.com; 177 (LO CTR RT), Shirley Hu/Dreamstime.com; 177 (LO RT), Sebastian Kaulitzki/Dreamstime.com; 178-179 (Background), Take 27 Ltd/Photo Researchers, Inc.; 179 (A–E), David Aguilar; 180-181 (UP), David Aguilar; 182, David Aguilar; 183 (UP), David Aguilar; 183 (LO RT), NASA/JHUAPL/SwRI; 184, Mondolithic Studios; 185 (CTR RT), Tony and Daphne Hallas/Photo Researchers, Inc.; 185 (Background up), Gabe Palmer/CO; 185 (UP RT), Walter Myers/Stocktrek Images/CO; 185 (LO RT), NASA; 189 (UP), Ralph Lee Hopkins/NGS; 189 (UP CTR LE), Visuals Unlimited/GI; 189 (UP CTR RT), Visuals Unlimited/GI; 189 (LO CTR LE), Doug Martin/Photo Researchers, Inc.; 189 (LO

CTR RT), DEA/C. Dani/GI; 189 (LO LE), Michael Baranski/SS; 190-191 (a), Jeff Goulden/IS; 190 (B), Hans Neleman/Photodisc/GI; 191 (C), Dirk Wiersma/Science Source; 191 (D), Alexander Bark/SS; 191 (F), Giovanni Rinaldi/IS; 191 (G), Dr. Ajay Kumar Singh/SS; 192 (CTR), James A. Sugar/CO; 193 (UP), Bruce Omori/EPA/ Newscom; 193 (CTR), Bruce Omori/EPA/ Newscom; 194-195, Prisma/Superstock; 196 (UP), Cynthia Turner; 196 (CTR), Brand X/GI; 196, NASA; 197 (UP), AVAVA/SS; 197 (LO), Chris Gorgio/ IS.com

Wonders of Nature (198-221)
198-199, Frans Lanting/Robert Harding World Imagery; 200 (1), Brad Calkins/Dreamstime; 200 (2), F1online digitale Bildagentur GmbH/ Alamy; 200 (3), Cultura Science/Jason Persoff Storm- doctor/GI; 200 (4), Melinda Fawver/ SS; 200 (5), Clemmesen/Dreamstime; 200 (6), Cholder/Dreamstime; 200 (7), Anatoly Maltsev/ epa/CO; 200 (8), Alex Fieldhouse/Alamy; 201 (9), Isselee/Dreamstime; 201 (10), Daisy Gilardini/ Masterfile; 201 (11), Maxim Petrichuk/ Dreamstime.com; 201 (12), Paul Chesley/NGC; 201 (13), Ali Ender Birer/Dreamstime; 201 (14), Steshkin Yevgeniy/SS; 201 (15), Edwin Giesbers/ NPL/CO; 201 (16), Eric Isselee/Dreamstime; 201 (17), David R. Frazier Photolibrary, Inc./Alamy; 202 (CTR), Humming Bird Art/SS; 203 (UP), Stuart Armstrong; 204 (LO), Richard Peterson/ SS; 204 (1), Leonid Tit/SS; 204 (4), Lars Christensen/SS; 204 (2), Frans Lanting/National GeographicStock.com; 204 (3), Daniel Loretto/ SS; 205 (UP RT), Richard Griffin/SS; 205 (UP CTR), GrigoryL/SS; 205 (UP LE), Lori Epstein/ NGS; 205 (LO LE), Lori Epstein/NGS; 205 (LO RT), Lori Epstein/NGS; 206 (UP), Dan Kitwood/ GI; 207 (UP LE), Sunil Pradhan/NurPhoto/CO; 207 (LO LE), Gavin Gough/NurPhoto/CO; 207 (LO RT), Lindsay Dedario/Reuters/CO; 208 (UP), Lori Mehmen/Associated Press; 208 (LO), Jim Reed; 209 (UP LE), Gene Blevins/LA Daily News/ CO; 209 (LO LE), Neil Bookman/National Geographic My Shot; 209 (UP RT), Susan Law Cain/ SS; 209 (UP CTR RT), Brian Nolan/IS.com; 209 (RT CTR), Susan Law Cain/SS; 209 (CTR), Judy Kennamer/SS; 209 (LO RT), jam4travel/SS; 209 (LO CTR), jam4travel/SS; 210 (UP), FotograFFF/ SS; 210 (LO), Craig Tuttle/CO; 211, VisionsPictures/MP; 212 (LO LE), age fotostock RM/GI; 212 (LO RT), Photo Researchers RM/GI; 212 (CTR RT), Anneka/SS; 213 (CTR RT), Ed Reschke/GI; 213 (UP LE), Edwin Giesbers/NPL; 213 (UP RT), Claus Meyer/MP/NGC; 213 (LO), Inga Spence/Visuals Unlimited/CO; 214 (UP), AVTG/IS.com; 214 (LO), Brad Wynnyk/SS; 215 (A), Rich Carey/SS; 215 (B), Richard Walters/IS.com; 215 (C), Karen Graham/IS.com; 215 (D), Michio Hoshino/MP/ NationalGeographicStock.com; 216-217 (UP), Jason Edwards/NationalGeographicStock.com; 216 (LO LE), Brandon Cole; 216 (LO RT), Reinhard Dirscherl/Visuals Unlimited, Inc./CO; 217 (LO LE), Dray van Beeck/SS; 217 (LO RT), Brandon Cole; 218-219, Enric Sala/NGC; 218 (LO LE), Rebecca Hale/NGC; 219 (UP), Danita Delimont/Alamy; 219 (CTR RT), Dan Burton/NPL; 219 (LO), Brian J. Skerry/NGC; 220 (UP), SS; 220 (CTR), age fotostock RM/GI; 220 (LO), Brian J. Skerry/NGC

History Happens (222-253)
222-223, Danita Delimont/GI; 224-225, Jose Fuste Raga/CO; 225, 145/Marcaux/Ocean/CO; 226-227 (Background), age fotostock/SuperStock; 227 (LO RT), North Wind Picture Archives/Alamy; 228 (UP LE), DEA/G. Carfagna/ GI; 228 (UP RT), Somyote Tiraphon/SS; 228 (LO), Robert Cravens/GI; 229 (UP), DaleBHalbur/GI; 229 (LO LE), DEA/G. Dagli Orti/GI; 229 (LO RT), alex83/SS; 230 (3), Richard T. Nowitz/NGC; 230 (1), Nick Kaloterakis/NGC; 230 (7), Geoffrey Robinson/Rex Features/AP Photo; 230 (5), The Print Collector/CO; 230 (6), Daniel Gale/SS; 230 (2), viti/IS; 231 (14), joshblake/IS; 231 (9), Mark Payne/SS; 231 (10), Culture Club/Hulton Archive/GI; 231 (12), carrollphoto/IS; 231 (16), Allkindza/IS; 231 (17), Lebrecht Music and Arts Photo Library/Alamy; 232 (LO), M Kathleen Schamel; 232 (LE), Doug Allan/NPL; 232 (RT), Atlantide Phototravel/CO; 233 (UP), Art By Mondolithic; 233 (CTR), Art By Mondolithic; 233 (LO), Art By Mondolithic; 234 (Various), Cidepix/ dreamstime; 234 (RT), Cloki/dreamstime; 234 (Various), Byjeng/Dreamstime; 234 (LO), Andrey57641/dreamstime; 234 (Various), Luba V Nel/dreamstime; 234 (LO RT), Kupka/Mauritius/ Superstock; 235, Jason Hawkes/CO; 236-237 (LE), AP Images/Adam Butler; 237, NSA (Public Domain); 238 (UP), Scott Rothstein/SS; 239 (UP), AleksandarNakic/IS.com; 239 (LO), Gary Blakely/SS; 240 (UP), Robert Harding World Imagery; 240 (CTR), Wolfgang Kaehler/GI; 240 (LO), Education Images/UIG/GI; 241 (B), WHHA; 241 (C), WHHA; 241 (D), WHHA; 241 (E), WHHA; 241 (G), WHHA; 241 (H), WHHA; 241 (I), WHHA; 241 (A), WHHA; 241 (UP CTR LE), Layland Masuda/SS; 242 (A), WHHA; 242 (B), WHHA; 242 (C), WHHA; 242 (D), WHHA; 242 (E), WHHA; 242 (F), WHHA; 242 (G), WHHA; 242 (H), WHHA; 242 (J), WHHA; 242 (CTR RT), cbenjasuwan/GI; 243 (A), WHHA; 243 (B), WHHA; 243 (C), WHHA; 243 (D), WHHA; 243 (E), WHHA; 243 (F), WHHA; 243 (G), WHHA; 243 (H), WHHA; 243 (I), WHHA; 243 (J), WHHA; 243 (CTR LE), Krissi Lundgren/SS; 244 (A), WHHA; 244 (B), WHHA; 244 (C), WHHA; 244 (D), WHHA; 244 (E), WHHA; 244 (F), WHHA; 244 (G), WHHA; 244 (H), WHHA; 245 (A), WHHA; 245 (C), WHHA; 245 (D), WHHA; 245 (F), WHHA; 245 (G), WHHA; 245 (J), The White House; 245 (K), The White House; 245 (I), WHHA; 245 (LO), Mary Anne Fackelman-Miner/GI; 246-247, CTON; 248 (LO), Bettmann/ CO; 248 (UP), Bettmann/CO; 249 (Background), Reuters/Mannie Garcia/CO; 249 (CTR), Division of Political History, National Museum of American History, Smithsonian Institution; 249 (LO CTR), Charles Kogod/NGC; 250 (UP LE), Archive Photos/GI; 250 (UP RT), Bettmann/ CO; 250 (LO LE), Michael Ochs Archives/GI; 250 (INSET), Underwood & Underwood/CO; 250 (LO RT), Patrick Faricy; 250 (UP CTR LE), Stuart, Gilbert (1755-1828)/Art Resource, NY; 251 (UP RT), Jason Reed/Reuters/CO; 251 (LO RT), 2011 Silver Screen Collection/GI; 251 (UP LE), New York Daily News Archive/GI; 251 (LO RT), EPA/ Chema Moya/Alamy; 252 (UP RT), North Wind Picture Archives/Alamy; 252 (UP LE), Somyote Tiraphon/SS; 252 (CTR RT), The Print Collector/ CO; 252 (LO RT), M Kathleen Schamel; 253 (UP RT), Michael Frost/Disney Publishing Worldwide

Geography Rocks (254-337)
254-255, Angelo Cavalli/Robert Harding World Imagery; 261 (RT), Mark Theissen/NG Image Collection; 261, NASA; 262 (CTR CTR), Maria Stenzel/NationalGeographicStock.com; 262 (LO CTR), Bill Hatcher/NationalGeographic Stock.com; 262 (UP), Carsten Peter/National GeographicStock.com; 262 (RT CTR), Gordon Wiltsie/NationalGeographicStock.com; 262 (LO LE), James P. Blair/NationalGeographicStock .com; 262 (CTR LE), Thomas J. Abercrombie/ NationalGeographicStock.com; 262 (LO RT), Bill Curtsinger/NationalGeographicStock .com; 263, fotoVoyager/GI; 264, Johan Elzenga/ GI; 265 (UP CTR rt), Flickr RM/GI; 265 (LO RT), Glowimages/GI; 265 (UP LE), Dennis Walton/ GI; 265 (LO LE), Letiziag84/Dreamstime.com; 265 (UP RT), keyvanchan/GI; 265 (LO CTR RT), mihtiander/GI; 268, Keith Szafranski/GI; 269 (lo ctr rt), Colin Monteath/Hedgehog House/ MP; 269 (LO RT), Achim Baque/SS; 269 (UP LE), Izzet Keribar/GI; 269 (LO LE), Alex Tehrani/CO Outline; 269 (UP RT), Dean Lewins/epa/CO; 269 (UP CTR RT), Wayne Lynch/All Canada Photos/ CO; 272, Shin Yoshino/MP; 273 (CTR LE), Arsgera/ GI; 273 (UP LE), narvikk/GI; 273 (UP RT), VPC Animals Photo/Alamy; 273 (UP CTR RT), David McLain/Aurora Photos/CO; 273 (LO CTR RT), Universal Images Group/GI; 273 (LO CTR), ullstein bild/GI; 273 (LO RT), Jon Arnold Images/Danita Delimont.com; 276, Karen Graham/GI; 277 (UP LE), Jon Arnold/Alamy; 277 (LO LE), Michael Lidski/Alamy; 277 (UP RT), Stuart Hannagan/ GI; 277 (UP CTR RT), Fairfax Media/GI; 277 (LO CTR RT), Allan Seiden/Robert Harding World Imagery; 277 (LO RT), robertcicchetti/GI; 280, sborisov/GI; 281 (up ctr rt), ollirg/SS; 281 (UP LE), Alexander Klemm/GI; 281 (LO LE), Brian Lawrence/GI; 281 (UP RT), Bob Krist/CO; 281 (LO CTR RT), Nikada/GI; 281 (LO RT), Roy Pedersen/ SS; 284, JoseIgnacioSoto/GI; 285 (LO CTR RT), FLPA/Chris and Tilde Stuart/MP; 285 (LO RT), Chris van Rijswijk/Buiten-beeld/MP; 285 (UP LE), Tony Gervis/GI; 285 (LO LE), Horse Mandible; Canadian Museum of History MgVo-3:65-90, D2007-12648; 285 (UP RT), Janie Blanchard/ GI; 285 (UP CTR RT), SusanSerna/GI; 288, 482094263/GI; 289 (UP LE), Photononstop/ SuperStock; 289 (CTR LE), David Tipling/Alamy; 289 (LO RT), Soberka Richard/hemis.fr/GI; 289 (UP RT), Ricardo Ribas/Alamy; 289 (UP CTR RT), DPK-Photo/Alamy; 289 (LO CTR RT), Cristina Mittermeier/NGC; 295, Mark Carwardine/ NPL; 296, Chris Cheadle/GI; 300, Mark Conlin/ Alamy; 303, blickwinkel/Alamy; 304, Tim Gerard Barker/GI; 308, Thomas Dressler/GI; 311, Hans-Peter Merten/Robert Harding World Imagery; 316, krivinis/SS; 322 (UP RT), Courtesy Yunak Evleri Cave Hotel; 328 (UP RT), Panoramic Images/GI; 328 (UP CTR LE), SS; 328 (UP CTR RT), SS; 328 (LO RT), PhotoDisc; 329 (UP), James Anderson/GI; 329 (UP CTR), NPL/Alamy; 329 (LO CTR), Jan Butchofsky/CO; 329 (LO), Nik Wheeler/ Alamy; 330 (UP), istore/Alamy; 330 (CTR), Ashley Cooper/Alamy; 330 (LO), Ashley Cooper/Alamy; 331 (UP RT), Michael Jenner/Alamy; 331 (UP LE), Arcaid Images/Alamy; 331 (LO LE), CB2/ ZOB/Newscom; 331 (LO RT), John Robertson/ Alamy; 332 (UP LE), Courtesy Yunak Evleri Cave Hotel; 333 (UP LE), Matt Cardy/GI; 333 (UP RT), Uwe Zucchi/dpa/CO; 333 (LO), Reuters/ Lucy Nicholson; 334 (1), HPuschmann/IS; 334 (8), Islandstock/Alamy; 334 (5), targovcom/IS; 334 (6), Stock Connection Blue/Alamy; 334 (2), isitsharp/IS; 335 (11), Kim Jae-Hwan/GI; 335 (17), Abel Uribe/Chicago Tribune/MCT/GI; 335 (10), David Zalubowski/AP; 335 (16), Jason Childs/ AsiaPac/GI; 335 (14), JB-2078/Alamy; 335 (15), Uli Deck/dpa/CO; 336 (UP RT), Thomas Dressler/ GI; 336 (UP LE), Mark Conlin/Alamy; 336 (LO RT), fotoVoyager/GI

Want to Learn More?

Find more information about topics in this book in these National Geographic Kids resources.

Brain Games
Jennifer Swanson
2015

Dirtmeister's Nitty Gritty Planet Earth
Steve Tomecek, Fred Harper (illustrator)
2015

Extreme Planet
Carsten Peter, Glen Phelan
2015

How to Speak Cat
Aline Alexander Newman and Gary Weitzman, D.V.M.
2015

National Geographic Kids By the Numbers series

National Geographic Kids Everything series

National Geographic Kids 5,000 Awesome Facts (About Everything!) series

National Geographic Kids Funny Fill-In series

National Geographic Kids Get Outside Guide
Nancy Honovich, Julie Beer, Richard Louv
2014

National Geographic Kids Just Joking series

National Geographic Kids Mission Animal Rescue series
kids.nationalgeographic.com/mission-animal-rescue

National Geographic Kids Ultimate Adventure Atlas of Earth
2015

National Geographic Kids Ultimate Explorer Field Guide series

National Geographic Kids Ultimate Weird But True series

Ultimate Bodypedia
Patricia Daniels, Christina Wilsdon, Jen Agresta
2014

Since 1888, the National Geographic Society has funded
more than 12,000 research, exploration, and preserva-
tion projects around the world. The Society receives
funds from National Geographic Partners LLC, funded in
part by your purchase. A portion of the proceeds from
this book supports this vital work. To learn more, visit
www.natgeo.com/info.

For more information, visit www.nationalgeographic.com,
call 1-800-647-5463, or write to the following address:
National Geographic Partners
1145 17th Street N.W.
Washington, D.C. 20036-4688 U.S.A.

Visit us online at nationalgeographic.com/books

For librarians and teachers: ngchildrensbooks.org

More for kids from National Geographic:
kids.nationalgeographic.com

For information about special discounts for bulk
purchases, please contact National Geographic Books
Special Sales: ngspecsales@ngs.org

For rights or permissions inquiries, please contact
National Geographic Books Subsidiary Rights:
ngbookrights@ngs.org

NATIONAL GEOGRAPHIC and Yellow Border Design are
trademarks of the National Geographic Society, used
under license.

Art Directed by Jim Hiscott, Jr.
Designed by Ruthie Thompson

Paperback ISBN: 978-1-4263-2417-8
Hardcover ISBN: 978-1-4263-2418-5
Scholastic edition ISBN: 978-1-4263-2660-8

Printed in the United States of America
16/QGT-QGL/1